आ नो भद्राः क्रतवो यन्तु विश्वतः ।

ā no bhadrāḥ kratavo yantu viśvataḥ

Let noble thoughts come to us from every side

\- Ṛg Veda I - 89-i

BHAVAN'S BOOK UNIVERSITY

STORIES OF VIKRAMADITYA

[SIMHASANA DWATRIMSIKA]

by

V. A. K. AIYER

BHAVAN'S BOOK UNIVERSITY

STORIES OF VIKRAMADITYA

[SIMHASANA DWATRIMSIKA]

V. A. K. AIYER

2019

BHARATIYA VIDYA BHAVAN
Kulapati Munshi Marg
Mumbai - 400007

First Edition	:	*1960*
Second Edition	:	*1963*
Third Edition	:	*1969*
Fourth Edition	:	*1974*
Fifth Edition	:	*1981*
Sixth Edition	:	*1988*
Seventh Edition	:	*2001*
Eighth Edition	:	*2008*
Nineth Edition	:	*2019*

Price : ₹ 470.00

Typesetting by Samir Parekh,
at Creative Page Setters

PRINTED IN INDIA

By Nilesh Parekh, Paras Prints, at Gala 32, Singh Indu. Estate-3, 1st floor, Ram Mandir Road, Goregaon, Mumbai - 400104 and Published by P. V. Sankarankutty, Joint Director, Bharatiya Vidya Bhavan, K.M. Munshi Marg, Mumbai - 400007.
E-mail : bhavan@bhavans.info - Website : http://www.bhavans.info

KULAPATI'S PREFACE

The Bharatiya Vidya Bhavan – that Institute of Indian Culture in Mumbai – needed a Book University, a series of books which, if read, would serve the purpose of providing higher education. Particular emphasis, however, was to be put on such literature as revealed the deeper impulsions of India. As a first step, it was decided to bring out in English 100 books, 50 of which were to be taken in hand almost at once.

It is our intention to publish the books we select, not only in English, but also in the following Indian languages: Hindi, Bengali, Gujarati, Marathi, Tamil, Telugu, Kannada and Malayalam.

This scheme, involving the publication of 900 volumes, requires ample funds and an all-India organization. The Bhavan is exerting its utmost to supply them.

The objectives for which the Bhavan stands are the reintegration of the Indian culture in the light of modern knowledge and to suit our present day needs and the resuscitation of its fundamental values in their pristine vigour.

Let me make our goal more explicit:

We seek the dignity of man, which necessarily

implies the creation of social conditions which would allow him freedom to evolve along the lines of his own temperament and capacities: we seek the harmony of individual efforts and social relations, not in any makeshift way, but within the framework of the Moral Order; we seek the creative art of life, by the alchemy of which human limitations are progressively transmuted, so that man may become the instrument of God, and is able to see Him in all and all in Him.

The world, we feel, is too much with us. Nothing would uplift or inspire us so much as the beauty and aspiration which such books can teach.

In this series, therefore, the literature of India, ancient and modern, will be published in a form easily accessible to all. Books in other literatures of the world, if they illustrate the principles we stand for, will also be included.

This common pool of literature, it is hoped, will enable the reader, eastern or western, to understand and appreciate currents of world thought, as also the movements of the mind in India, which, though they flow through different linguistic channels, have a common urge and aspiration.

Fittingly, the Book University's first venture is the *Mahabharata,* summarised by one of the greatest living Indians, C. Rajagopalachari; the second work is on a section of it, the *Gita,* by H. V. Divatia, an eminent jurist and a student of philosophy. Centuries ago, it was proclaimed of the *Mahabharata:* "What is not in it, is nowhere." After twenty five centuries, we can use the same words about it. He who knows it not, knows not the heights and depths of the soul; he misses the trials and tragedy and the beauty and grandeur of life.

The *Mahabharata* is not a mere epic; it is a romance, telling the tale of heroic men and women and of some who were divine; it is a whole literature in itself, containing a code of life, a philosophy of social and ethical relations, and speculative thought on human problems that is hard to rival; but, above all, it has for its core the *Gita*, which is, as the world is beginning to find out, the noblest of scriptures and the grandest of sagas in which the climax is reached in the wondrous Apocalypse in the Eleventh Canto.

Through such books alone the harmonies underlying true culture, I am convinced, will one day reconcile the disorders of modern life.

I thank all those who have helped to make this new branch of the Bhavan's activity successful.

Publisher's Note

THE Stories of Vikramaditya are among the oldest collection of folk tales centering round the personality of King Vikramaditya of Ujjain. First written in Sanskrit, a number of slightly differing versions are extant in all the major languages of India. The stories are most interesting.

The main purpose of these stories is to illustrate the generous deeds of a model king and emphasize moral lessons. In this light they are didactic, but in their ingenious plots, dramatic situations, portrayal of real life and correct appraisal of human character, they are superb. As the reader can easily notice, human nature has not changed a whit after a thousand years at least.

The original authorship of these stories is unknown, even as their date; but they are generally believed to have originated during the period 11th to 13th centuries.

"Simhasana Dwatrimsika" or Thirty-two Tales of the Throne, is a series of stories related by the statuettes on the throne of King Bhoja. They were first published in the *Bhavan's Journal* and proved very popular. A sister volume to these "Stories of Vikramaditya" is also published under the caption of "Vetala Panchavimsati."

CONTENTS

1

Bhoja Discovers the Throne

DHARMAPURI was famous for its colossal temples, high buildings, large tanks, beautiful gardens and rich fields. King Bhoja who was learned in all *shastras* ruled over it in the manner laid down in them. His fame as a just ruler spread far and wide.

One day King Bhoja sent word to his Chief Minister, Nitivakya, and expressed his desire to go for a hunt. Nitivakya, accordingly, made all preparations for the royal hunt. On an auspicious day Bhoja set out in full panoply accompanied by the fanfare of a royal retinue.

The party roamed over hills and dales and deep forests for several days and accounted for many lions, tigers, boards and what not.

Quite satisfied with the results of the hunt, the party made its way back to the capital. On the way it had to pass through the maize fields belonging to a brahmin, Saravana Bhatta by name.

The latter had pitched a tent in the midst of his field high on a scaffold and was on watch. On seeing the King's party rather tired, he called out to them and said "Friends, you seem to be tired. Help yourselves to the tender maize-corns over here. There on the other side, I have grown cucumber. Please help yourselves to them and allay your hunger and thirst."

When the King heard the entreaties of the brahmin, he was much pleased and permitted his followers to help themselves to the timely food so generously offered.

While the King's party was engaged in eating the luscious cucumber and green corn with great relish, the brahmin came down from his high perch and after walking a few yards towards them for driving birds away, raised a hue and cry and shouted "By what right do you enter my field and do havoc to my corns and cucumber? Is there no one to check this depredation?"

King Bhoja was stunned by this accusation of the brahmin and immediately ordered his army to quit the field.

On this, the brahmin traced his way back to his howdah. But no sooner did he reach his seat than he started shouting "Raj, how is it that you do not eat my corns? Do you not like them?" and entreated the King's party to partake of them and wear away its tiredness.

On hearing this, King Bhoja turned round sharply and beckoned to his Chief Minister, and said "Nitivakya, did you notice the change in the brahmin's behaviour when he was on the perch and when he came down?"

"Yes, your Majesty", replied Nitivakya.

"And what do you think of it?" asked the King.

"Your Majesty, I guess there must be some mystery in the perch or the ground underneath it. Or else there appears to be no reason for his sudden change", replied the Minister.

"I suppose so. I agree with you", replied the King thoughtfully.

"If your Majesty permits me, I shall have them examined", said the Minister.

"Oh, brahmin!" called the King and said, "We are extremely sorry for damaging your crops. But we have decided to offer compensation to you with larger and richer fields and presents, provided you agree to give this field to us in exchange."

The brahmin grinned ingratiatingly and clasping his hands in prayer, replied "Your Majesty, it will be my privilege to do so. How can I go against the wishes of your Majesty? and fidgeted with his nails.

The King immediately signed orders granting the brahmin alternative fields and cash presents, and despatched workmen to examine the seat and excavate the brahmin's old field thoroughly.

The digging went on for several days.

One day deep down in the field, the workers stuck against a metallic structure which was unearthed carefully and burnished. Ultimately it turned out to be a very precious throne made of gold and inlaid with silver and innumerable precious stones. It had thirty-two steps and each step was borne by a statuette of great beauty.

When the King heard of this precious find, he came post-haste to the spot in the company of his ministers and saw the precious throne. He was greatly pleased with its luster and workmanship. He decided then and there to install the same in his *durbar* and make it his official throne.

The King ordered elaborate arrangements to be made for its ceremonial carrying to his palace and its proper installation. The throne was purified with sacred waters drawn from the four seas anointed with fragrant unguents and decorated with flowers and worshipped by priests with Vedic chants in the prescribed manner. After mass feeding and sixteen-fold gifts of gold, cows etc., the King called the *durbar* on an auspicious day and in the presence of ministers, ambassadors, plenipotentiaries and his subjects, decided to ascend the throne.

He prayed to God and after receiving the blessings of brahmins and the good wishes of those assembled, he placed his right foot on the first step when, lo! as one man, all the thirty two statuettes bearing the throne became animated and burst into a peal of laughter and clapped their hands in derision.

The King was dumbfounded as he stood back, even as the

august assembly before him. He was a picture in stone for a brief moment.

The King, however, collected his senses immediately after the shock and addressed the statuettes: "Oh statuettes, what made you laugh when I set foot on the throne? Will you explain?"

Said the statuette holding the first step "Listen, King Bhoja! You must be thankful to us for stopping you thus from ascending this throne, else your head would by now have been blown into smithereens, because it never occurred to you to examine if you were fit enough to occupy this throne."

After, a pause it added "This throne was occupied by King who has no parallel. He was charitable, gentle, brave, knew even the eye-languages of ants, was learned in the Vedas, *Shastras* and *puranas*, could leave one body and enter another, was a *siddha* and above all a great king, valorous and just. With Bhatti as his Minister, he lorded over 56 Kings for 2,000 years earning the name of the Indra of the Earth. He was Emperor Vikramaditya. Do you think you are a thousandth part as wise or great as Vikramaditya? If you can say yes, you can ascend this throne; otherwise quit."

Replied King Bhoja, "O Statuette! I am much obliged to you for reminding me of those great Maharajadhiraja Vikramaditya. Can you tell me in a detail all about him–his ancestry, capital, and the various great deeds he performed?"

Then the Statuette started telling King Vikramaditya's story from his very early ancestry.

2

A Quartet of Brides

SAID the Statuette:

Listen, Bhoja. There was a city called Nandipur where lived a brahmin by name Chandravarman. He was learned in the four Vedas, Six *Shastras*, eighteen *Puranas*, twenty-eight *Agamas* and the sixty-four arts.

Not being content with what he had learnt, Chandravarman went out in search of a *guru* who could impart him further learning.

As he was passing through a forest based on the slopes of a hill, he came across a large lake on whose bank stood a huge peepul tree. He quenched his thirst in the pellucid waters of the lake and lying on his back, slept.

It so happened that an erudite Brahma-rakshas[1] was occupying that peepul tree doing penance. On seeing the brahmin fast asleep, the Brahma-rakshas became inquisitive. So rousing the brahmin from his slumber, it asked "Oh, brahmin! Who are you and where are you coming from? Why were you asleep here?"

On waking up, the brahmin prostrated before the Brahma-rakshas and replied: "I am a brahmin by birth and come from Nandipur. I have learnt a small bit of the *shastras* and I have been wandering in search of a *guru* but not finding one, I was nearly broken-hearted. I sat down exhausted when I fell asleep. You seem to be a learned person. If you will be kind enough to teach me higher knowledge, I shall be highly obliged to you."

1. Ghost of a learned man

Said the Brahma-rakshas: "I have no objection to teach you; but unless you follow my instructions carefully, the knowledge imparted by me may not be of any use to you."

"I promise to follow your instructions very carefully," assured Chandravarman.

"Now, listen. You will have to go without food and sleep throughout the course of my instruction. What do you say?" asked the Brahma-rakshas.

"Agreed," replied the brahmin. Whereupon the Brahma-rakshas taught him the *mantra* whereby one could go without food or sleep for an indefinite period.

Each day the Brahma-rakshas wrote down the lesson on a leaf of the tree atop which it had its abode, and dropped it down. The brahmin picked up the leaf and studied it carefully day and night. Thus within six months, he mastered higher knowledge and became thoroughly conversant with the eight-fold *siddhis* or accomplishments.

When the course of instruction imparted by the Brahma-rakshas was over, a heavenly chariot came from heaven to fetch the Brahma-rakshas. The parting between the *guru* and disciple was heart-rending. The Brahma-rakshas blessed the brahmin saying "You have proved an ideal *shishya*. Now that you have mastered higher knowledge. I want you to go back to your native place and marry the girl of your choice."

On his way to his native place Chandravarman had to pass through the streets of a city by name Kannyapur. Having been released from his *vrata* of no-food and no-sleep by his master the previous day, he felt very tired and took shelter under the roof of a palatial building and soon fell asleep.

It so happened that the house was owned by a danseuse by name Alankaravalli who was devout and greatly attached to the deity of the local temple where she danced everyday, at the appointed hour of worship.

Late at night, while she was returning from the temple, she saw the brahmin lying like a log of wood, consumed by the tiredness and hunger of the past six months. He was completely inert but for his deep breathing. His condition evoked pity in the dancer and a genuine fear whether he was seriously ailing. So she immediately sent for the *vaidya* who came on the scene in an instant.

After examining the brahmin, the *vaidya* said: "Madam, this man appears to have taken no food for six months at least; unless therefore we help him with something immediately, his life may soon part from his body."

Oh *vaidya*! What can I do? However much I rouse him, he wouldn't sit up! Tell me, what should l do?" asked the woman.

'Don't worry! I will send a *rasayana* which you should rub in all over his body and head, thrice a day, for eight days. In this manner the essence of food will get into his system through the pores of his skin. After eight days he will regain his consciousness," replied the *vaidya*.

She thanked him profusely and sent a messenger with him to fetch the *rasayana*. She nursed the brahmin for eight days in the manner prescribed by the *vaidya* and to her great relief he sat up on the following day.

Recollecting his wandering, his meeting with the Brahmarakshas and his learning, he quickly tried to slip away from the place. But the woman stopped him saying "Oh brahmin! I have nursed you all these days into life and yet you do not even have the courtesy to thank me?"

The brahmin did not reply but again looked wistfully seeking a way of escape from that house.

The woman would not let him go. She closed in on him and said "Why do you think, Oh brahmin, have I taken infinite pains to bring you back to life when it was hovering on the border? Was it not because I want you to marry me?"

The brahmin uttered "Siva! Siva!" and closed his ears.

He then protested: "I am utterly unworthy of marrying you, madam."

The woman would not agree. This brought about a mild scuffle at the end of which the woman dragged him to the King's court and filed a complaint.

The King hearing the statements of both, and realising its complication, sought the advice of his ministers and the Palace Priest.

The latter said "Your Majesty! The man being a brahmin, he can marry a brahmin girl, a kshatriya girl, a vaishya girl and a shudra girl – all at the same time, but not otherwise."

Thereupon the King said: "If that is so, O priest, if you are willing, I propose to give your daughter, my daughter, my vaishya friend Somasekhar's daughter and this lady together in marriage to this brahmin!"

To this, all, except the groom, were agreeable. But the King ultimately prevailed upon the brahmin by various means to agree to his proposal.

Accordingly, on an auspicious day Kalyani, Chitrarekha, Komalangi and Alankaravalli were married to the brahmin amidst great pomp. The King presented the brahmin with plenty of riches and robes and sent him home with his quartet of brides.

3

The Perfidious Queen

BACK home Chandravarman had little to complain against fate or life, for, he lacked nothing. When he was spending his life thus, all his four wives in due course gave birth to a son each. He named them Vallabh, Vikramaditya, Bhatti and Bhartruhari, born respectively of the brahmin, kshatriya, vaishya and shudra brides.

These four boys had their due education and even in early age, showed themselves to be uncommonly intelligent and valorous.

In the meantime, the King of Kannyapur, Shuddhavarman, who was Chandravarma's father-in-law, became too old to hold the reins of his government. Having no other issue he called upon his son-in-law Chandravarman and installed him as king and retired. Soon after, Shuddhavarman left this world.

Chandravarman, with all his great erudition ruled the kingdom in an exemplary manner.

The Crown-princes, in their new environment, got plenty of opportunity to develop their talents. Each one vied with the other in the acquisition of skill and knowledge in the arts and sciences.

In due time, Chandravarman too became old, and as he was preparing to quit the world, all four sons gathered round him.

Looking around, Chandravarman's eyes stopped on Bhartruhari. The dying man's eyes became moist and soon watery as he thought within himself that he would be denied *moksha* if Bhartruhari, born to him through a *shudra* woman, married and begot children. The other three sons, however, interpreted the old man's tears as his partiality for Bhartruhari. But being highly accomplished, Bhartruhari was quick to sense the development, and in order to clear the air, addressed the dying man: "Father, it is natural that you should feel unhappy that I, born of a dancer, would be instrumental in denying you *moksha*, should I marry and beget issues. I therefore solemnly promise that I shall not marry; even if I do, I won't beget children. Please therefore be disabused of your fears."

On hearing this assurance, the old man was overjoyed, particularly at the sense of responsibility showed by Bhartruhari. He therefore smiled and in a faint voice, ordered his other sons; "My sons, you know very well that it was Bhartruhari's mother that made it possible for your mothers to marry me. Hence you should all crown Bhartruhari first as king of our country and you can follow him on the throne later."

All three agreed and after seeing Bhartruhari crowned as King, the old man breathed his last.

The funeral and other ceremonies over, the brahmin wife's son, Vallabh, being greatly learned in the Vedas, went away from home to perform *tapasya* in the forest, resolved on a hermit's life.

Bhartruhari married 360 women but never forgot his promise to his father, which he maintained.

One day, a sage came to have audience with King Bhartruhari. The latter showed him due respects and when asked about the purpose of his visit, the sage gave him a pomegranate which, he said, he brought from heaven specially for him. Its virtue was, whosoever ate it will remain eternally young. The King received it gratefully.

After the sage was gone, Bhartruhari hurried to his *zenana* and calling his senior Queen, Mohana, told her of the divine qualities of the pomegranate and with a mischievous twinkle in his eyes, his desire to make her young forever. He continued "Don't start eating it straight now, for I have to consult the astrologer for an auspicious day for it. You hear?" and caressed her fondly.

The Queen placed it carefully inside the cupboard, but after a few days, sent for the stable-keeper who happened to be the secret lover. As soon as he came in through the secret door, she pressed the fruit into his hands and said "Here hold this; this is divine fruit given me by the King. By eating it, one can become eternally young. So take it home and eat it; don't give it to anybody else." And she literally showed him out before anybody knew it.

As the stable-keeper was returning to the stables, he met a woman on the way picking cow-dung from the street. She happened to be the maid-servant of a public woman with whom he happened to be chummy. He caught hold of both her hands and thrust the fruit into them as a gift to her *mem-saheb.* The maid-servant pushed the fruit rakishly over to the dung-basket on her head, atop which it shone with brilliance.

It was dusk and it so happened that the King was looking out of the balcony at the time. As the woman was passing by the palace gate the brilliance of the fruit caught his eyes. He immediately recognized it and sending his aide, got the woman with the fruit, brought before him. He asked her how she came into possession of the fruit.

Frightened out of her wits, she told him: "The stable-keeper from yonder gave me this fruit to be given to my missis" and began to cry.

The King immediately ordered the stable-keeper to be brought before him. When he came he asked him. "How did you get this fruit?"

Shaking all over the body the stable-keeper replied "I did not steal this, Saheb, T-t-t-to tell the truth, your Queen Mohana gave me this.... She is-is-is sweet on me and she wanted to make me always young. And, and, I sent the fruit to my-my woman, through her maid-servant. This is the truth, Saheb."

The King's wrath knew no bounds, but being very highly cultured, he cooled down, realising the futility of putting the culprits to death.

He decided then and there to give up his love of women, and indeed, the entire material world.

Deciding upon a life of *tapasya*, he ate the fruit himself and with the new buoyancy so acquired plunged into the forest, after releasing all his queens from his harem and providing for them all.

4

Vikrama Inherits the Throne

WHEN Bhartruhari became a *sannyasi*, Vikramaditya came to be crowned King of Kannyapur and Bhatti, his brother, became his minister.

While he was ruling the country to the satisfaction of all sections of his people, Vikramaditya called Bhatti one day and said, "Bhatti, somehow I don't feel content to rule over this small principality. I want to expand my kingdom, and with God's grace, would like all other kings pay homage to me. As a first step I want to construct a new capital for my empire, on a rather large and high altitude with mountains and rivers nearby and temples with exalted deities to worship."

"I entirely agree with you, your Majesty, in your natural desires. If only you order me, I will straightaway go and make arrangements for building a new capital", replied Bhatti.

"Please do it", ordered King Vikramaditya.

Bhatti travelled far and wide, along mountains and forest and crossed many cities in search of an ideal site for the new capital, commanding all the conveniences required by his King.

At long last, he sighted a spot near river Gunapati, south of the Vachana Giri slopes. It was a large one on a high altitude, and surrounded by forests and hence bereft of human habitation.

There was also a large temple dedicated to Bhadrakali by the side of which was large lake surrounded by trees reaching up to the sky.

He went round the temple thrice and stood before the image of the diety which had an imposing appearance. Bhatti was struck by the sight.

Casting his eyes a few yards from the temple he noticed an inscription on a stone-pillar near the lake. He read it with interest. It said:

"Right above this spot hang seven pitchers on hangers. Whosoever cuts them asunder with one stroke, and before they fall, dives into the lake in such a way that his head strikes against the javelin standing in the centre of the lake, Bhadrakali will appear in person before him and bless him with all he wants."

This statement on stone sent a thrill through the body of Bhatti and it took no time to assess that King Vikramaditya alone could perform that feat.

Bhatti returned to Kannyapur hastily and lost no time in reporting to King Vikramaditya of the site he had chosen for the new capital and the inscription on the stone.

Vikramaditya decided then and there to visit the place and thinking that it was really a call to greatness, set about to perform the feat mentioned in that inscription.

Handing over the governance of his country to his ministers, Vikramaditya made for the spot on a richly-caparisoned steed followed by Bhatti and a small retinue.

No sooner did he sight the temple than Goddess Kali herself was amazed at the loveliness of Vikramaditya and she made a resolve to help him, found a kingdom.

Vikramaditya got down from his steed and followed by Bhatti went into the temple and prostrated before the Goddess. He then went to the lake-side to have a look at the javelin in the middle of the lake, stemming the waves.

"How is it, Bhatti, this javelin stands by itself all alone in the midst of water which must be pretty deep? Is there any mystery about it?" asked Vikramaditya.

"Yes, my lord", replied Bhatti. "This javelin is connected to the sanctum of the deity and it is said, it activates with sacredness on account of it", he continued.

Vikramaditya put away his garments on the shore, and bathed in the lake muttering a prayer. Being thrilled by the prospect of the adventure before him, he prayed soulfully before the Goddess and went up the tree where the seven pitchers hung.

Finding that they were hanging from a large circular beam, he asked Bhatti "How can I possibly cut all of them with one stroke?"

Bhatti scanned them from below and called out: "Your Majesty! Mount on one of the pitchers and swing a circular motion so that all the seven chords will roll themselves into one; then cut them with your sword and drive simultaneously into the lake."

Acting upon Bhatti's advice, Vikramaditya cut the seven chords which had twisted themselves into one with one stroke and himself dived on to the javelin-spike. But before his head touched the sharp tip of the javelin, Goddess Kali appeared before him, held him in Her arms and took him, into Her temple.

King Vikramaditya fell on all fours before Mother Kali and prayed in grateful terms for her infinite mercy.

Goddess Kali said "Vikrama, I am greatly pleased with your courage. Ask of me whatever you desire."

"O Mother, I want nothing but your grace. May I build a capital in your august presence. May I be blessed with all the riches needed for it. May all the Kings of this country pay homage to me, Your servant."

"So be it", replied Mother Kali and disappeared.

It did not take long for King Vikramaditya to build an ideal capital at that site. He found the wherewithal to do that mighty task with the grace of Goddess Kali. He named the city as Ujjain after the name of the Goddess, and after installing one of his ministers as King of Kannyapur, Vikrama installed himself as Emperor at Ujjain, on an auspicious day, appointing Bhatti as his Chief Minister, besides a number of other ministers. Soon the population grew.

With the grace of Goddess Kali, he prevailed upon the kings of 56 other states to pay homage to him in course of time.

Emperor Vikramaditya's fame spread far and wide. Even the *devas,* sages, *gandharvas,* etc., came to look upon him with respect.

Vikrama at Devaloka

At this time a dispute arose in the heaven between Rambha and Urvashi as to who was the better dancer. None of the *devas* was able to adjudge between them. Indra was at his wit's end. Then Sage Narada said: "Listen, Indra. In the earth there lives a King by name Vikrama. He is a master of all the arts. In particular, he is an expert in the science of music and dancing. I think he alone will be able to adjudicate on the issue before us."

On hearing it, Indra at once sent his charioteer Matali to fetch Vikrama to his *durbar.*

Matali entered Ujjain with his divine chariot and ushered himself into the palace unhindered. Locating the King he bowed before him and said: "King Vikrama, my master Devendra has asked me to fetch you to his *durbar.* I am Matali, his charioteer. The divine chariot is waiting for you outside."

Vikrama consulted Bhatti. The latter told him *tete-a-tete* "My lord, this invitation is the forerunner of your future greatness. Please àccept it and start for Devaloka immediately."

Vikrama dressed himself appropriately and taking hold of his weapons, he prayed devoutly before Goddess Kali and later stepped into the divine chariot. Matali who at first had a poor opinion of a mere man ascending the divine chariot had to change his opinion on seeing Vikrama.

Within a short time the chariot entered the clouds; before he knew, Vikrama was at the portals of Sudharma, the Council Hall of gods. He was immediately ushered into the presence of Indra, Lord of the Devas, who very kindly enquired about Vikrama's health and his subjects.

Vikrama stayed at Indraloka for fifteen days as the guest of Indra. He went to the Council in the company of Indra and occupied a distinguished seat in the assembly as an august visitor witnessing the deliberations with great interest.

On one of these days the divine danseuses Rambha and Urvasi, exhibited their unrivaled skill in dancing to the utter bewilderment of the audience.

Indra, by whose side Vikrama was seated, gently stated: "King Vikrama, these danseuses are our best exponents. We are at a loss to adjudge who is the better of the two. It is in this connection that I invited you, having heard of your great erudition in and expert knowledge of music and dancing."

King Vikrama smiled in embarrassment, but promised to give his verdict the next day when the assembly dispersed.

Early in the morning, Vikrama arranged to bring two beautiful bouquets in which he embedded a scorpion each in such a way that when you held it in hand without the least shaking, the scorpion would not be able to sting you.

That evening, the two rival danseuses were called to exhibit their skill in a private show. The two vied to excel each other. In the course of it, Vikrama called them and said "It will look much better if you dance with this bouquet in hand" and handed them one each.

Quickly the scorpion did its work in the case of Rambha who lost her sense of timing and faltered in her steps, as the pain became unbearable. But Urvasi, however, was apparently unaffected by the bouquet or the scorpion imbedded in it. She did her footwork amazingly well and the sequence was a perfect success.

King Vikrama winked at Indra and the latter agreed that Urvasi came out of the trial with colours. Not knowing the cause of the other woman's poor show that day despite her accredited talent, he was in half wonder.

The show over, Vikrama called the rival candidates to return the bouquets given by him. He asked Indra to untie them when lo, a scorpion fell from each!

King Vikrama explained: "I had imbedded them in the bouquets. Because Rambha mishandled it, the scorpion stung her with consequences you know. Urvasi, on the other hand, had perfected her art so well that the bouquet continued to be a bouquet in her hands. Indeed, the manner of her handling must have sent the scorpion to sleep! Result, she has vindicated herself."

Lord Indra was greatly pleased with the ingenuity of the test and the verdict. Urvasi was crowned the best danseuse and Rambha too was rewarded for coming as a close second.

All the *devas* were immensely pleased with King Vikrama. Indra presented him with *this* divine throne which was given to him by Lord Shiva when Indra first came to power. Indra also blessed Vikrama that he would rule from that throne for a thousand years.

Calling Matali, Indra asked him to carry King Vikrama and the divine throne to Ujjain. With the blessings of all, Vikrama returned to Ujjain.

5

Kali's Boon to Bhatti

THE statuette continued: The first act of Vikramaditya on arrival at Ujjain was to hurry to the temple of his favourite deity. Bhadrakali, before whom he prostrated full of gratefulness for her grace in giving him an opportunity to go to Indraloka and for becoming the recipient of Indra's gift of the divine throne which he placed before Her.

Reaching his palace, he retired for a few hours and came out dressed for the *durbar*. Bhatti was waiting for him to come out. Beaming broadly, Vikramaditya ordered Bhatti to bring the divine throne from Bhadrakali's temple which was done.

Vikrama recounted in detail what he saw and heard in Indra-Sabha and related in modest terms how he adjudicated in the case of the rival danseuses and how Indra complimented him.

Bhatti replied: "I congratulate you, Your Majesty, on this unique distinction conferred by the King of Devas," and turning aside, put on a thoughtful face.

Vikrama asked: "What ails you Bhatti? You wear a look of disappointment! Tell me."

"You are right in your presumption, my Lord, I wanted to know what your majesty has brought me, your poor servant and brother, from Indra," replied Bhatti.

"Oh, I am so sorry, I completely forgot to ask anything for you! But, surely, whatever is vouchsafed to me, is yours as well!", said Vikrama.

"You are right, perhaps", replied Bhatti, crestfallen.

Bhatti despite his learning and affection for his brother could not help feeling that he was let down by his august brother and therefore became twice intent on earning the blessings of Bhadrakali.

At about 10 p.m. that night Bhatti started towards the temple of Bhadrakali, sword in hand. At that time the Deity had gone out in Her routine round of the town. In her absence, the minor deities were on parole about the temple. Dodging them cleverly, he entered the sanctum and started praying.

In the meantime Bhadrakali Herself returned and on seeing Bhatti prostrate before the sanctum, She raised him and asked solicitously "Bhatti, what made you come here at this time of the night?"

"Oh Mother!" cried Bhatti and said "Whoever can help me besides You? My brother went to Indra-Loka and obtained for himself everlasting fame and a thousand years of rule. But he did not ask of Indra anything for me!"

"So what?" interjected Kali.

"May it please you, Mother, to bless me with two thousand years of life and equal prestige, as the Minister to Vikrama for the duration?" asked Bhatti.

"Oh no! That is going to be a very difficult task for me," protested Kali.

"But you must bless me, Mother, or else who can help me", replied Bhatti.

"If help I must on the above terms, it will be on this condition that you place before my feet the head of your King Vikrama, after beheading him", said Kali.

Bhatti said "Yes" and walked in the direction of the palace.

The King was fast asleep. On his side lay Queen Mandakini and on the opposite side lay King's famous sword in its sheath.

Without raising the least suspicion or opposition Bhatti entered the King's bed-chamber. Walking on tip-toe, he took hold of Vikrama's sword and with his fingers roused Vikrama. Vikrama woke up immediately but Bhatti signalled him not to make noise and rouse others.

"What brings you here now?" asked Vikrama in a whisper.

"I want your head for an important purpose," replied Bhatti nonchalantly.

Laughingly Vikrama lay down and asked Bhatti to cut his head asunder and take it off. Bhatti, after cutting it off, took the head in hand and hurrying to Kali's temple, offered it at the feet of the Goddess, and fell down prostrate.

Pleased with the offering, the Goddess blessed Bhatti with 2,000 years of life and equal glory.

As soon as he rose up, Bhatti laughed. Kali was visibly annoyed and asked him, "What made you laugh?"

"Oh, Mother! Indra gave my King-and-brother Vikrama a thousand years of rule the day before and here his head lies before Your feet! And now you are pleased to bless me with 2,000 years of life. I don't know how far this is going to prove effective," replied Bhatti.

"Oh, you mean that," said Kali smiling. "Don't think I am

as effete as Indra. Take it from me, my boon will never go wrong. You may put it to test if you like," challenged Kali.

"Mother! No that I doubt Your powers. But under the circumstances, my belief in gods has been shaken to its foundations. However, I can believe your boon if you kindly revive my King this instant before my eyes!" asked Bhatti.

"Take this *bhasma* and the head back. Put the head and trunk together and smear the *bhasma* all over and Vikrama will come back to life," replied Kali.

Bhatti literally ran to the palace with the head in hand and placing the head and trunk together and smearing the sacred ashes, saw to his immense joy Vikrama rousing as if from deep slumber.

"What is all this about?" asked Vikrama rubbing his eyes.

Then Bhatti related to him his adventure and the blessing of Kali and how it came about. Vikrama embraced Bhatti in sheer joy saying "I was really much worried that I did not ask of Indra any boon for you. And now you have by your ingenuity earned 2,000 years of life whereas mine is only 1,000 years!"

Bhatti rejoined, "My Lord, you need not worry; you will also live for 2,000 years. I shall guarantee it!", said Bhatti flourishing his hand.

"How is it, Bhatti? You cannot possibly improve on what Indra has thought fit to confer?" asked Vikrama doubtfully.

"I shall tell you how, my Lord. What Indra gave you was 1,000 years of *rule*. Now I am going to advise you to sit on this throne for six months and rule and go away to the forest for the next six months! Thus you will extend your life to 2,000 years!" explained Bhatti.

"Well said!" agreed Vikrama and praised Bhatti for his wisdom.

Thus did King Vikrama and his minister Bhatti love and appreciate each other and for the full span of 2,000 years rule over Ujjain in a manner that was the wonder of all countries and ages to come.

"Do you think, Bhoja, you have a hundredth part of the valour of Vikramaditya, to be able to rule from this throne?" asked the first statuette concluding the story of Vikramaditya.

It was dusk by then and King Bhoja and his minister who heard this story were wonder-struck by it. They returned home for the day.

NOTE: King Vikrama's encounter with the second statuette on the second day is published in a separate volume, being a long and complete story by itself. In this story, a vetal or ghoul becomes King Vikrama's personal valet.

6

Vikrama and the Whale

ON the third day again, King Bhoja came to the throne-room followed by his minister Nitivakya and after worshipping the divine throne in the prescribed manner, set his foot on the steps. The first two statuettes let him go up but the statuette bearing the third step stopped him derisively and asked: "Whence this haste King Bhoja?"

Bhoja's cheeks became flush with shame and he bent his head low.

"I am surprised", continued the statuette, "that even after hearing the exploits of King Vikramaditya related by my sister, the second statuette you do not seem to realize your limitations to rule from this throne. Would you like to hear more of Vikrama's exploits, when you might, perhaps, see reason?"

"Do tell me, O statuette, more of King Vikramaditya's exploits", entreated King Bhoja.

Said the third statuette:

When King Vikramaditya was ruling in the manner suggested by Bhatti, and as sanctioned by the *shastras,* there lived in his capital a brahmin by name Ved-Govinda who was well-versed in the Vedas and *Shastras.*

Being denied the pleasure of having a son, the brahmin performed intense *tapas* before the Lord who, pleased with the brahmin's *tapasya,* blessed him with a beautiful son. A chip of the old block, the young boy too was quick in learning the Vedas.

While the boy was seven years old, the brahmin took him for a bath in the sea on auspicious occasion. The father and son got down into the sea and were waist-deep in water when he dipped his son in the sea. Suddenly a huge whale swam to them and swallowed the boy! The brahmin was stunned by the speed of the whole occurrence and seeing the whale disappear into the sea, ran ashore beating his breast and wailing for the loss of his only son.

The justice and fairness with which King Vikramaditya ruled his country was reflected on his people, none of whom died ere they reached the full span of a hundred and twenty years. The brahmin, learned and devout as he was, was sure that none of his actions nor those of his forbears could in any way have been responsible for his present calamity. He concluded it was due to some fault in the administration of King Vikramaditya that he had this misfortune.

He decided then and there to seek the King's audience and accuse him of some misdeed as a consequence of which he lost his son; if he failed to get redress, the brahmin decided to end his life before the King.

The brahmin rang the complaint bell of the palace and King Vikramaditya who had never before occasion to hear it ring, sent Bhatti post-haste to fetch the complainant.

Running to the palace-gate, Bhatti saw the desolate-looking brahmin. He put his arms round him and quieting him asked, "What is your trouble O brahmin, please tell us."

The brahmin related all that happened to him and ended "If I fail to get back my son, I shall end my life here itself, for the cause lies entirely at the King's door!"

"Please calm down", entreated Bhatti. "We shall surely restore your son."

Bhatti conducted the brahmin to King Vikrama's presence where he rated all that transpired between him and brahmin.

King Vikrama was at first surprised how, in his reign, a whale would swallow a human child. This wonder immediately turned to anger, and jumping down from the throne, he ran in the direction of his favourite deity – Bhadrakali's temple.

Going round her temple thrice, he stood before her and sought her blessings for the success of his mission. Kali appeared before him and placed *bhasma* in his hands.

Returning to the palace, the King learnt that the six months of his rule for the year would end on the next day. Handing over the governance of the country to Bhatti for the next six months, the King put on hermit's robes and repaired to the forest hiding his weapons inside the robes. Taking the brahmin along with him, he first went to the seashore where the misfortune occurred.

King asked the brahmin to identify the locality and on his doing so, sent him away, assuring him that he would bring back his son hale and hearty within six months, and that he had little to worry thence forward.

After the brahmin was gone, King Vikramaditya was touched to the quick. What was his valour worth if he was unable to restore the boy? So thinking, he jumped into the sea at the spot and searched for the bloody whale which had swallowed the boy.

After some time, he came against a whale which, even before he could make up his mind, swallowed the King too!

To his astonishment the King found himself on the streets of a big town within the bowels of the whale. King Vikrama was looking with curiosity at the large buildings and temples, streets and humanity that lived there.

In a corner of a street, he found a cluster of urchins playing, among whom was a boy of about seven years, who fitted with the description given by the brahmin. King

Vikrama went directly to him and catching hold of his hand, asked him who he was.

The boy replied: "I come from Ujjain; I am the son of Ved-Govinda, a brahmin of that town. While bathing in the sea with my father, I was swallowed by this whale. That is how I came here."

Holding the boy by his left arm, Vikrama drew his magic sword from its sheath. With it, he tore open the womb of the whale and emerged out of it, along with the boy. Closing the opening and smearing Kali's *bhasma* over it, lest the city inside the whale should tumble down, he swam ashore with the boy.

7

The Curtain Tells a Story

THE shore which King Vikrama and the boy reached turned out to be an island. Handing over his magic wand and other personal accoutrements to the custody of the ghoul which had become his invisible personal valet, King Vikrama went into the interior taking the boy along with him.

He soon found out that a King by name Shambhunath ruled over it and that, he had an extremely lovely daughter by name Ela and for whose *Swayamvara* all the eligible Kings and princes of the land had come over. The capital was gaily decorated for the occasion and was humming with activity.

On seeing the gala appearance of the city, King Vikrama too wanted to participate in the function. Being a King without his retinue that he was, he thought of a plan whereby he could make known his identity appropriately. Accordingly he ordered the faithful ghoul to bring valuable gems, pearls, diamonds, rubies, jewelleries and other fascinating ornaments suitable for kings which was instantly done. After entrusting the boy to the care of a city-dweller for a consideration, he went to the bazzar and in one of the street squares spread his carpet on which he displayed the valuable gems for sale.

Soon crowds gathered round him. The princes who had specially come seeking the hand of Ela, hearing of this merchant and his fabulous wares, swarmed round him. Countless were the purchases. By his miraculous powers the fake merchant was able not only to satisfy each princely customer, but continued to make the whole lot of them stay round him, unmindful of the purpose of their island-visit.

When, therefore, the time came for the *swayamvara*, the King of the island found the hall deserted; he sent out messengers to fetch the royal suitors but heard, instead, how a funny merchant had inveigled them.

The King himself could not contain his desire to visit the merchant and so, postponing the *swayamvara* by a few minutes, went to the square where the merchant was selling his fabulous wares with infinite charm and eloquence. The King too could not resist purchasing a decent lot.

Finding that the crowd had no mind to melt, the King did the wise thing of inviting the merchant too to his palace, to participate in the palace-function of *swayamvara*, of course as a distinguished visitor.

The merchant agreed and collecting his wares, accompanied the royal troupe to the palace where he was a silent witness to the function.

Princess Ela in her maidenly beauty was bewitching and in the ordinary course, King Vikrama would have been a highly eligible suitor; but in the special circumstances in which he found himself that day, he had to invoke his special powers.

When Princess Ela had gone round the assembly twice with the garland in hand, accompanied by her retinue and was about to enter on the third, King Vikrama spelt certain *mantras* which had been vouchsafed to him by his favourite deity Kali, which immediately attracted Ela towards him.

Ela too felt attracted to this stranger and impelled by a force within her, she moved close to him and garlanded the fake merchant to the astonishment of all kings and princes assembled, and fainted.

There was wide commotion and not a few uttered uncomplimentary remarks about the King's daughter marrying a commoner. King Shambhunath was greatly agitated but put on a brave face till the august visitors departed.

Meanwhile Ela was taken to her bed where, after first-aid, she recovered and saw before her mind's eyes the whole episode and the face of the fabulous merchant. She could not explain his strange attraction, at that time.

King Shambhunath came into her room and seeing her conscious, wanted to express his disapproval of her choice stating "Ah frailty, thy name is woman!"

But Ela was quick to perceive what was passing through his mind and said "Father, I don't think I can make a mistake. I am sure the merchant is more than what he looks. I cannot conceive of an ordinary man possessing such fabulous wealth. Something tells me that he comes from a very high royal family and is a person of high attainments. I shall make it all clear to your satisfaction. Will you kindly send him to my apartment tonight, for after all, he has become my husband?"

"Yes, my dear, I hope you are right," replied the King.

"Daddy, you, mummy, and others keep listening to our conversation, by posting yourselves round my apartment," added the Princess.

The King agreed and departed.

When the King communicated the desire of his daughter that he should visit her apartment that night, the fake merchant smiled within himself that his plans were working satisfactorily, and of course, consented to do so.

Princess Ela, in her wedding dress looked adorable that night as she rose up from her couch to greet her strange husband.

After partaking of the sweets and fruits she held out for him, Vikrama seated himself on a beautifully decorated couch to which the Princess led him. In between them, she laid a curtain and retired to her own couch without a further word.

Vikrama felt that, if he did not make his identity known soon, his stay in the palace would become impossible. For, building, on top of which he made the couple stay, far from the ken of human eyes.

But who can avoid destiny? While the young couple were thus having the best of time high above the earth, one full-moon night, the divine Seven Virgins happened to roam in the sky in that part of the city. Roused by curiosity by the seven-storied building, they hovered round it and peered through the balcony of the top floor, where the princely couple lay asleep on the exquisitely decorated couch.

On seeing them, the Seven Virgins became dumbfounded as to whether such beautiful pair was ever created by Brahma! This wonder soon turned into desire on their part and so, they carried away Kantarupa to their celestial abode, in an attempt to possess him for themselves for ever.

"What happened afterwards I cannot say," said the Curtain, "for I do not know it."

On hearing this absorbing story, Princess Ela and all other invisible ears that listened to it were genuinely disappointed.

The fake merchant Vikrama then intervened: "Oh Curtain! This is certainly unkind of you. How can you stop at this most interesting place? Please do continue."

Replied the Curtain: "Oh, great King, honestly, this is all that I know of the story. If you want to hear its continuation, please ask the Chandelier hanging above, it will oblige you."

The fake merchant took his cue and invoking the ghoul on the Chandelier, addressed it: "Oh, Chandelier, if you happened to know what happened to Kantarupa after he was abducted by the Seven Virgins, kindly tell me."

The wonder of all those who were hearing, including the Princess, rose a high pitch. Could ever a Curtain and Chandelier speak? They awaited in anxious expectation.

8

The Chandelier's Story

THE Chandelier said:

Hear Great King! When the Seven Virgins decoyed Kantarupa, the young bride was fast asleep. She had absolutely no knowledge of what had happened. Hence when she awoke in the morning, she was at first surprised not to find her husband by her side.

Dressing properly she went about the rooms and the baths. He was not to be found. She ran all about the seven stairs only to meet with the same result.

She was then alarmed and started wailing. Her attendants hearing her cry, came running to her, only to find her sobbing more and more. With great difficulty they were able to gather that the Prince was missing. They made a thorough search of the entire palace with no different result.

In great fear, the attendants ran to the King and informed him of thc disappearance of the Prince. The King too sent out messengers to search for the Prince throughout the capital and made enquiries at the exits of the capital. None seemed to have noticed his escape.

The King thereupon consoled his daughter stating that her husband would soon return. In the meantime he took great care to protect her properly in the absence of her husband.

The Seven Virgins on the other hand, had a swell time in the company of Kantarupa, with whom they lived by turns.

One day their conscience began to prick them. They felt that the Prince's bride was also a woman like them and that it would be a great sin to separate her forever from him.

On seeing this, Sundaravalli jumped to her side and pulled her away by the hand. The Princess was at first scared, but subsequently calmed down, at her human looks.

"My girl! What has driven you to take this mad step?" reprimanded the courtesan affably, after allaying her fears that she was no more an apparition than the other was.

Wresting her hand, thc Princess protested, "Why do you stop this wreteched life of mine finding solace in the all-too-kind fire?"

"Oh my! You adorable creature! Are you a princess or a celestial being? And, with the child in the womb? No, no I will never allow it. Now listen to me," she continued, wiping the tears from her eyes. "There lies on the pyre my daughter, my beautiful daughter, consumed by the flames. She died – Oh, she died – giving birth ... to a child ... Now, won't you become my daughter and I will forget I have lost her? Please say yes; come with me. You seem to have no one to care for you. I will shower my love on you."

After great persuasion, the Princess went with the courtesan to her house and to her enquiries about her past, told her a yarn that would fit in with her then predicament, revealing neither her identity nor the true circumstances of her exit from home.

The courtesan called in the midwife when labour started for the Princess, but true to her colour, gave secret instruction that, should a male child be born, it should be killed, but if a female child, it should be carefully amended to.

The midwife tied the Princess's eyes with cloth when the time came, as precaution. A male child was born, and the midwife immediately secreted it out. Placing a wooden doll on the cot, she untied the cloth that had been wound round the Princess's eyes and said "Look at the child you have given birth, look" and stood with her arms folded.

The Princess could not believe her eyes. It was a wooden doll! She was dumbfounded as she wondered if ever a thing like that could happen.

Princess Kantarupi was convalecing. In the meantime, the midwife who took away the child, which looked marvellous, could not reconcile herself to the thought of putting an end to its life. She felt, if she did so, her entire line for generations to come, would perish. Consequently she took it out into the deep forest and left it in a basket by the side of an ant-hill where serpents were reputed to live in large numbers.

"O, great King I know only this much of the story and no further", concluded the Chandelier.

"Oh Chandelier, you have left the story at a most pathetic stage. Kantarupa is a captive in heaven, Kantarupi is languishing in the house of a courtesan and their child is at the mercy of cobras! I am very anxious to know their future," observed the fake merchant.

Said the Chandelier: "Ask the Cushion on which Princess Ela is reclining for the rest of story and it will continue the story."

Taking the cue, the fake merchant Vikrama invoked the invisible ghoul on Ela's Cushion which replied: "O King, why do you want me to tell a story? I have been packed full with silk-cotton, and on top of it, this lady is putting her full weight on me, making me pant for breath. How do you expect me to speak?"

Ela reacted as if she received an electric shock and placed the Cushion right between herself and the fake merchant. She was, by now, also clear in her mind that the fake merchant who could make a Curtain, a Chandelier, and a Cushion speak, could be no other than the great King Vikramaditya of Ujjain.

Sensing that all the listening ears wanted to hear the rest of the story, the fake merchant spoke: "Oh Cushion, this lady appears to be very kind and intelligent. Now that she has unburdened you, could you oblige me by completing the story?"

9

The Cushion's Story

SAID the Cushion:

Listen, Great King to the rest of the story. As soon as the midwife went out of sight, the child, left near the anthill, started crying vociferously.

A five-hooded cobra lived in that anthill. When it heard the child's cry, it came out to see. Finding the child resplendent in its lustre, the cobra divined who the child was.

The cobra thought: "For several generations past, the family of King Gandeswara had been feeding and worshipping me and it is but meet that I should do them a good turn by restoring this child to his grandfather, Gandeswara."

Accordingly the cobra, carrying the child on its hood, set out in the direction of the Kali temple were King Vikramaditya came to worship everyday. The cobra reached the temple before daybreak. Depositing the child at the feet of the deity, it returned to its abode.

When early in the morning, King Vikramaditya, followed by his ministers and priests, came to worship before Kali, he was surprised to hear a child's cry emanating from the sanctum. He ran thither and on seeing the child at the feet of Mother Kali shining like the morning sun, he could not contain his joy. He gathered the child in his arms and pressed it to his heart thinking that it was Mother Kali's gift to his desolate home.

Worship over, he literally ran to his harem and pressed the child into the hands of his Queen saying "My dear, we need no more to sorrow, for Mother Kali has bestowed this child on us. Look at it, what beauty! Look, he laughs. Do you notice how he resembles our dear Kantarupa? God's ways are inscrutable indeed!"

The child grew like the waxing moon at the hands of the aging royal couple. No comfort or convenience was deemed too much for him. They named him, Madan Kesari and gave all the education needed for a future King. The boy took to them all like fish to water.

One day, when he had become a well-grown youth, he was going round the streets of his metropolis in the royal manner accompanied by his friends. While passing through the streets inhabited by courtesans, he happened to notice the courtesan Sundaravalli. With her stood, out of curiosity, Kantarupi, who continued to be at her protection.

As soon as the prince set eyes on Kantarupi, he was strangely fascinated by her. On her part, Kantarupi, on seeing him, missed a beat of her heart, because he resembled her husband Kantarupa so much. But for the fact the prince was very young, she would have sworn that it was her husband.

Having looked at a different man made her so wretched that she became quite flush and ran inside the house uttering "Ram, Ram."

Prince Madan Kesari on seeing the lady run away abashed felt a pang in his heart. His associates did not fail to notice the Prince's attention and his subsequent embarrassment. Winking their eyes merrily, they poked fun at the Prince and said that it was but natural and he need not be so coy about it.

As soon as the Prince reached home, he made up his mind to visit the lady who fascinated him. Picking a couple of confidants and a bag of thousand gold coins, he repaired to her house at nightfall.

The Prince and his confidants had to negotiate a blind

alley before entering the courtesan's house. Guided by his followers the Prince felt his way along.

At the courtyard was tied a cow and her young one. The Prince, in darkness, stumbled upon the calf and went ahead, after jumping over it as it lay on the ground.

The calf was brushed in the act, and so it complained to its mother. "Mother, this fellow has no eyes: he not only hurt me but jumped over me!"

"My dear," replied the cow, "what more do you expect of this fellow, he who in his madness, is going to make love to his own mother! Idiot! Come on, suckle me, you will get over the pain."

Now, the Prince was an adept, among other things, in interpreting the language of birds and beasts. As soon, therefore, as he heard the conversation between the cow and her young one, he was thoroughly non-placed. King Vikramaditya was his father and the Queen, his mother, for all that he knew. "How could the woman of this house be my mother? And yet I have not known the birds and beasts to lie", he wondered. Leaving it at that, he entered the house, much perturbed.

The royal messengers informed the courtesan Sundaravalli of the arrival of Prince Madan Kesari. As soon as he heard it, she became flurried and started turning the house upside down for receiving the august visitor.

She was extravagant not merely in the lush welcome she gave him, but in the exhibition of her false teeth as well!

The Prince conveyed his intention of seeing the other lady.

Sundaravalli thereupon collected herself and ran inside, not so vivaciously. She sought out Kantarupi and harangued on the virtues of royal patronage and tried her best to persuade her to meet the Prince.

Kantarupi had till that time escaped the mortification of such pressure and had been living a life of purity and virtue. Impossible to escape and relying, as the ultimate help, on

God's own direction, she entered the room occupied by the Prince with head bent with shame.

On entering the chamber which was floodlit, she could not help the temptation of looking up at the man and when she did so, she got a strange sensation and her breasts began to spout milk which shot at the Prince's face.

The Prince was completely paralysed of thought, for the apartment seemed to reel before his eyes. He literally ran out of the chamber towards the palace, followed by his confidants.

Sundaravalli who had been building castles in the air to install herself at the royal household at the earliest opportunity, was taken aback by this sudden development as she realised that the pot had broken when butter was collecting.

She took Kantarupi severely to task for having spoiled a golden opportunity and what was worse, she feared reprisal at the hands of the crown for the disrespect shown.

At the palace, the King and Queen waited for the Prince to turn up as usual in the court-room. Not seeing him come for quite some time, they sent word to him. Unable to find him in his apartment, the messengers searched and found him sleeping hurdled in corner of a forsaken room on bare floor. They woke him up and brought him before the King.

The royal couple were alarmed on seeing and hearing what the messengers said. They expostulated "My son, what ails you? How did you happen to sleep on the floor? Do tell me."

"Yes, dad, I shall tell you. But do you promise to answer me without reservation?"

"Yes, my son, what makes you doubt that?" replied the King.

"I shall tell you presently, and if I don't get the correct reply, I have decided to forgo my food for ever!"

"Ha, ha," chuckled the King. "You need not have to do that."

"I want to know if you are my real parents."

The King was at first dumbfounded to hear that question, for he never expected the secret to peter out but decided in the circumstances to tell the truth in the most palatable manner possible for he was not prepared to lose this child too.

"Hear, my son," started the King. "We had a son by name Kantarupa who married Kantarupi, the daughter of King Mahendra. When they were living happily, my son disappeared. But my daughter-in-law became pregnant providentially. On hearing it, we disinherited her out of respect for public opinion. Kantarupi was banished according to law and I have no further knowledge of what happened to her.

"While I was sorrowing their loss, I found one day, a divine child lying at the feet of our family deity Kali. It has a striking resemblance to my son. I brought the child home thinking it was God's gift to solace us in our old age. That is you. And now I have decided to coronate you as King and retire."

On hearing these words, Prince Madan Kesari thought: "It is clear that I am not the son of this King. I must now find out my parents and that can be done only through the help of the lady in the courtesan's house."

"Father, please summon the courtesan Sundaravalli living in our city and another lady living in her house; for, I expect I will learn something about my real parents", said the Prince.

The King accordingly sent his messengers to the house of the courtesan to fetch them. Sundaravalli who was already fearing the King's displeasure was trembling now. However, not being able to refuse the King's orders, she went to the palacc along with Kantarupi.

On setting eyes on Kantarupi King Gandeswara immediately recognised her as his daughter-in-law, but decided to put on a stern face till the truth was out.

"Now tell us, asked the King of Sundaravalli, "who is this lady? Is she your daughter, or your foster-daughter? You must tell us the truth or you will be punished."

"Hear me, O King, I will tell you the truth. My daughter died giving birth to a still-born child. While I was setting fire to her corpse, this lady came from I don't know where and tried to leap into the pyre. Finding that she was pregnant, I persuaded her to come with me. She has been living with me since then.

"When the time came, she gave birth to a son, but I foisted a wooden doll in its place asking the midwife to kill the child as it was not a girl. The lady has been consistently and obstinately refusing to follow my profession and I can vouch for her purity and chastity. This is all what I know of this lady."

The King ordered the midwife to be produced before him immediately. When she came the King asked her: "How did you dispose of the child born to this lady? Tell us the truth or you will be punished."

"O King, when the other lady asked me to kill the child, I had no mind to kill it lest the act should exterminate my entire family. So, I left it in a basket near the anthill of the five-hooded cobra. That is all I know," she replied trembling.

The King addressed Kantarupi: "Tell me, O lady, who are you and what is your name?"

Kantarupi replied: "I am the daughter of King Mahendra of Mahendrapuri and my name is Kantarupi. I was married to Kantarupa, son of King Gandeswara. While we were living happily, my husband vanished one night and I lived in the custody of my father. I don't know how, but I conceived – but I swear I have never to my knowledge been unfaithful to my lord. On hearing my state, my father-in-law disinherited me and my father banished me. In the frost I perceived this lady near a burning pyre; thinking that she was a demoness, I tried to leap into the fire; but the lady took me to her house where I have been living since. I was told I gave birth to a wooden doll, which I accepted. I have been living there cursing my fate but I have never lost my chastity."

King Gandeswara who was by now shedding tears asked the Prince "Now, how do you propose to move further out of this stalemate?"

"Yes, father, the only point to be clarified is whether the child left by the midwife near the anthill and the one you found at the feet of Mother Kali are one and the same. I think if we go and pray at the feet of Mother Kali, she will help us," replied the Prince.

All of them thereupon went to the temple of Kali and prayed before her that further light should be thrown on the knotty problem.

Mother Kali appeared before them and said, "King Gandeswara, the child left by the cobra and the one you found at feet are the same. The lady yonder, Kantarupi, who is pure and chaste, is your daughter-in-law."

"Oh, Mother," exclaimed King Gandeswara, tears of joy rolling down his cheeks "kindly enlighten me on this point only. If my son had vanished much longer before the child's birth, how did Kantarupi conceive him?"

"Oh, you mean that!" smiled Kali. She continued: "The Seven Virgins decoyed your son, having been enamoured of his beauty. But later on, they decided to bring him once a week to Kantarupi's place and leave him with her for the night after throwing her into a spell. Now you understand? You did a grave wrong by disowning her who is a priceless gem of chastity. Now, if she wants to get her husband back, let her observe *Vrata* on Mondays and at midnight, let her worship the Seven Virgins. When pleased, the Seven Virgins will restore her husband."

Mother Kantarupi and son Madan Kesari embraced each other sobbing for sheer joy while the aged parents and attendants stood on looking with watery eyes.

The King disposed of the courtesan not merely by pardoning her, but by presenting her with valuables for protecting his daughter-in-law. The midwife was presented with valuables for her act of compassion.

Of course, Kantarupi lived with her parents-in-law observing the *Vrata* ordained by Kali, as a result to which her husband was restored and all of them lived happily.

"We would not have cared to relate the story but for you, the Great King Vikramaditya," concluded the Cushion.

There was no doubt left as to the identity of the fake merchant now, and Princess Ela as much as her parents were really worried that they had not behaved properly towards the great Vikramaditya.

Princess Ela thereupon, immensely happy about her choice rose and fell at the feet of Vikramaditya and prayed to be forgiven for all the disrespect shown to him out of ignorance.

King Shambhunath expostulated: "There was absolutely no need for Your Highness to come in this garb! A word from you would have brought us all at your feet!"

When the other kings assembled but disappointed, heard who the fake merchant was, they all came post-haste and stood on guard and saluted King Vikramaditya.

After receiving the presents of King Shambhunath, Vikramaditya started towards his country along with his wife Ela. On the way he took the brahmin boy from the place he had left him, after rewarding the custodian.

All three mounted the faithful ghoul which took them to Ujjain in no time.

After worshipping before his favourite deity Kali and leaving Ela at the harem, King Vikramaditya sought out the brahmin Ved Govinda to whom he restored his son.

"Listen Bhoja", concluded the Statuette, "do you really think that you are as good and as valorous and great as King Vikramaditya? If you think you are, you may go up."

On hearing these words King Bhoja and Nitivakya got down from the steps full of praise for the great King Vikramaditya, and returned to the palace at sunset.

10

Lady of the Perfume

ON the fourth day, King Bhoja and his minister Nitivakya came to the throne-room after completing their morning duties. They worshipped the divine throne in the prescribed manner and King Bhoja ascended it in the hope that he would no longer meet with any heckling.

But as soon as he set his foot on the fourth step, the statuette holding it became animated and rolling its eyes in derivasion, clapped its hands and shouted at the King, "Stop!"

King Bhoja was taken aback, but having become accustomed to this sort of setbacks, he asked the statuette: "May it please you, O Statuette, do tell me the reason why you stopped me from going up?"

Replied the Statuette: "You really are a guy; don't you know that on this throne the great King Vikramaditya sat and dispensed justice in a manner that was the envy of gods? How dare you, you who do not even possess a hundredth part of his valour and wisdom, ascend it?"

"I beg your pardon, Statuette," apologized King Bhoja. Continuing, he asked "Can you tell me why and how he ruled to the envy even of gods?"

"Hear then," started the Statuette:

You know perhaps that King Vikramaditya ruled his country for six months in the year and went out to the forest for the rest of the year. Once while living in the forest, King Vikrama and his faithful minister Bhatti happened to take shelter in a choultry in mid-forest. No sooner did they seat themselves on its steps than they were regaled by the sweet aroma of the *champaka* flower! The smell was so exotic that the King sent Bhatti to find out were it came from.

Bhatti naturally thought there must be a garden or at least a cluster of *champaka* trees near about wherefrom the perfume emanated. He searched the entire surroundings up to quite a few miles but failed to discover any *champaka* tree. He therefore returned and reported to his master that no *champaka* tree could be found.

They inhaled the perfume again and again and the aroma continued to regale them. Consequently, they wondered where possibly could it be coming from.

At that time a group of travellers happened to pass that way, rather in a hasty manner. The King beckoned to them to stop for a second and asked them about the mystery of the *champaka* scent, when there were no *champaka* trees around.

The travellers, on the other hand, beckoned to them to follow them a few yards away when they would tell them.

Accordingly King Vikrama and Bhatti followed them nearly a mile when they said;

"Not far from this choultry is the city of Vijayanagar where rules King Vijaya Ranga Raja. He has a daughter by name Champakavalli. She was born with the perfume of *champaka* flower on her body and that is why she was named like that. This aroma is natural to her. She came of age at twelve and from that time – now she is twenty-two – she has taken a vow not to see a man. On Fridays she comes over to this choultry with a big retinue and she stays for the day. She bathes in the lake younder, dresses up her hair and wear gay flowers. Among her maids-in-waiting, she gambols like a she-elephant and by evening she repairs to her palace where she is under strict surveillance. On the day previous to her coming, royal messengers mounted on elephants tom-tom on these roads and scare away all vestiges of men. None therefore dares to stay in these parts and should anyone chance to see you, woe unto you, so begone!" Saying this, the travellers departed.

King Vikrama then said: "Bhatti, when her body should be so bewitchingly aromatic, how much more lovely should her person be? I am now determined to make the girl break her vow and marry me. Tell me, how can I set about it?"

"Quite right, my Lord, your will shall be done. Come to think of it, it is necessary, first of all, to find out the cause of her vow and then seek to break it. Tomorrow is Friday and the Princess will come over here. We should take that opportunity to find out the truth.

Continuing, Bhatti said: "You must assume the form of an aged decrepit and I shall assume the form of a young maiden. While you may watch the Princess from afar hidden in the bushes, I shall mix with the maids-in-waiting and find out what could be found."

At 10 a.m. on Friday the Princess came to the spot with all the fan-fare of a royal party which consisted of a thousand maids-in-waiting. They sported in the lake beyond, took their food, played and after siesta, departed homewards. Bhatti, disguised as a maiden, had no difficulty in dissolving himself into the party. He went with the party far into the city in the hope of finding something.

There were seven gates to the city at each of which part of the retinue melted and at the last gate, only a pick of them went in. Bhatti had half a mind to go inside but fearing that he would be spotted out, turned his way back feeling sorry all the time, that, after all the troubles he took, he was not any the wiser about the Princess. Rather than go to the King empty-handed, he decided to go to mother Kali's temple at Ujjain to fall at her feet, seeking guidance. Throwing off his disguise, Bhatti walked briskly towards Ujjain.

On the way it became noon and unable to proceed further, Bhatti saw a big banyan tree and a lake by its side. Quenching his thirst in the cool waters of the lake he lay down beneath the cool shade of the banayan tree trying to woo sleep.

It so happened that an ascetic couple lived nearby. They were practising penance. The ascetic came to the lake to take his midday bath. On seeing Bhatti's comely appearance it made him think on these lines: "This young man seems to be of a royal origin. He is so beautiful that if my wife sees him, she is likely to err. So, to be on those safe side, I shall transform him into a woman." So thinking, he picked up a herb and uttering a *mantra*, threw it on Bhatti, who became a handsome woman instantaneously.

After the ascetic had gone, his wife came to the lake with a pitcher in her hand to fetch water. Like her husband she too happened to notice the young woman that was Bhatti, lying beneath the banyan tree. She thought: "My husband has so far not set eyes on other women, much less a young woman of this beauty. It will prove dangerous if he does so, so I shall transform her into a man." So thinking she pulled another herb and uttering a different *mantra* cast it on Bhatti, who once again became a man.

Bhatti was at first wonder–struck by these phenomena. But his synthetic mind immediately jumped at the fact that he was in possession of two herbs and the formulate by which one could turn a man into a woman and *vice versa*. And this knowledge, he thought, was providentially put into his hands by Mother Kali in the prosecution of his plans. Taking hold of these herbs, he ran post-haste to where his royal master was anxiously waiting for him.

King Vikrama has lost his patience waiting for Bhatti. Appending trouble for the latter, he had almost decided on raising hell in Vijayanagar in that eventuality and taking the Princess by force. When Bhatti returned by nightfall, it was such a relief to both.

Bhatti related all that happened since the morning and the precious possessions of the herbs and their formulae.

"What do you propose to do now?" asked Vikrama of Bhatti rather petulantly.

"Listen, my Lord, to my plan. By the power of this herb, I shall convert you into a young lady and I shall somehow manage to leave you in the Princess's harem, where you can find out the secret of the Princess's vow after which we shall connive at the marriage.

The King agreed.

King Vikrama became a young lady and Bhatti, calling himself King Salya, went to King Vijaya Ranga Raja, followed by Vikramaditya in the disguise of a young woman. Let us call her Lady Vikrama.

Bhatti sought the audience of King Vijaya which was immediately granted. Bhatti told King Vijaya: "I am King Salya and by a series of misfortunes, have come into bad days. King Vikramaditya of Ujjain whose vassal I happen to be, would not leave me if I don't pay his annual dues. The worst part of it is that I have married his own sister, here this lady, and I do not want to be under any obligation to him. If you can kindly lend me a thousand gold coins, I shall pledge my wife to your care and shall soon redeem her."

"Oh no," protested King Vijaya. "I shall of course give you the money you need, but don't take the trouble of pledging this lady. That is not necessary at all."

"I quite appreciate your point", replied Salya, 'but you see, I am fighting for principles.'

Salya received the money, but while departing told King Vijaya, "Oh King, this lady has not known any hardship. Her birth as well as married life was paved with maximum comforts. I would therefore request you to treat her as your own daughter. I hear you have a daughter. If you leave this lady too to the care of your daughter, they will each find a good companion in the other."

"Exactly," returned King Vijaya, "that was what I wanted to do and now you have given expression to it. Please be assured that your wife will be looked after just like my own daughter."

After signalling a farewell to his fake wife, Salya returned.

King Vijaya escorted Lady Vikrama to his daughter's palace where he entrusted her to Champakavalli's personal care stating that no effort should be spared to make her stay happy. The two girls immediately took to each other and their friendship became so fast that it was impossible to see them separately.

Bhatti, on the other hand, dug up a pit near the slopes of a mountain and after burying the gold coins, invoked his extraordinary powers by which he cast off his human frame and entered the body of a squirrel. Leaving his human frame to the care of the faithful ghoul, he jumped his way into the Princess's harem. At nights, when the girls slept together, the squirrel used to perch itself on the canopy unnoticed and listen to their conversation. During days it went outside through the windows or ventilators.

For a long time, the Princess did not of her own accord, reveal either the cause of her vow, or anything at all connected with her. Lady Vikrama, therefore, one day feigned a weary face and sought a forsaken room where she lay with careworn face. Princess Champakavalli, not finding her anywhere, spotted her there and started importuning her for her sudden carewornness.

"What is the use of telling you about my worry? Can you remove it?" asked Lady Vikrama dejectedly.

"By all means, yes, what makes you doubt that? Listen to a story where two people were so friendly that one proved to be of invaluable help to the other", replied Champakavalli.

Lady Vikrama nodded consent and Princess Champaka started: King Saindava ruled over Chaturgiri. A son was born to him who was named Chitrasena. At about the same time was born a son to a hunter in the same kingdom who came to be called Simha. It so happened that Chitrasena and Simha developed fast friendship while at school and so, when the old King expired and Chitrasena became King, poor hunter Simha was the happiest man; for he dreamed that the new King, being his friend, would offer him riches and make him happy.

He went so far as to stay all day long at the gates of the palace so that the King might look at him and recognise him, but although the King passed before him several times, he did not even nod acquaintance.

Blasted of all hopes the hunter returned home. Having been educated in the modern manner, he was poor in his traditional vocation of hunting. When all means of livelihood were exhausted, he went to the forest for hunting. While all others bagged rich quarries, he could not even get a sparrow.

Disheartened he went along the way his legs took him. The way took him to the mouth of a cave where, to his astonishment, he saw a very attractive woman on whose lap a bearded ascetic lay fast asleep!

On seeing him, the lady warned him. "Flee back, if the ascetic wakes up he will make short work of you. For heaven's sake fly for your life."

Simha came aside and thought: "This young lady is so beautiful that she must belong to a royal household. Apparently she is wrongfully confined by this ascetic." With a snap of his finger he came to this decision: "I shall run to my friend, King Chitrasena, who will be the ideal match for her and shall inform him of this girl. He will reward me for my labour."

So thinking, he ran to King Chitrasena and after gaining audience related to him his find. The King was charged with the proposition. The King immediately said he recognized his old friend and profusely apologized for forgetting him all those days. He promised to make amends for his default.

Riding on his best steed, the King armed himself suitably and accompanied by the hunter came to the cave and found the girl much prettier than what he had imagined her. The ascetic was sleeping on her lap.

Beckoning the hunter aside, Chitrasena said: "Go inside and place the head of the ascetic on your lap and send the girl to me. After deposing her safely, I shall come and kill the ascetic and release you."

The hunter agreed, first, at the chance given to him to help his old friend and secondly, because his poverty would for once be banished.

When the hunter entered the cave, the girl once again persuaded him to go away before the ascetic woke up, but Simha told her, "Oh woman, you, in your prime of youth, should not languish in the clutch of this old wretch. You must live in a royal harem and enjoy all the comforts and sports of the age. Outside, I have brought the matchless King Chitrasena who is waiting for you on his steed. Go and marry him and live happily."

The girl heaved a sigh of helplessness, but Simha offered, "I know why you despair. Allow me to hold the old man's head on my lap while you depart. I shall take care of myself while you can make good your escape."

The girl agreed and gently handing over the old man's head to the hunter, went out of the cave. King Chitrasena who was mad with joy, lifted her bodily and depositing her beside him on the steed, whipped him in the direction of his palace. All the way, he could not help lavishing his love on the divine girl.

King Chitrasena while doing so, never thought of his friend, the hunter, nor of his promise to rescue him from the ascetic, who would doubtless kill him. Indeed, he made light of the entire promise, thinking "Why do I care what happens to the hunter as long as I have my love?" He completely forsook him.

"What happened to the hunter, my dear?" asked Lady Vikrama anxiously.

Princess Champaka continued:

"The poor hunter, not finding the King return for a long time knew that the King would never return and find his own days, rather hours, were numbered, for, the ascetic on waking up would surely kill him. The thought brought torrent of tears of his eyes and his entire body shook with fear."

11

The Perfidious Princess

AT last the ascetic woke up and finding that his head was lying on the lap of an uncouth youth instead of the cosy young woman, his face contracted and eyes reddened. The poor hunter's body shook like a reed in the wind.

"Who are you and where is the lady? Tell me the truth or your life will separate from your body," roared the ascetic.

The poor youth's tongue stuck on his palate and he was too dumbfounded to reply, while tears flowed from his eyes profusely.

The ascetic thereupon concentrated for a few seconds and divined what had happened. On realizing that the youth before him was but a scapegoat in this drama, his heart warmed up towards him. Patting him on his shoulders the ascetic asked him in soothing terms, "Don't be afraid, I won't kill you. Now tell me the truth, who are you and where is the young lady?"

The hunter-youth thereupon prostrated before the ascetic and said whimpering, "I come from Chaturgiri and King Chitrasena rules there. He was my childhood friend, but forgot me completely after he became King. Not being successful in my hereditary profession, hunting, I was coming along this way dejected when I saw your young woman. I went to King Chitrasena and told him about her in the hope that he will reward me for the information but the ungrateful King put me in this predicament and ran away with her. This is the truth."

"Hm", said the ascetic as he shook his head with a sardonic smile.

"What you did was irresponsible", he continued, "but what your royal friend did was worse. When you went out of your way to oblige him, it is quite wrong of him not to have helped you. What is worse, he has left your life in jeopardy. On the contrary he should have helped you even with his life. I have heard a story of old, in which two royal friends were so faithful to each other that one brought back the life of the other with his own. Hear it!"

The ascetic stated:

In the South there was a king who had a son by name Sanmarga and his minister too had a son, Gunabhadra, who were approximately of the same age. The two sons took to each other so well even from childhood that their parents gave them equal education in the royal arts and sciences. When they came of age, they were duly married but as their education had not concluded, they had left their wives at their (wives') parents' home.

One day, however, these two princely pals felt that they should fetch their brides home. After informing their parents, they started towards their brides' country, Sanmarga riding ahead and Gunabhadra following him.

On the way a bird chirped in its language: 'The one who rides ahead is heading for his death."

It so happened that the minister's son Gunabhadra knew the language of the birds and the beasts whereas the other did not. So he thought, "It is the Prince that goes ahead. What shall I do if he dies? Surely I can't allow it. Let me then go in front and make it safe for my friend on whose greatness lies my future, indeed, my all."

Gunabhadra cleverly persuaded the Prince to follow him while he himself led.

After some distance, however, the same bird chirped: "The man who follows will meet with death."

Gunabhadra was now flabbergasted. His position was like that of a stork, which was so sure of its feed until a few hours back, finding the lake suddenly dry! But he resolved that, come what might, he should protect his friend's life. So thinking, he rode on the flank of Sanmarga, holding him by one hand and keeping the other on his sword.

When they reached the outskirts of the city where Sanmarga's wife, Suratha, lived they sent word to her father King Kusa, of their arrival. Soon King Kusa came to receive the royal pair with due honours.

The King offered them each a palanquin to ride, one made of emerald to his son-in-law and another made of ivory for his friend.

Gunabhadra who was obsessed with the evil omen suspected that there might be some fraud in that arrangement and somehow managed to occupy the emerald planquin himself and caused his friend to ride on the one earmarked for himself.

The rest of the journey was uneventful, except that it went round the city in a procession.

As soon as they arrived at the palace, the Prince was directed to an apartment and the minister's son to another.

The doubting Thomas that Gunabhadra became, after the declared ill-omen, he decided at the last minute, to occupy the chamber allotted to the Prince and persuaded his friend to occupy that which was earmarked for himself. Thus, he thought he was stalling fate.

There was some comment in the capital about these sudden changes and the enormous influence which the friend wielded on the Prince.

After supper, the royal household retired and Princess Suratha followed by her maids entered her husband's chamber with delightful dishes and sweet scents. There, on the cosy bed, the Prince lay fast asleep, having become tired by the strenuous journey of the day.

Gunabhadra, on the other hand, after ostensibly retiring pulled a cover over himself and arming suitably, walked briskly towards Sanmarga's bed-chamber. After dodging, the sentries cleverly he managed to hide himself besides his friend where he kept all-night vigil.

Princess Suratha looked around and seeing the lights down and her husband snoring, bade her maids adieu. When they had gone, she pulled herself up and with supreme contempt spat on the ground before her husband, uttering "Tut! The fool that he is!"

Turning round with a swing of her body, she placed the tray of sweetmeats on a table nearby and collecting half of them in another tray walked out of the room after closing the door behind her.

Gunabhadra lost no time in jumping out of his hideout and trailed behind her with the shadows.

The Princess walked swiftly out of the palace to the north of the city until she came to a dilapidated mutt, where lay a cripple, before whom she laid the delicacies she had brought. He was her secret lover.

"Why so late?" questioned the cripple.

"Excuse me, dear! My husband came today unexpectedly, and how can I come before sending him to sleep?" replied the Princess cringingly.

"Oh! that is it? I had all along been thinking you were not married; now that I know you are, you shouldn't come to me. I wouldn't touch a married woman. If you come, note, yours and my life will be in danger", said the cripple.

"Oh dear! How can I live without coming to you even for a day? Please don't say that," remonstrated the Princess.

After a few minutes, the cripple said "If you are so insistent, you must kill your husband and then only can I reverse my decision."

"Agreed," replied the Princess.

The cripple then took out his sword and gave it to her. He then partook of the declicacies brought by the Princess and became his old self.

"I shall not only make short work of my husband, but see that his close friend too is indisposed of, thus killing two birds with one stone." Saying this she walked back to the palace jauntily.

Not a single word of this conversation was missed by Gunabhadra who had shadowed her to the strange rendezvous and its meaning was not lost on him.

He, however, entertained a legitimate doubt if the Princess said what she meant, for he felt, it was her infatuation for her lover that made her say fantastic things. However unfaithful a woman might be, it was too much to expect her to put the dagger into her husband's neck with her own hands, he thought.

Yet, when he remembered the bird's ill-omen he could not confidently leave things at that. He therefore hurried back to his hideout beside the Prince, before the Princess arrived and was ready for any emergency.

The Princess turned the latch of her husband's bedroom and softy walked towards his cot, not stopping to look back or think.

No sooner did she reach it than she whipped out the dagger and thrust it into her husband's neck and so Sanmarga lay dead in a pool of blood! It was all quick like lightning and Gunabhadra, who was spellbound, was a second too late when he clutched her hands uttering: "How dare you murder your own husband and that too when he has not done you any harm and while asleep?"

Princess Suratha was quick to realise the seriousness of her situation and clever like the devil that she was, cried "Oh! Is there no one to punch this outrage! This man not only murdered my husband but tries to outrage me!"

The entire royal household was stirred by her hue and cry and came withering to the Princess's bedroom.

The scene before them was so realistic and needed no explanation that the guards beat Gunabhadra blue on the spot and put him in the lock-up.

On seeing her father, the Princess embraced him and let flow a torrent of tears, exclaiming "What shame! That wretch not only killed my husband but committed treachery. How can you tolerate this atrocity to your dear child? Father! What shall I do now?"

People were not wanting there to remind the King how Gunabhadra had, from the beginning, been planning, this atrocity by changing palanquins and rooms.

The King immediately ordered that Gunabhadra be beheaded and the Minister for the North be entrusted with the execution of this order.

The guards took Gunabhadra to the concerned Minister after clamping the fetters on him. The guards related to the Minister the circumstances of the arrest and also conveyed the King's orders.

The Minister who was mellow with age and wisdom asked the prisoner: "You seem to come from a noble family and look intelligent. How is it that you committed this dastardly crime? By this act you not only suffer by yourself, but have brought a bad name on your family!"

"Sir, what you say is correct and I am fully aware of them. But who is exempt from the decrees of fate? Since I have been found committing the crime, it is but natural that I should suffer the consequences. You may kindly expedite the execution of the King's decree," replied Gunabhadra.

The Minister was too shrewd to take the prisoner at his word. The physiognomy and other indications of the youth clearly showed that he was innocent, particularly, as the Minister thought a woman was involved in the incident. At any rate he was not willing to take risks. So he paid the guards handsomely and sent them along with the prisoner to the Minister for the West for the execution of the King's orders.

Accordingly the guards took him to the latter to whom they related the circumstances of the tragic events and also what transpired between the tragic events and also what transpired between the prisoner and the Minister for the North.

The Minister for the West too had his own doubts about the veracity of the incident and he had too great a regard for the Minister for the North and his great intellect to take independent action. So he sent them to the Minister for the East after rewarding the guards.

It was daybreak when the East Minister heard the case. Under the circumstances, the latter arranged for a meeting of all the four Ministers in connection with the King's orders on Gunabhadra.

The four Ministers seated themselves in a secluded spot where they called Gunabhadra and after putting him at ease that they were favourably disposed towards him, persuaded him to tell the truth.

Said Gunabhadra: "My master Prince Sanmarga and myself have been fast friends since our childhood. We came here, he to fetch his bride and I to fetch mine on the way. On our way a bird uttered the ill-omen of impending death to my friend. I tried to protect him by offering to change my palanquin to his and his room to mine. I lay hidden in my friend's bedroom last night when the Princess came in. Finding him asleep, she not only ignored him, but taking hold of the delicacies meant for them, went at dead of night to the dilapidated mutt where she gave them to the cripple, her secret lover, and made merry. On his initiative she took the sword from him and without thought thrust it into my friend's neck, while alas, I was late by a second in catching her hand. In order to save herself, she has put the blame on me now. This is the whole truth."

Continuing, he said, "One request I have to make to you. Kindly see that my friend's body is not burnt."

The Ministers were impressed by the prisoner's statement, and decided to verify it and in the meantime, agreed to keep the Prince's body intact.

It was not difficult for the Ministers to convince the King that his orders had been carried out by showing some blood.

As pre-arranged the four Ministers, guards and Gunabhadra lay in ambush at night on the way looking out on the palace and the dilapidated mutt.

When it was past midnight, Princess Suratha's silhouette appeared on the far horizon climbing down from her balcony through an improvised ladder. She was carrying a tray of delicacies and the sweet scent on her apparel sent a chill into the bodies of those who lay in wait.

At a signal from Gunabhadra, the party threw a cordon round the mutt and all of them pipped their ears into the stillness of its walls so as not to miss even a single syllable of the conversation.

Little suspecting and confident that her enemies had been razed down, she made straight for the mutt and stood before the cripple self-consciously.

The cripple asked pugnaciously "Did you carry out my instructions?"

"Sure as anything, I not only killed my husband, but sent the other fellow to the gallows by implicating him in the crime!" she replied proudly.

"I know you will do it," saying this, the cripple stroked her cheeks and partook of the dainties brought by her.

The four Ministers and guards who listened to the conversation quickly collected into a tete-a-tete and swooped on the offenders. The guards tied them with ropes and straightaway brought them before King Kusa, although it was still early in the morning.

The King saw his daughter and the cripple bound up before him, and Gunabhadra too, who surprised him most.

"How is it, friend, that you, who were beheaded yesterday, stand before me now?" asked the King.

Gunabhadra related from beginning to end, all that happened during the past two days and cited the four Ministers as his principal witnesses.

The King bent his head in shame, but did not swerve from his duty by ordering the beheading of his daughter and the cripple.

The ascetic explained, friendship to be true, should be like that between Sanmarga and Gunabhadra and not like that of King Chitrasena.

Lady Vikrama at this pause asked "My dear, you seem to end the story at a most inopportune moment, for you have not told me what happened in the end to the hunter-youth, the Prince whose dead body was not, by request, consigned to the flames and finally of Gunabhadra himself!"

"I shall tell you presently", replied Princess Champaka.

12

Secret of Champaka's Vow

"WHAT happened to Gunabhadra and the dead Prince?" asked the hunter-youth of the ascetic.

The latter said:

The four Ministers thereafter took Gunabhadra to their place and after praising him for his devotion to his friend, asked him "Now what do you propose to do?"

Gunabhadra replied: "Kindly embalm the dead body of my friend in such a way that it will not deteriorate for months to come. Place it in a box and hand it over to me. I shall go on a pilgrimage to sacred shrines and *tirthas* praying for his life. If at the end of it he does not come back to life, I too shall give up my life."

The Ministers praised him for his determination, and after providing him with funds and facilities for his travel, bade him farewell.

Gunabhadra in the course of his pilgrimage turned his thoughts on his own wife and wanted to know how she fared, especially after his last experience. And so he went to Kalinga where his father-in-law, a minister of that country, lived.

The Minister, on hearing the approach of his son-in-law, made elaborate preparations for receiving him. Accordingly, Gunabhadra with his precious luggage – the box containing the embalmed body of his royal friend – was taken round the city in royal procession amidst get pomp, to the accompaniment of music and dance.

On arrival at the Minister's residence, Gunabhadra gave orders that the box should be carefully carried to his chamber and kept respectfully and soon following it retired for that day.

Supper over, he lay on the luxurious bed elaborately prepared for him and felt like sleeping, when his wife Amrita, looking magnificent in the bloom of her youth, approached him shyly.

Amrita was greatly devoted to her husband and was praying for her husband's arrival all these days.

She held in her hand a tray of delicacies prepared with her own hand while her maids came behind her carrying fruits and *tambul*.

Although Gunabhadra noticed their approach, he feigned sleep. Thinking that her husband was asleep, Amrita ordered her maids to retire.

Closing the door gently behind them, Amrita walked towards her husband and touching him reverentially with her hands, went round him thrice and prostrated before him. Untying her braided hair, she did it again in the heroic manner. Taking hold of a dagger and a ripe lime, she walked back towards the door as though she was possessed.

Gunabhadra noticed her action from the corner of his eyes and somewhat astonished, leapt on his toes as she closed the door behind her. Out of the palace, he scanned her outline frisking rapidly through the street. Keeping his own sword in readiness Gunabhadra shadowed her.

Amrita's steps took her to Bhadrakali's temple, where, after bathing in the tank attached to the temple, she went into the sanctum. Going round the deity thrice, she prostrated before it and uttered "Mother, as a result of my prayer, my husband has come to me. Now please accept my head, being my part of the contract." So saying she placed the sword on her own throat.

At that moment a miracle happened. Bhadrakali herself appeared before her and stopped her from self-immolation saying: "My child, I am pleased with your devotion. There is no need of taking out your life. Take this my boon: you and your husband shall be eternally young and live happily for ever. Hear further. Your husband was greatly devoted to his royal friend who now lies dead in the box brought by your husband. That friend died out of the perfidy of his own wife. Now, your husband has vowed his own death if that friend does not come back to life, in which case, you will attain widowhood, which is against my blessing. So take the *bhasma* and smear it on the dead body enclosed in the box and the prince will come back to life."

Gunabhadra could not believe his ears or eyes. He was greatly pleased with the fidelity of his wife.

When he noticed her returning to the palace after prostrating before Bhadrakali, he reached it before her arrival and lay down in his bed feigning sleep.

Amrita, like the dutiful wife she was, finding her husband still asleep, stood by his side with folded hands, awaiting his waking.

Soon Gunabhadra opened his eyes and after yawning loudly saw his wife standing near. He drew her fondly to his side and seated her on the bed uttering words of endearment. After the first few words enquiring after her, he confided: "My dear, I just had a strange dream, would you believe it? A girl entered my room and afterwards went to Bhadrakali's temple while I followed her. After bathing in the tank, she tried to offer her own head to Mother Kali, who appeared before her and blessed her with a boon. The look of Kali frightened me which woke me up, when I saw you standing by my side! Isn't that strange?"

"Suppose that girl was I and the dream real?" she asked coquettishly.

"I will be the happiest man!" replied Gunabhadra disarmingly.

"Then, please take this *bhasma* Mother Kali gave me," requested Amrita which he took and applied on his forehead.

"My Lord!" continued Amrita, "Mother Kali told me, further that you have brought the dead body of your royal friend. She asked me to apply this *bhasma* on it when, she said, the prince would come back to life!"

"Is that so? How wonderful? I do have that body here. Come, let us open the box. Oh! How I want my friend come back to life!"

Gunabhadra feverishly opened the box and smeared the *bhasma* on the wound, after putting the head and trunk together, when lo! the prince woke up as if from sleep!

Gunabhadra could not contain his joy. He danced for sheer happiness and going round the prince thrice, prostrated before him, shedding tears of re-union.

After the first few moments when he appeared to be dazed, Prince Sanmarga recognised his friend Gunabhadra and asked him: "Where are we now? Who is that lady yonder? What happened to me? Please explain all!"

Gunabhadra asked his friend to take rest for some time, and after giving him some milk and food, satisfied himself that the prince was out of danger. Then, seating themselves together on the bed, the minister's son, Gunabhadra, related to Sanmarga all that happened to them since they started from home to fetch their brides. He continued: "This lady is my wife;" and the prince saluted her with gratefulness.

After staying there for a week, the royal friends felt it was time to return to their country. Accordingly Amrita's father made all arrangements for their departure. The Prince and Gunabhadra accompanied by Amrita, departed. Cart-loads of presents and other essentials of a long journey followed them.

After returning to his capital, Prince Sanmarga married another Princess with whom he lived happily for long. "You must befriend men like Gunabhadra and not like Chitrasena. And now, don't look at his face again. Here, take all these riches and live happily." Admonishing him thus, the ascetic sent away the hunter-youth with all riches.

At the conclusion of this story Princess Champaka said, "My dear Lady Vikrama now you will realize the value of real friendship. Will you now at least reveal the cause of your anxiety?"

Replied Lady Vikrama: "You are indeed a clever girl. You have really changed my mind to confide in you. To tell you the truth, I am not at all anxious on my account, about my husband or my people at all! What I am concerned about now is only you – you, who though full of the bloom of youth, languish without the joy of life. The *Rita* of life is that all women should, on coming of age, marry; for in marriage alone consists the joy of life. A woman unmarried is like a country without a king or a crop without a fence. Women alone will appreciate this point and this thought has been on my mind ever since I befriended you."

"Ha! ha!" laughed Champaka at first. But soon she assumed a serious face and replied: "Yes my dear, you may be right, but I have my own reasons for not marrying. In fact, I was also of your opinion, but later, circumstances have made me change that: I have now come to the conclusion that the male species as such, is treachery incarnate."

Lady Vikrama smiled understandingly and asked, "And what were those circumstances that put the stupid idea into your head, may I know? I do not suppose that anybody dared to make love to you in this life and jilt you, for, ever since you came of age, you have scorned the male?"

"You are right, my dear, it is not in this life. It all happened in my previous birth. Don't laugh before you hear the full story." With this she related the following story.

Long time back two pigeons lived in a jungle as husband and wife. They didn't have a child for quite a long time. The pair prayed to Mother Goddess as a result of which, the female bird laid an egg. They built a nest in a cluster of bamboos and protected their progeny with the greatest care. One day when the pair went out in search of food, the bush in which the young one lay, caught fire of its own accord, which killed the child. When the parent-doves returned they were heart-broken at the calamity. Disgusted with life, they both made a suicide pact to make an end of their lives by leaping into the same fire which burnt their young one.

As they sorried over the fire, the female pigeon noticed her mate turning his back on the fire, contrary to the pact and so, calling him, she accused him of treachery. But he did not listen to her but took to his wings. The female pigeon then went to Mother Goddess's temple and after bitterly complaining against the treachery of her erstwhile partner, prayed: "Mother, should I happen to be born as a female in my next birth, let me be born to a king and let my body have the natural aroma of *Champaka* flower and let me be blessed with the memory of my past life. Above all, let me not touch a male."

"You will by now have guessed that I was the female pigeon, and my vow stands there. Do you understand my pigheadedness now?" asked Champaka.

Bhatti who did not miss a single word of this interesting conversation from his hideout on the canopy in the form of a squirrel, jumped out of the ventilator stating: "Now I know. I shall see that my king marries this girl within eight days!"

The squirrel went to the mountain slope where it had hidden the gold coins lent by King Vijaya. Calling the faithful ghoul, Bhatti asked his human body to be brought which he entered and taking hold of the money, sought the King of Vijayanagar under the old name of King Salya.

13

Vikrama Weds Champaka

BHATTI in the garb of King Salya went to the palace of King Vijaya and sought his audience which was granted.

King Vijaya welcomed him with great joy and offered him all the respects due to a brother King.

After preliminary talks, the fake King Salya said, "I have come to repay the thousand gold mohurs which I had borrowed from you."

King Vijaya thereupon took the bag of coins from him and handed it over to his treasurer. He then entertained Salya to a lavish dinner. After some rest, they together went to the harem.

Asking Salya to wait outside, King Vijaya entered the apartment of his daughter Champaka and asked her to send her companion back to her husband who was waiting outside.

The news was unbearable to Princess Champaka, but conscious that the place of a wife was by her husband she reluctantly permitted the fake lady to join her husband. On her part, Lady Vikrama showed great distress at the parting but promised to visit her friend once in a month.

King Vijaya presented the couple with rich gifts and bade them goodbye.

As soon as the two were out of bounds of the city, Bhatti asked his companion of all that had happened during his stay in Champaka's harem.

King Vikrama who had by then cast off his disguise recounted all that had happened and he explained the secret of Champaka's vow, as he had heard.

Bhatti replied midst laughter: "I know all these, for, do you know I did not miss even a single syllable of your conversation? I was listening to it from my perch on the canopy – transformed as a squirrel!"

King Vikrama hugged his counsellor and friend for his ingenuity.

Suddenly turning grave, Bhatti said: "Your Majesty, I have just calculated that your six-monthly self-exile in the forest is almost come to an end. You must hurry up to your post."

"What happens to Champaka?" asked King Vikrama dejectedly.

"Of course, you are marrying her before we start home!" replied Bhatti.

Just at that moment a party of street-jugglers was passing in front of them. Asked Bhatti of them: "Hey! whither bound ye?"

"To Vijayanagar, to exhibit our skill before King Vijaya and win his applause," replied they.

"Is that so?" asked Bhatti. He added: "I have in my home an athletic girl who is a great adept not only in physical feats, but in the legerdemain of the highest order. If you like, I shall bring her to you now and you can make her one of your party. Your rewards will be still greater. What so you say?"

The jugglers consulted among themselves and agreed to take the girl.

Asking them to wait there, Bhatti and King Vikrama went a little further away when Bhatti disguised himself as an athletic girl and addressed King Vikrama: "I am a street-juggler and you are my *Guru*. I shall go with this party and awe King Vijaya with my performances. He will come to meet you later. This is the position."

After instructing him thus, the girl Bhatti joined the party which entered the city and sought audience with the King.

On the next day in the palace foregrounds the party started the performance amidst a huge concourse of human faces. The entire city had assembled there to witness them. On the opposite side where stood the harem, ladies of the royal household collected on the balcony, among whom was Princess Champaka wearing *purdha*, in view of her vow.

The performances grew in tempo and each item was more breathtaking than the one before. The illusions, sleight-of-hard and physical feats came in rapid succession to the utter bewilderment of the audience.

Bhatti who was disguised as the girl offered the star performances. Being a pastmaster in all the eight *siddhis*, he could effect almost any illusion. Human heads were hurled from above and blood showered like rain in a projected fight between the gods and devils.

Her final trick was this. The girl Bhatti threw up a rope towards the heaven which stood there erect and for all their straining of the neck, the audience could not discern the other end! Together with a man whom she called her spouse, she walked adroitly up and down the rope.

Saying that her husband had a telephonic call from heaven she sent her husband along the vertical rope. The man walked up the rope and vanished high above. After some time, to the utter dismay of all, a human head oozing with warm blood fell before her with a thud. On scrutiny it was found to be that of her husband! Girl Bhatti, then started wailing that the gods had murdered her husband out of malice against her powers, and that, as a dutiful wife, she would in the circumstances, enter the sacred fire.

King Vijaya intervening protested and pleaded with her that such a talented and young girl like her should not immolate herself and offered to maintain her luxuriously. But girl Bhatti would not listen.

To the utter consternation of all, she scratched the earth with her toe when a huge fire started roaring before her scorching the standers-by. What was worse, she entered it coolly carrying the head of her husband with her. The entire assembly stood aghast unable to do anything.

But within a few minutes, the girl Bhatti walked out of the fire holding the hand of her husband! There was not a soul who did not cheer the girl.

When King Vijaya complimented the girl on her extraordinary powers, she replied: "I know only a hundredth part of what my *Guru* knows! You should see him at work!"

The King's curiosity was kindled and he asked her: "Where, young lady, is he living?"

"Oh, he never comes into the city, he lives in the forests only.

The funny part of it is that he would not touch women and he taught me all this with a stick," replied she.

"Would it be possible for us to see him at his abode?" asked the King.

"Yes, Your Majesty, you can come with us tomorrow," replied the girl-athlete.

As arranged, the party, followed by the King, his Ministers, and ladies of the harem started. Champaka who was greatly taken in by the feats of the girl, desired to see the girl's master also at work, so she too followed under *purdha*, of course.

In the forest, comfortable tents were put up for the royal

retinue. Champaka occupied a separate tent which was covered all round except for an eye-hole through which she could peep.

Bhatti after briefing King Vikramaditya fully as to what he should do and say, introduced him to King Vijaya. The King bowed before the fake *Guru* Vikramaditya and praised the great feats exhibited by his *chela.*

The *Guru* grunted satisfaction.

King Vijaya asked: "If I may ask you, *Guruji,* how is it that you don't enter the city but prefer to live in the jungle? I shall be too happy to provide your holiness with all comforts in my city if only you deign to come."

The *Guru* replied: "Thanks for your kind offer, O King, but I am afraid I won't be able to accept it. I have my own reason, you will pardon me for it."

"May I know it, *Guruji,* if you don't mind telling?" asked the King solicitously.

"That is a long story", started the *Guru.* "Long back a pigeon couple lived in a jungle. They did not have any issue for a long time, but after praying to Kali, they got a young one. One day they left the youngster in their nest in a bamboo cluster and went out in search of food. As ill-luck would have it, the bamboo caught fire and the nest including the young one was burnt out. When they returned, they were overwhelmed by the tragedy. They then vowed among themselves to commit suicide by falling together in the same fire. As they flew over it, the male pigeon noticed the female one ducking against the pact, and ultimately flying away, while the male fell and lost its life. At the time of its death, the male pigeon vowed that should it be born again, it should never touch a female, for the female species as such was treacherous. I was the male pigeon and hence my reason for being misogynist."

Princess Champaka who was hearing this account could not contain her anger at this perversion of truth and tearing herself away from her secrecy, she came before the *Guru* and said "Don't lie, the female was never treacherous; it was the male pigeon which deserted and I know it personally, for I was the female pigeon."

The *Guru* replied "No: you are lying. You may be the King's daughter, but I can't swerve from truth."

Instantly a scuffle ensued between the two, Champaka and the *Guru*, and both were badly mauled by each other before others could intervene and separate them. It was some time before peace could be restored.

The King and his ministers who had come to meet the *Guru*, assembled together and lobbied things over. As a result of it, King Vijaya proposed: "Now that it is established beyond doubt that you two were the pigeon couple, I propose that whatever might have happened, you should be married together in this birth."

On hearing this, Princess Champaka bent her head when the corner of her mouth could be seen curling with a smile while the *Guru* was all smiles.

The entire party then moved on to the capital where unprecedented enthusiasm prevailed. The King celebrated the marriage in a grand manner and all the jugglers were richly rewarded.

The *Guru* in his bridegroom's attire sat on a richly camparisoned steed while the bride sat by him coyly on a mare and priests blessed them.

At that moment, Bhatti, in his official robe as Chief Minister appeared before the bridegroom and prayed. "Oh Great King Vikramaditya, the time is come for you to return to Ujjain, for your self-exile period comes to a close today!"

It was not possible at that time to measure who was most pleased at the announcement. "Hail unto Vikramaditya!" rose the spontaneous cry from all assembled. King Vijaya became most solicitous and reluctantly bade adieu to his daughter and son-in-law who started on their journey to Ujjain followed by faithful Bhatti and cart-loads of presents.

"Do you think, Bhoja", asked the statuette holding the fourth step, "that you are half as resourceful and valiant as King Vikramaditya who ruled from this throne? If you think you are, you can ascend."

On hearing this King Bhoja and his minister Nitivakya were greatly pleased and repaired to their palace and retired for the rest of the day.

14

The Rival Courtesans

WAKING up with the sun on the fifth day, King Bhoja went through the morning routine and after breakfast walked into the throne room where his Ministers and other officials were waiting for him.

As usual he worshipped the throne and started ascending the steps. As soon as he set foot on the fifth step, the statuette holding it broke into violent laughter and exclaimed "O Bhoja, I thought you were intelligent. Even after hearing the stories of my four sisters you do not seem to have become any wiser. How do you think you are qualified to sit on this throne from which the Great Vikramaditya and his unequalled minister Bhatti ruled this vast continent? Would you like to hear more of their exploits?"

"If you please," replied Bhoja.

The fifth statuette started:

In one of his half-yearly self-exiles from the kingdom, King Vikrama with Bhatti came across a pillar in the midst of a forest in which there was an inscription. It read: "If you go along the northern route you reach Alakapuri where Alakesa rules. This ruler has two courtesans in his *durbar*, Dhanavati and Gunavati by name. They are most beautiful and rivals in profession. They keep the company only of the richest people of the world. If you go south, you go to Pataliputra, where lives an incredibly beautiful girl born of a *tapaswin*. She is kept within a series of barricades of insuperable nature and she is offered in marriage to anyone who overcomes them and also succeeds in making her, who is not dumb, speak at least three words. But not more than one person can walk along either of these two routes."

The King's curiosity was roused by that tell-tale inscription and it did not take long for Bhatti to find it out. So he offered: "Your Majesty may proceed northward and tackle the courtesans while I shall move southward. We shall try to meet later."

King Vikrama agreed and went along the northern route, followed of course, by the faithful ghoul. On reaching Alaka, Vikrama entrusted his royal robes to the ghoul and dressing himself as an old weather-beaten mendicant, he wended his way to the house of Dhanavati.

On reaching the doors of her house, he coughed profusely and thumped his walking stick on the footsteps by way of announcing his arrival. On the door on a copper plate was written that whosoever was willing to part with a thousand gold coins for a day, might knock at the door. King Vikrama knocked.

On hearing the knock, Dhanavati instructed her aides: "If the man has the necessary cash, let him in. If it be a poor man give him food and water and send away; if it be the temple-bull give it grass and water."

The attendant opened the door. On seeing the old man she offered food and water. But Vikrama protested: "I want the mistress of the house, I have come to stay with her."

The attendant had one of her heartiest laughters for a long time and reported to her mistress of the old man's audacity.

Dhanavati became furious and taking hold of a wooden pestle meant for de-husking paddy, ran towards the door. Vikrama had to act the old man's part to perfection. He tried to parry the blows but got away with a few, swearing underneath his breath that she would have them doubly back.

Wisened Vikrama turned his way to the other lady's,

Gunavati's, which was not far off. There too, he read the writing on the copper-board, demanding a thousand gold coins as her fee. Mendicant Vikrama swallowed the lump that rose in his throat before he knocked.

On finding it to be an aged mendicant, the house attendant offered food and water, as was the wont. But the old man wouldn't have them. He said: "I don't want this food, but I want the companionship of the mistress of this house. Go and tell her." Making one of those wry faces that piqued women alone do, she turned her back on him with profound contempt and reported the old man's "indignity" to her mistress.

On hearing it, Gunavati, instead of taking the cue from her servant, raised her brow and with knitted forehead said, "Is that so? I feel privileged to entertain such a venerable old man. Please bring him in."

Although vexed, the servant conveyed the orders of her mistress in no uncertain terms. Yet, old Vikrama was not fully convinced, what with his late experience. Coughing profusely, he walked inside, thumping his walking stick often than was necessary.

Contrary to his expectations, Gunavati welcomed him with folded hands, washed his feet and went round him thrice. Leading him by the hand, she seated him comfortably and gave him excellent food and drink. She made him wear fine robes and generously entertained him in royal manner, saying all the while "I am greatly privileged by this visit of your venerable self."

What little doubt old Vikrama had of her intentions, vanished and he confided to her, "My dear, I have come from a faroff place, at this age, only to have the pleasure of your company and I feel so glad that you reciprocate my love with equal fervour. It is now your responsibility to feed me well and cure me of this wretched cough, and make me your suitable and constant companion," and twitched her cheek as he laughed open-mouthed.

Gunavati bowed again and promised she would do all that and more. True to her word, Gunavati lived with him in a manner that was the envy of gods.

Dhanavati, the other courtesan, in the meantime, had become frightened at the prospect of the old man whom she had beaten, meeting with any accident, and thereby causing further trouble. So she had sent out one of her men to follow him and report. When the man returned and reported the royal reception the ramshackle mendicant had at the hands of her rival Gunavati, she became greatly piqued and then and there vowed to put Gunavati to shame by hook or crook.

On the next day, when, as usual, the two courtesans attended the *durbar*, Dhanavati taunted Gunavati for keeping an old wretch as her companion. The latter retorted that the brahmin priest on whom Dhanavati noted, was not better than her man. Thus a heated altercation arose, resulting in a duel between them which attracted the attention of the King and all his courtiers. They interceded and separated them.

After that, Dhanavati who prided on her wealth, emptied a bagful of gold coins before the King as her penalty for the quarrel she picked up before him and challenged her rival to pay as much, stating that if she defaulted in doing so, she would call her slave.

Gunavati who had only her nobility to boast, returned home sadly, not knowing how she would meet the challenge. Old Vikramaditya noticing her sorrow importuned her to tell him why she was so crestfallen.

"What shall I say, my lord? My rival Dhanavati has challenged me to pay a bagful of gold to the King as she has done," and related to him the whole episode that transpired before the King. Old Vikrama consoled her saying that God would help her.

Calling the faithful ghoul, secretly ordered it to bring a costly jewel made of emeralds. It was brought within the batting of an eyelid. Holding it in his hand, he said to

Gunavati, "My dear, have this, which is the result of my life's savings. It is very costly and I guarantee, its value far exceeds the value of gold which your rival has deposited. Go and pay this up to the King as your penalty."

Gunavati who was dazzled by the brilliance of the jewel, could not believe her own eyes at first. Soon gratefulness began to shine in her eyes as she fondly embraced the old man for his timely help. At the same time Vikrama grew in her estimation a hundred-fold.

Saying "ta-ta" to the old man she ran like a doe to the palace and placed the valuable jewel before the King's feet stating that it represented her penalty for the previous day's quarrel.

The King was taken very much by the emeralds and he sent for the state-jeweller who estimated it as several times costlier than what Dhanavati had paid.

On the next day, Dhanavati was completely put out at finding Gunavati occupying her old seat as her equal! On enquiry she found out what had happened, and that knowledge sent her head in a swish. But that was only for a moment, and she renewed her resolve to humiliate her before the King somehow.

At the close of the *durbar*, Dhanavati invited the King with all his courtiers, members of the royal household, the entire four-fold army, including animals, for a lavish party to be thrown by her the next day. The King agreed and accordingly attended. The party turned out to be a great success.

On hearing of this, Gunavati too felt that if she did not throw a party to the King likewise, she would become the object of ridicule for her rival. But not having the wherewithal to do so she decided to tap the old man, who, she now realized, was something of a superman.

15

Princess who Would Not Speak

WHEN, therefore, on that night, Gunavati was more than usually entertaining, old Vikrama did not fail to notice it. So he asked impishly: "I guess, my dear, as you are in a very cheerful mood today, you expect some of your rich friends to drop in tonight?"

Gunavati was touched to the quick: "You are very much mistaken, my lord. Once I promise I never back out. You will come to know me better by and by."

In the meantime, old Vikrama had sent the invisible ghoul on a check-up of what transpired at the palace that day and felt relieved for he was able to divine the cause of her behaviour. Ultimately he asked her, "Now tell me, what do you want, for I feel you are in some difficulty."

Gunavati faced him up and reported faithfully what happened that day at the palace, and expressed her desire to entertain the King and his hosts in a manner that would outshine her rival. Old Vikrama again said that God would help her and went to sleep.

At dead of night he woke up and conjuring up his faithful ghoul ordered that Gunavati's house and the route from her home leading to the palace should be decorated most beautifully and all equipments and men should be installed before dawn for the entertainment of the King, his courtiers, palace inmates and the army personnel.

Gunavati's home was decorated like a palace and the garden shone like Indra's Nandana. The halls were spread with posh carpets and the catering arrangements were superb. Music and dance reverberated along the corridors and the city as a whole took on a gala appearance. The courses to be served were endless. Numberless women were there to attend to the comforts of the invites and everything was spick and span before daybreak.

When Gunavati awoke, she felt like Alice in the fairly land! She ran about the house like a lost child but every arrangement made her gape with wonder. She looked out of the balcony and the gay festoons fluttering loftily above the entire street and beyond beckoned welcome to her. She ran back and hugged the old man and wept, stating he was her god!

"Now, be a good girl. Go and invite the King and his entourage to dine with you. Hurry up," comforted old Vikrama patting her on her shoulder.

Changing into her best attire, Gunavati ran up to the palace and invited the King and his party including the army to dine with her. Already the royal household had got scent of this invitation by the elaborate arches that welcomed passers-by on the route to her house, and everybody put his finger on his nose.

"How is it, Gunavati, that you have managed these elaborate preparations so quickly?" asked the King.

"Your Majesty, if Dhanavati offered the choicest food to you, please be good enough to partake of the humble food which I am able to give," replied Gunavati.

The King agreed and as he walked, he was astonished by the wealth of decorations and the army of servers engaged for the occasion. The King and his party had never known such preparations and the food they ate was so delicious that they longed to stay there for more days. It was something like Sage Bharadwaja's feast. After food and *tambul*, Gunavati placed at the feet of the King a lakh of gold coins as her presentation to the King. The King rolled his eyes in wonder.

Dhanavati, the rival, when she heard the report her messengers brought of her rival's party, felt like a volcano.

On the next day the two rival courtesans were seated in the King's *durbar.* Dhanavati who was bent on disgracing her rival made the following proposal to the King.

"In the city of Pataliputra lived a King by name Panchasena. He died leaving a daughter behind. This girl is of extraordinary beauty. The Queen has now assumed rulership and has kept her daughter in a place which is utterly inaccessible by all human standards. She has proclaimed that whosoever hazards all the contraptions on the way successfully and makes the Princess speak three words will win the hand of the girl. Now I shall make by brahmin-lover to do it when my rival Gunavati should agree to be shaved bald and be my eternal serf. If, however, my man fails and her old mendicant succeeds in the mission, I agree to be so disfigured and become her eternal slave."

King Alakesa looked askance at Gunavati who had no other option but to accept the challenge.

On return home, therefore, Dhanavati called her brahmin lover and reported in toto the conversation that took place in the royal *durbar* and ended: "My dear, you are unrivalled in your qualities of the head and heart. So, it is up to you to go straightaway to Pataliputra and fetch the Princess dragging her by the apron!"

The brahmin, on hearing this assignment, became visibly pale and his tongue parched. He knew it was impossible for him to accomplish what had cost many a stalwart King his might and reputation. Yet his refusal to undertake the perilous task would bring no better result and so he replied with feigned boldness, "Go and tell the King that I am equal to the task! And tell him too that I want three months to do the job."

"That is just like you, my dear," replied Dhanavati smacking him on his near-bald head.

At the instance of Dhanavati the King placed at the disposal of the old brahmin a few elephants, horses, visa and provision for the journey. Dhanavati also gave him a lakh of gold coins for his expenses.

The brahmin reached the city of Pataliputra lumering. He took up lodgings at a fashionable place and rested on the first day. On the next day, carrying some money he repaired to the palace where the Princess-who-would-not-speak was said to be living.

He rang the bell at the entrance to the fort. Then men in attendance there demanded a thousand gold coins as the price of entry into the first gate which the brahmin gave. They took him from there to the second gate where a door opened and three statuettes appeared. One of them drew a chair for him, the second conducted him to the chair and the third seated him on it and shaved his head clean with a barber's razor!

The old brahmin disgraced thus ran back to Alaka overnight and reported to his darling Dhanavati all that happened.

Dhanavati heaved a big sigh but did not lose courage. She said, "What you could not accomplish can never be accomplished by the ramshackle mendicant. Don't worry," and the old man's courage which had ducked returned with renewed vigour at the assurance. He added: "Not by that mendicant alone, none whosoever, can do it; I can guarantee that."

After consoling each other in this wise, Dhanavati went to the King and duly reported the failure of the mission on the part of her lover, and added: "I now call upon my rival Gunavati to send her mendicant on this mission."

The King thereupon sent for Gunavati and told her: "You will remember Dhanavati sent her man to Pataliputra. He has returned disgraced and he confesses the failure of his task. Now, it is your chance to send your man to do it. If he turns up with the Princess successfully, all glory to you, for Dhanavati will forfeit to you not only her freedom, but her entire wealth. I think you are in honour bound to send your man on the mission."

Bowing acquiescence, she returned home and told her old man all about the Princess of Pataliputra, the conditions for winning her and the failure on the part of Dhanavati's brahmin. She ended: "The King has ordered me to send you on that quest. If you return successfully, all glory to me. If you fail, I have to remain a slave to my bitterest enemy."

"My girl! Don't you know that the quest for this Princess is more difficult than that of the Golden Fleece and many are the Ulysseses who have lost their all at it? You have been a fool to agree to it and the worst part of it is that I am the party that is involved most in this game," replied the old man.

"My lord, don't try to fool me thus. Whoever has measured your capabilities? I am not concerned with any other reason except this; in the event of your failure, I shall, from being your slave, have to become the slave of Her Excellency Dhanavati. If you are willing to accept that position for me, you are perfectly at liberty to fear as you do," said Gunavati.

"Well said!" patted the old man on the shoulders of Gunavati and continued: "For your sake I shall no doubt attempt the difficult task, but mind you, I can't guarantee success, for it is on the lap of gods. Now, go and tell the King that I am going to Pataliputra tomorrow and get from him a palanquin, a few horses and other necessaries. Tell him I will require 45 days for the work."

"I am going this instant, but listen, if you do not return on the 46th day, you may be certain that I shall have become food for *agni*', said Gunavati.

According to plan, on the morrow, the old man put on new robes of ochre colour and ascending the palanquin, left for Pataliputra in quest of the Princess-who-would-not-speak.

16

Mysteries of the Fortress

MENDICANT Vikrama had to pass through deep forests and across mountains before reaching Pataliputra. The faithful ghoul kept him company during the journey along with his *entourage.*

Tired and thirsty, the party arrived at the destination by nightfall. The city was a huge one and was so designed that numberless streets ran concentrically, and in the centre was the palace where the Princess-who-could-not-speak lived with her mother. At the outer entrance was mounted the challenge and before it, hung a marathon bell to announce any challenge that might be forthcoming.

Bhatti, as already told, had gone to this same city. Without disclosing his identity, he stayed in the house of an old woman who happened to be extraordinarily well-informed on matters of the moment. Besides, Bhatti freely mixed with the nobility of the town by his winning manners and was literally clearing the ground for his boss, King Vikramaditya, whom he was expecting every moment.

When, therefore, Vikrama the mendicant, entered the bazaar, he was not surprised to find Bhatti engaged in a game of dice with three others before a shop which was not crowded. Bhatti's roving eyes caught a glimpse of his master and recognised him. A code message passed between their eyes, as a result of which Bhatti brusquely left his game and walked in the direction of a choultry at the far end of the town and disappeared. Old King got down at that choultry along with his party. Paying his followers enough money to hold on for a month, he asked them to stay there and wait for him to return which might take about that time.

Bidding the party good-bye, he went a few yards further and by the side of a dilapidated house, changed his clothes to his usual robes. After that, he walked towards the bazaar where, at the other end, he saw Bhatti walking towards him. When they came near, they embraced each other fondly. Not finding the thoroughfare the proper place for talking things over, Bhatti took King Vikrama to the house of the old lady were he was staying.

On reaching it, he told the landlady: "*Maji*, here my brother has come from our place to meet me. I hope I am not troubling you if I ask you to prepare meals for him too."

"Oh, not at all; I am very glad to see him. Wait for a minute and I shall have cooked", replied she with a toothless smile as she walked inside briskly.

When she was engaged in her culinary work, she did not fail to notice the brothers counting a thousand gold coins out and tying them up into a big bundle.

Roused by curiosity the old woman came towards them and with her hands clasped together behind her back, asked them with a sheepish smile "What, my child, do you intend to trade with all that gold?"

"*Maji*, it is not for trading; my brother intends to meet the Princess-who-would-not-speak tonight, and this money is for paying the entrance fee", replied Bhatti.

"My goodness!" exclaimed the old lady. Continuing she said, "Don't you know that countless are the kings that came seeking her hand and had to return with shaven heads and battered reputation? Whoever would venture on this mad pursuit?"

"*Maji!*" interposed King Vikramaditya, "can you tell us all about how this Princess manages to disgrace all her suitors?"

"Oh, yes, listen, children. The harem in which the Princess lives is surrounded by ten fortresses. The entrance to the outermost fortress carries a copper-plate on which the terms are written. Before that plate hangs a monster bell. A suitor has to chime that bell. Then will come a few officers out of the fort and to them must be paid the entrance fee of a thousand gold coins. After payment they treat the suitor to a feast in which cooked and uncooked food, ripe and unripe fruits will be mixed and served. It should be eaten as it is and nothing should be left behind.

"They will then take you to the second fort. At the gate you have to push a button. Three statuettes will come out of it. One will draw a chair for you. Another will seat you on it and the third will shave your head bald. If you escape from them, you will be conducted to the third fort where two formidable boxers will offer you battle. If you floor them, you will be taken to the forth fort. There a giant ape will challenge you to a bout. After conquering it, you have to go to the fifth fort across whose gate a hungry tiger will lie in wait. You have to escape it to enter the sixth for where a rogue elephant will be on guard at the gate. You have to escape from it also to reach the seventh gate which is surrounded by a very wide and deep well which has to be jumped. At the eighth gate a deep marshy waterless canal runs, across which you have to walk and cleanse yourself of the mire with water contained just in the shell of a snail and a tiny piece of palmleaf scroll. You then walk across the ninth gate and enter a hall paved with extremely slippery marble when, more often than not, you will batter your head against the floor. After escaping that fate, you have to enter the tenth fort which is dark as ink. That hall has innumerable giant pillars made of rocky stones against which you are sure to knock your head squarely.

"If you escape that too, you will enter the harem of the Princess. You have to enter the reception room which is very artistically decorated with painted curtains and pillars inlaid with gold and gems. The hall is lighted night and day with a thousand oil lamps. At the centre is a cot made of the five metals. You have to lie down on it, but correctly, i.e., with the head at the head-end and the leg at the leg-end. If you make a mistake in doing so, some statuettes will emerge from below, one of which will pour a solution of cowdung on your head, another will shave your head, leaving five patches and a third will paint you over with bizarre colours and a fourth will further disgrace you.

"If, however, you lie down on the cot correctly, another set of statuettes will emerge, one of which will place before you a large mirror, another will smear you with fragrant sandal-paste and *attar*, a third will offer you *pan-supari*, two more will waft tender breeze from cowrie fans. A fourth will twang the *tambur* and raise exquisite melody and a few more will delight you with celestial dance sequences. In short you will feel as though you were seated in Indra-*sabha*.

"Then comes the last part of the assignment which is to make the Princess speak at least three words. I may tell you that she is pastmaster in *indra-jala* and she may put you to any number of inconveniences. After escaping from them all, you have to succeed in making her speak!"

When the old woman paused here, Bhatti intervened and asked "Mother, you have given us the correct perspective of the risk involved. But you haven't yet told us who that Princess is and what she looks like!"

Replied the woman: "She is the daughter of King Panchasena and her mother's name is Amrita. The King and Queen performed long and austere penance and as a result of it she was born. When the King died, the Queen took over the reign and taught her daughter all the arts and sciences and she took to them like fish to water and today she is unrivalled in her knowledge of the *shastras* and other arts. It is impossible to describe her beauty even by the thousand-tongued Adi Sesha. Briefly speaking, there is nobody as beautiful as she is in all the three worlds. And yet she is very devout and never fails even for a single day to propitiate God. Although she has endless jewels, her character is her brightest jewel. She is equally clever in the sphere of sports and pastimes that are indulged in by women."

On hearing this King Vikrama and Bhatti replied in chorus; "We have now understood the magnitude of the risk involved in our mad pursuit, and as a result, we feel it won't be advisable to go after her any more."

The old woman felt happy her guests had become wise as a result of her narration. She gave them excellent food. After partaking of it and eating *tambul* the two left by nightfall saying they would have a look at the bazaar.

When they went out, Vikrama did not fail to take with him the faithful ghoul with him. Bhatti had the bundle of gold coins they had counted out that morning.

After crossing many streets, they stood before the outermost fortress surrounding the Princess harem and King Vikrama chimed the huge bell hung before the copper plate thereby throwing down the gauntlet.

17

Vikrama Jumps the Hurdles

AS soon as Vikramaditya chimed the bell, the gates of the outmost fort flung open and from that emerged a man. He was the treasurer and he asked, "What may you require, sir?"

"I have come to see the Princess-who-would-not-speak", replied Vikrama.

"You have read the conditions on the copper-plate, yonder?"

"Yes".

"Then you may pay the entrance fee of thousand gold coins."

"Here they are," and Bhatti handed the bag over to the treasurer.

After counting and locking it up carefully, the treasurer took them inside and after making them wash their hands, served the customary food before Vikramaditya.

By that time the treasurer began to fidget because a second man had no further business there. Vikrama quickly sensed it and by his winning ways befriended the treasurer with his jokes and entertainments.

As reported by the old woman, the food served before Vikrama was a mixture of cooked and uncooked vegetables. King Vikrama was wrestling with a piece of sugarcane trying to munch it.

Bhatti who looked askance found the King's difficulty and in code words said, "O King, keep the uncooked food away and eat the cooked food alone. I shall take the former away at a suitable moment."

While the King was thus engaged in eating, Bhatti regaled the treasurer with his fanciful yarns. Vikrama called for some water and when the treasurer was away, Bhatti quickly tied the uncooked food in his uppercloth and hid it under his armpit.

The treasurer expressed satisfaction at Vikrama's performance in leaving a clean plate behind. He offered him water to wash his hands and subsequently sandal-paste, *pan-supari*, etc.

The three of them then started for the second fort. Bhatti was keeping the treasurer in a highly slated mood with his sweet banter.

On reaching the gate, they pushed the button and the gate opened, out of which a statuette emerged and offered a seat.

Close by the gate, the treasurer's stable-boy was waiting to escort his master. Bhatti in the twinkling of an eye, bumped against the stable-boy and pushed him into the chair when the second statuette clamped the boy securely in it.

"Oh, I am so sorry! I was so engrossed in talking to you, that I did not notice the boy standing in my way. I hope there is nothing that could be done about it now," grieved Bhatti.

The treasurer who, by now, was quite chummy with Bhatti, made light of the incident and proceeded further. Meantime the third statuette shaved the stable-boy bald and dismissed him. Turning a blind eye to this incident all three proceeded further and neared the third gate, walking hand-in-hand. On reaching it the treasurer said, "We have to stand back here and the competitor alone can go inside to meet the boxers."

As they stood before the open gate Bhatti signalled to Vikrama to collar the treasurer inside the gate. In a split second the poor treasurer found himself buffeted by the two mighty boxers who started attacking him from opposite directions and he ran between them like a shuttlecock and was beaten up like jelly.

Turning their back on this scene, King Vikrama and Bhatti, followed, of course, by the invisible ghoul, proceeded to the fourth fort. At that gate a mighty ape was standing on patrol. Bhatti on seeing it, threw the packet of uncooked food he was hiding under his armpit, towards it. In the ordinary course, the ape should have started eating it, but it did nothing of the kind but was sitting idle.

Bhatti became suspicious and from a safe distance examined the ape carefully only to discover that it was not a real ape, but a mechanical robot. He, therefore, ordered the ghoul to smash it to smithereens.

The fourth gate thus made safe for passage, they crossed it and proceeded to the fifth fort, talking all the while on the consummate artistry with which the ape had been made.

Across the fifth gate was lying the tiger with glowing eyes. Bhatti had the fifth gate opened for meeting that menace too. From a distance he threw the lump of meat which he had carefully preserved in the folds of his dress. His plan was, being half-starved, it would avidly eat when both of them would gain an entrance. Unfortunately, however, that tiger was more keen on looking at the trespassers than devouring the meat. So they hid themselves for a time to give it an opportunity of relishing the meat alone. No, the tiger's eyes roved in their direction alone.

Bhatti's keen eyes again scrutinized the tiger carefully and in a few moments, he snapped this fingers saying, "Oh, King, this again is not a real tiger, but cleverly made to look like one. I really marvel at the ingenuity of whoever has planned this nightmare." And as in the previous instance, he ordered the ghoul to break it to powder.

Wondering, the two proceeded to the sixth fort where an elephant was standing guard. Bhatti who had by now formed an idea of the working of the mastermind that created all these and the hallucination of its being an impregnable fort, was now more than ever confident of his own abilities to counter the traps, whatever they might be.

He made sure, by throwing pieces of sugarcane he had preserved, before the elephant at the gate, that it was one more dummy and a trap. Without wasting much time he asked the ghoul to make short work of it and proceeded further.

They were now before the seventh gate and there was a huge well yawning like a monster. It was impossible to cross it. Even if one tried a long jump, Bhatti suspected, deep down there might be some contraption that might swallow up anybody who falls.

He therefore picked up a big stone and threw it into the well and when it struck something below, lo! two planks of wood emerged from the sides and closed the well. King Vikrama and Bhatti looked at each other in wonder and walked safely across the well by the bridge so unexpectedly improvised.

Before the eighth gate lay the marshy canal across which King Vikrama walked while Bhatti did so on the shoulders of the faithful ghoul. On reaching the shore, Bhatti removed the mire from Vikrama's feet by the scroll of palm-leaf provided, and dipping his handkerchief in the water of the snails' shell, he removed the leftover from Vikrama's feet, thus leaving half the water back.

Together they walked into the ninth fort, after crossing the eighth. They had to walk on slippery marble of a portico when

Bhatti said, "O King, you have to walk across this floor very carefully or you will fall down. Ask the ghoul to bring some wax and a lighter. By smearing melted wax on the soles of your feet, you will get some grip which will help you to have some sort of balance."

Accordingly, he asked the ghoul to bring the materials and King Vikrama smeared a thick coating of melted wax on the soles of his feet before he walked. Bhatti, on the other hand, rode on the shoulders of the ghoul. Thus they successfully negotiated the ninth fort and entered the tenth.

The inside of it was enveloped in inky darkness and Bhatti said, "See, King, the inside has reputedly many pillars and the way will be zig-zag and you must avoid knocking against promontories. I shall take the form of a wasp and shall lead the way buzzing. You must listen to the buzz and follow it."

King Vikrama agreed and strictly followed the above advice and successfully negotiated the long and tortuous alley, as Bhatti went ahead buzzing.

The journey terminated before a wicket-gate which, too, they entered. On getting inside, they were agreeably surprised by the scene of a large and well-lighted hall, very tastefully decorated. A thousand oil lamps were burning.

At a short distance from the entrance lay the tell-tale cot, made of the five metals, brilliantly burnished. All around that cot, a number of female attendants were asleep. The King was admiring the whole set-up.

Bhatti in the meantime discarded his wasp form and taking his original form, reminded the King that he had more hurdles to overcome. He said, "Your Majesty, this is the cot mentioned by the old lady. Now, take this lime-fruit and place it on the cot when you will know the correct ends."

King Vikrama placed the lime on the surface of the cot which looked quite horizontal to a superficial observer. But to his surprise the fruit rolled towards one end which he concluded was the leg-end. So King Vikrama lay on it with his head at the head-end and legs at the leg-end.

As though by magic, a few statuettes appeared from nowhere, one of which showed a mirror before the King, another offered him *pan-supari*, a third gently wafted the cowrie fan, a fourth offered fragrant sandal-paste, another started dancing and yet another raised an exquisite melody with suitable accompaniments. Another set of statuettes started shampooing Vikrama.

Bhatti in the meantime went about like an imp tying the braids of the sleeping attendants, two together at a time, and before they rose up, extinguished all the lights. As a final stroke, he pinched the thigh of one of the sleeping girls and himself ducked beneath the cot whereon the King lay.

When the attendants awoke, disturbed by the dance-music and the screech of the pinched girl, they tried to rise up, but as each one was tied to the other by her braids and as it was dark, they knocked their heads against one another's. For about an hour there was a *melee.*

When at last some order was restored, they realized their predicament and untying the knots of their hair ran dazedly inside. All the while, more than even their own condition, they feared that of their mistress, the Princess, whom they feared the miscreant should have abducted. So they ran straight to the Queen's apartment raising a hue and cry.

In the inner sanctum of her apartment the Queen and the Princess were having a siesta. So when they heard the hullabaloo, they woke up with a start and asked the attendants what had happened. After several attempts, the attendants succeeded in communicating their fears, although gratified at the sight of the Princess. The Queen and the Princess who heard the story were agreeably surprised. Said the Queen, "The man who has so far evaded all the traps must surely be extraordinary. My girl, now it is up to you to do your best to outwit him, if you want to stop him."

The Queen Mother held a small conference at the close of which a beautiful girl dressed in richest garments set out from the apartment to meet the visitor, escorted by attendants holding lighted lamps, and followed by dance and music. Vikrama did not believe his own eyes at the sight; for the whole episode appeared fairy like.

As the party drew near, King Vikrama asked his invaluable aide, the faithful ghoul, if that girl was the Princess, for, he was not sure, as things stood, that she was not a fake.

Replied the ghoul, "O King, I shall draw the wick of the lamp she holds lower. If, after rekindling it, she rubs her fingers on a duster, you may be sure that she is the Princess. If, on the other hand, she does so on her hair on the head, you may reckon she is an attendant."

Immediately the wick of the lamp held by the girl started receding and the girl, after kindling the lamp, rubbed her fingers on her head! King Vikrama was not surprised, but bit his lips, deciding to teach the girl a lesson.

When she stood before him, he taunted her: "Naughty girl, is your mistress too beautiful to appear before me? Go, this instant, and send her here and tell her, I am not such a fool to be so lightly pushed aside."

The girl was thoroughly put out by this exposure and admonition. The whole party returned and reported what transpired before the man.

The Queen and her daughter held another conference and as a result, another girl, more beautiful than the first and better dressed, left to meet King Vikramaditya. She took with her a tray in which she carried endless varieties of food dishes.

On seeing her, King Vikrama asked the ghoul, if that new girl was the Princess. The ghoul advised: "She appears to bring food for you. Ask her to serve it. At that time, I shall overturn the cup containing ghee. If it is the real princess, she will order another cup of ghee to be brought. If, however, she is the cook or any other attendant, she will salvage the split ghee and serve it back to you."

When therefore the girl started laying the dishes before King Vikrama he did not demur. At the time of serving the ghee, the cup rolled over but the girl instinctively salvaged the split ghee and tried to serve it. But King Vikrama stopped her and said "Why is it, good madam, that you choose to leave the kitchen and try to deputise for your Princess? Do you think that a donkey can ever become a horse? Go and send your mistress to me and tell her I want no more of this fun."

The girl ran back abashed and reported to the Queen, of the newcomer's discovery and strictures.

The Queen thought for a while and heaving a sigh, addressed the Princess: "My child, we have so far never had any visitor who had crossed the second barrier. This man has crossed all ten, and is now before our portals. I thought I could put him off by the ruse of duplication. But apparently he is too clever for that too. It now rests entirely in your hands. The only way to make him lose his game is, not to speak the three words that have to fall from your mouth."

The Princess agreed to try.

The Queen mother thereupon walked into the drawing-room where King Vikrama was seated. She addressed him: "Valiant Sir, you have fulfilled all our conditions for the hand of my daughter except the last. Now, I shall place a cot here and ask my daughter to sit along with you, a curtain dividing you from her. If, before dawn you succeed in making her speak you shall have her hand. I may also tell you this, if in so doing, you resort to violence or touch her, your head will break into smithereens. You may perhaps know that we are great *tapasvins* and we are as good as our words. So don't belittle my warning."

"I am agreeable", replied Vikrama curtly and the Queen withdrew.

Returning to her apartment the Queen taught her daughter all the tactics to avoid being inveigled into conversation with the man.

18

Prince who Loved a Statue

A beautifully decorated cot was brought and placed at the centre, across which was drawn a curtain. Princess Amrita in her actual dress, occupied one side of it, with a sense of fatefulness and uncertainty not unmixed with a pleasurable sense of expectancy. Four of her attendants kept her company, all with sealed lips. The King sat on the other side.

After a time, King Vikrama addressed the Princess on the other side: "Oh Princess, I come from afar to win your hand and braved many a danger to meet you. The only distance between us now is three words which I request you to speak and show compassion on me."

Princess Amrita who had been steeling herself against all forms of poaching, could not so easily be made to resile from her determination.

Not finding any response to his direct approach, King Vikrama decided to play his trump-card – telling of stories – to make her speak. So, he invoked his dutiful ghoul on the curtain which divided them and addressed the curtain: "Oh Curtain, the Princess won't speak: sleep refuses to oblige me; the light is on and daybreak is not far off. So won't you at least oblige me by telling a story, helping me while away the time usefully?"

The Curtain started fluttering and in clear, ringing, human voice replied: "Oh King! I am so grateful to you for thinking of me. What shall I say except how I was born and how I now rot?"

"Oh, Curtain, tell me all about you, if you don't mind," decreed the King.

The Curtain said: "I was a small seed. A cultivator sowed me in his field, and tilled it. God rained and I sprouted into two, four and ten leaves. I grew one foot, two feet and so on; broke into branches. They called me King Cotton. I flowered, then fruited and ripened. I broke and emerged as cotton. The cultivator picked and sold me to girls who thumped on me and put me to innumerable tortures like ginning, carding and spinning. A weaver bought me as thread and starched and doubled me and put me into spindles and wove me through shuttlecocks into canvas. A cloth merchant stocked me. The Princess on the other side sent her men to purchase me and gave me to the tailor who tore me into pieces and stitched me into this curtain, chaining me to the ceiling with brass rings and holding me through eyelets bored into me. I do not mind all these travails but what pains me most is that I am used as the instrument of dividing you from the Princess. When I am so woe-bestruck, how do you expect me to tell any story that will interest you?"

The Princess who was first amused became very much interested in the curtain's account of itself. With a view to encouraging it to speak more, she ordered her attendants to untie the curtain, just to relieve it from the pain of hanging from the ceiling.

When the curtain came down, the King and the Princess had a deep look at each other.

Said Vikramaditya: "O, Curtain, the Princess appears to be very kind-hearted and that is why she has ordered you to be brought down. I hope you will appreciate her act and tell me a good story."

"Yes, now I shall tell you a good story, but you should listen to it carefully," said the Curtain.

"I promise I shall do so very attentively", replied King Vikrama.

The Curtain said:

In the city of Mandakinipura lived a King by name Manmathakara. He had a son by name Madanmohan. The King's minister had a son whose name was Tantraloka. These two boys were of the same age and they studied together. In course of time they became fast friends. Once the two boys went out to the forest for hunting. At mid-day they felt thirsty and so sought a lake, on whose banks happened to be a large banayan tree and a temple. After quenching their thirst, the two friends went inside the temple out of curiosity. As they were going round the *prakara* they noticed a statue of a girl holding a bouquet in her hand. The statue was so remarkable in beauty that the Prince immediately fell in love with the image. Tantraloka tried his best to wean him away from the foolish act, but the Prince would not.

As Tantraloka was thinking of a way out of the awkward situation he noticed the manager of the temple coming that way. So he approached him and asked him if he knew anything about the girl's statue. The manager told him the name of the sculptor who made it and the village he belonged to. After thanking him for the information, he told his friend, the Prince, "Please remain here for some days when I shall try to trace the original of this image and bring her to you."

The Prince agreed and Tantraloka went to the village to find out the house of the sculptor. Finding him at home, he asked the sculptor "Revered sir, are you the sculptor who made the statue of the girl with the bouquet at the forest-temple near Mandakini?"

"Yes", replied the sculptor.

"I think you must have had in mind a girl after whom you must have sculptured the image which was remarkably beautiful. I am interested in knowing who that original girl was, if you have no objection."

"Well, that is a big story. Sometime ago a potter from yonder village came to me at dusk with what looked like a gem. I was so taken up with it that I paid a large sum for it with the intention of setting it in an ornament for my daughter. I locked it up securely in a safe. But when I took it out in the morning, I found it to my utter dismay to be a human nail. I cursed the potter and myself for the bargain. However, I cashed on that tragedy by making the statue of the girl, to whom the nail must belong. You know, our *shastras* contain rules for such visualizations. And, I got my money back, but I have absolutely no idea of who that girl was."

Tantraloka thanked the sculptor for the information and went in search of the potter whose address the sculptor furnished. He succeeded in tracing the potter.

Tantraloka asked the potter: "Sir, did you sell a gem to the sculptor from yonder village?"

The potter who became afraid looked uncomfortable. But Tantraloka disabused him of his fear by explaining his purpose. Then the potter confirmed that he sold it, but added, "A couple of days before that incident, a hunter from the forest over there, brought to me at dusk what looked like an emerald. Poor as I am, I wanted to make an ornament out of it to my daughter and so exchanged it for a heap of earthen utensils which the hunter wanted. I had kept the thing safely, but when I took it in the morning, I found to my mortification that it was a piece of human nail. I could not afford to lose money and so I palmed it off to the sculptor!"

Getting a fair idea of where the hunter was to be found, Tantraloka repaired to the forest indicated and waited for the hunter to pass. He came and Tantraloka asked him: "Did you sell an emerald to the potter yonder? Please don't be afraid of telling the truth, for I have not come to take you to task for that."

The hunter said "yes" and Tantraloka asked him: "May I know were you got it from or who gave it to you?"

Replied the hunter: "I was sleeping beneath that distant banyan tree one night. When I woke up, something shining brilliantly appeared on the ground. I picked it up thinking it might be one of those fabled jewels that serpents are known to possess and felt glad I would become rich overnight. When I took it home in the morning and looked at it, it turned out to be a mere human nail-piece. I was very much disappointed but I cashed on it by passing it on to the potter!"

"But have you the faintest idea of who could have dropped the nail?"

"Not the least."

Drawing blank here too, Tantraloka went over to the shade of the banyan tree pointed out and waited for something to develop. As time went on, nothing happened, and the young man became disheartened. Night was approaching fast. He then decided, "Rather than go to the Prince empty-handed, let me perish here, in this forest itself by allowing myself to be eaten away by the animals."

As night set in, the birds started returning to their nests. That banyan tree happened to be the headquarters of a large number of parrots, one of which was the leader. The clamour of chatter they made diverted his attention to them. As it happened, the leader-parrot noticed Tantraloka lying beneath and it asked: "Young man, why are you staying behind here at night? This is a dangerous spot were wild animals abound. Unless you run away and seek asylum in the nearest village, you are sure to be eaten up by the wild ones."

"I don't mind being eaten up, for, the alternative in my case, is worse," replied Tantraloka.

"What brought you here, sir? If there is anything that I can do, I shall do with pleasure", replied the leader-parrot solicitously.

"Sometime ago a hunter found a piece of human nail right here and I am searching as to whom that belonged. If you know that, I shall be most obliged to know."

The parrot thereupon called on all the other parrots and asked them if they knew about the piece of human nail. Almost all of them denied knowledge. At the end, however, one parrot came before the leader and said, "You will remember, sir, sometime ago, I along with other parrots was on my return flight from far off island with our daily collections. On the way, at Mallikpur, in one of the island, was a seven-storied building, on the terrace of which a young lady was tying her hair. While so doing a part of her nail got clipped away and fell on the terrace and shone like a gem. I thought it to be a gem fallen from her crown or other jewels. So, when she went down, I alighted on the terrace, threw the fruit which I was carrying for your good self, and picked up the shining thing in my beak, thinking it will delight you. When in the morning, I presented it to you, you knocked me on the head – the scar is still here, see – chastising me for bringing the good-for-nothing human nail-piece instead of the fruit. Probably our friend refers to that nail-piece which you cast away."

"Right you are", replied the leader-parrot, recollecting the incident, and turning to Tantraloka said, "Now you know the source of the nail. But how would you get to the island, which is off the seven seas?"

"You are right", observed Tantraloka. "After all the troubles, my quest would appear to end here."

"I will help you here too", replied the leader-parrot. "About three miles from here is a huge peepul tree in which a roc couple, huge fabulous birds, live with their children. Everyday they cross the seven seas. If you can get into their good books, they can carry you bodily to Mallikpur."

Banking upon God, Tantraloka decided to approach the rocs. He thanked the parrots for their help and repaired to the peepul tree. He found out the tree and the nest where the young ones were playing. The parent rocs had gone out on their daily flight in search of food and so he waited.

Hardly had he been there a few minutes when a gigantic serpent came hissing in the direction of the tree and spotted the young rocs for its food. Quick as lightning, Tantraloka flashed his knife aiming it on the serpent which was cut clean into two. The young rocs which had become mortally afraid felt immensely grateful to Tantraloka for saving their lives and addressed him: "Sir, you have saved our lives at the nick of time and our parents who have gone out will be very grateful to you. But please don't stand here when they come, for they will mistake your intentions and harm you."

Tantraloka felt glad that Providence had given him an opportunity to earn the gratitude of the rocs and, may be, help in his quest.

The parent rocs returned at dusk and their young ones instead of clamouring towards them as usual stood aside with bent heads. The parents asked them why they were so and the young ones related how a serpent came to swallow them and how a man saved them by killing the serpent. The parent rocs saw the cobra lying slain into two. They therefore along with their youngsters sought out Tantraloka and found him lying huddled under a tree.

Addressing Tantraloka, they said, "We are glad that Providence brought you, sir, in time to save our young ones. We are eternally grateful to you. If there is anything that we can do for you, we are most willing to do."

Tantraloka then told them the object of his visit and the need for reaching Mallikpur.

The father roc said: "Oh, is that all? It is nothing for us. Please accept our hospitality and be our guest tonight, and tomorrow we shall take you to the seven-storied house at Mallikpur. Now you may forget your worries."

Tantraloka gladly accepted their invitation and after partaking of the food offered by them, slept soundly.

19

Mystery of Missing Daughter

TANTRALOKA got up early in the morning and walked out to where his steed was grazing. He rode along for a few furlongs and reached a small village. He met a villager into whose care he entrusted the steed till he return to the abode of the rocs.

Soon the parent rocs were busy preparing for their trans-oceanic flight. Bidding adieu to their young ones, they came to Tantraloka and asked him to jump on its back and cling tightly to its neck. He did so and the birds took off.

As they journeyed the birds described to Tantraloka the landscape below, the oceans they were crossing and what each was famous for.

One of the oceans, the birds explained, was famous for nine kinds of gems which it contained in abundance. On hearing this, Tantraloka expressed his desire to land somewhere so that he could lease himself. The birds agreed and landed on one of the many heaps of gems that lay scattered around. Tantraloka on alighting filled his pockets with valuable gems before seating himself once more on the back of the roc.

The rocs continued their aerial journey and in a comparatively short time touched down on the island of Mallikpur where they left Tantraloka. Before parting, they gave him one of their feathers and said, "When you have finished your business here and desire to return, think of us and fumigate this feather with incense and we will come to carry you back. Good-bye."

Tantraloka trudged on to the mainland and caught sight of the city itself. He dressed himself as a trader from foreign lands and made his way to the street where jewellers plied their trade.

At a crowded spot, he spread out his wares, the rare gems he had brought from the ocean, and started selling them.

The jewellers of Mallikpur saw the gems offered for sale by Tantraloka and were greatly struck by their quality, so they flocked to buy from him. They bought lakhs and lakhs worth of gems.

At Mallikpur lived Navakoti Narayana, a man who was far famed for his wealth. He was the richest merchant in the city and owned a seven-storeyed mansion fitted with all manner of conveniences. He had a daughter Rukmini by name, who was as beautiful as she was accomplished in the fine arts of music and dancing. She was of marriageable age.

This business baron heard of the foreign merchant and the fabulous gems he was offering for sale. Being the leading merchant of the city, his curiosity was aroused and so he came to the spot where Tantraloka was selling his gems. As soon as he arrived, all the other merchants bowed to him and stood aside respectfully. When he set his eyes on Tantraloka's gems, he was greatly fascinated by them and so, sitting down by the side of Tantraloka, asked him, "Where do you hail from, sir?"

Tantraloka replied, "I come from Mandakini. My father is a dealer in jewellery and I stepped here on my way round the world, taking a few gems to defray my expenses. My name is Bhairava."

Navakoti was greatly impressed by the young man's bearing and his pedigree and so he requested him, "I am most obliged to you for the details. Kindly be my guest during your stay in this city and accept my hospitality."

Bhairava readily agreed to the proposal and taking up his wares, repaired to the house of Navakoti.

On reaching home, Navakoti introduced him to the members of his family. Bhairava endeared himself to them all by calling them by appropriate epithets denoting relationship like uncle, aunt, cousin, etc. The merchant's daughter Rukmini too took to him fondly. In this manner Bhairava spent a few days in the household of Navakoti.

One day when they were alone, Bhairava addressed Navakoti thus: "uncle, I have been sufficiently long under your hospitable roof and I do not want to put you to further inconvenience. I have therefore decided to build a house for myself to stay by you and bring my wife too to live here for sometime. When the time comes for us to leave, we would like to present the house to you. You should not object to my proposal."

The old man, calculating as he was, readily agreed and offered the land adjoining his mansion free of rent. The best masons were called and in a short time, a palace equal in beauty to the old merchant's was constructed by its side.

In so doing Bhairava took a couple of masons into his confidence and after paying them handsomely, got a tunnel dug connecting his house with the ladies apartment of Navakoti's. This was done under cover of night with great secrecy.

Bhairava furnished his palace, adequately and lived there, taking his meals elsewhere. One night, he opened the gate of the tunnel and walked along the well-built passage holding a torch in his hand. He reached the other end which opened on the sleeping-room of Rukmini, the merchant's beautiful daughter.

Without making the slightest noise, he entered her room where she was fast asleep like a queen on her comfortable bed.

Making sure that no one was awake, he prodded the sleeping Rukmini with a stick and she woke up with a start. But as soon as she saw it was Bhairava before her, she was not sorry for the disturbance. Smiling approvingly, she asked him, "How did you manage to get in here?"

Bhairava explained to her about the tunnel along which he had come.

As they were conversing in whispers, the expression on the face of Rukmini was not lost on Bhairava in the dull red light of the torch he bore. So he told her: "Rukmini, I think you have thoroughly mistaken me. I have not come here for myself. Listen to me first. As you know, I come from Mandakini where reigns a king. He has a son by name Madanmohan. The minister of that State has a son of the name Tantraloka. That is me. Madanmohan and I are fast friends. Once when we were hunting, we happened to enter a temple in which an exquisite statue of a girl attracted our attention. My friend, the Prince, fell head over ears in love with that statue and started asking it, "Give me the flower you hold," not realizing that it was but a statue made out of stone. With all my powers, I was unable to cure him of his passion. So I decided to find out the real girl after whom the statue was made. With great difficulty did I find out, through the sculptor who had made the statue and I established that you were the model," and he explained the circumstance of her fallen nail-piece and the roc couple. Rukmini agreed that she did lose the nail-cutting on that particular day.

Bhairava said finally, "And now you know the purpose for which I came here. You must come with me so that I can carry you to where my friend is still waiting for us and without you he is sure to end his life forcibly."

Rukmini heaved a long sigh which was not altogether unpleasant and which indicated her acceptance.

The two of them then walked back along the tunnel to Bhairava's residence where they talked a long time about their plans for making good their escape and came to certain tentative arrangements. Bhairava then led the merchant's daughter back to her room and returned to his own room after locking the gates of the tunnel securely.

It was about eight in the morning when Bhairava emerged from his house and entered that of his neighbour Navakoti. The latter on seeing him enter, welcomed him profusely and conducted him into the drawing room where they sat on an exquisitely carved *jhoola* which started swinging gently.

Said Bhairava, "Uncle, my wife has come home this morning and I want you, aunt and your daughter to dine with us today."

"Ho, ho!" exclaimed the old merchant with boisterous laughter, mischief twinkling in his experienced eyes, and said, in a subdued tone, "of course, of course. Here comes your aunt, tell her yourself!" as though he was not sure of her answer.

Bowing gracefully to the merchant's wife, Bhairava repeated the request which was accepted to the great relief of the old man.

At Bhairava's kitchen, vessels clanged and the hearth was extremely alive, and a number of attendants flitted along the corridors.

At midday, Bhairava again stepped into Navakoti's, when he found the Navakoti family giving the finishing touch to their dress. Within five minutes they followed him.

"Where is Rukmini, uncle?" asked Bhairava seeing that she was not with them.

"Oh, she is not well, laid up with headache, stomach-ache and what not. We tried our best to persuade her to come with us if only to meet your wife, and not partake of anything. But she would not, and she is lying down with a bandage round her head."

"I am so sorry and disappointed," replied Bhairava.

"Don't worry, we shall bring her another day," replied Navakoti.

Bhairava conducted his guests along the well-carpeted corridors showing them some of his rare acquisitions – furniture, art-pieces, curios, etc. The merchant and his wife were manifestly delighted by everything they were shown.

They entered the dining hall. Bhairava called his wife and said, "Dear, come here, your uncle and aunt have come to see and bless you. Come and offer your obeisance to them."

In the dull light of the oil-lamps that shone from decorative arches, the silhouette of a young woman emerged which was covered in respectful *purdha* and prostrated before them.

As she stood up to receive their blessings, the merchant couple were struck with the resemblance of the girl before them in size and height to their own Rukmini and looked at each other meaningfully. The girl retreated clanging her bangles.

Dishes were laid and the guests took their seats. As Bhairava's wife was coming and going while serving the food, the illusion of the merchant and his wife that the girl was very like their daughter increased. At one stage Bhairava also appeared to have gone inside, when Navakoti asked his wife, "My dear, this girl looks like our Rukmini. What shall we do?"

"I also feel there is something peculiar about this business. You have got that *attar* with you? When she comes out next, sprinkle it on her *sari* and let us check up on our return home," replied the merchant's wife. Bhairava had returned by then.

When the girl came with the next dish, Navakoti sprinkled the *attar* without being noticed. Dinner over, Bhairava offered *pan-supari* to his guests who appeared to be rather in a hurry to return home.

Bhairava offered his guests the customary thanks and asking them to wait for a few minutes, he brought a bundle of rich presents for both of them and their daughter which he himself carried and walking with them delivered at their door.

On reaching home, Navakoti closed the door behind him and literally ran to his daughter's apartment and he found her fast asleep on her bed.

The merchant's wife also went inside the room and sniffed all over their daughter, but there was no trace of the *attar*. She returned and told her husband: "No, we have been foolish; there is no trace of *attar*. I have checked up. It cannot be our daughter."

With their suspicion thus cleared, the merchant settled down comfortably to his daily routine of the afternoon – sleep.

A couple of weeks later Bhairava came to the house of Navakoti and said: "Uncle, I and my wife are returning to our native place today. You have been very kind to us and I do not know how I am going to repay you. But I will have the satisfaction that I have given over this mansion and all that it contains in part return to your kindness. I have come here to bid you good-bye."

Navakoti's eyes became misty with tears. He protested: "We shall come with you to bid you good-bye."

As Bhairava and his graceful wife walked in front, the merchant and his wife followed them for quite a mile when Bhairava said: "Now, uncle, you must stop here. Please bless us," and addressing the girl he said "My dear, pay your respects to your uncle and aunt and get their blessings." As she did so, the party as a whole felt as though a part of their body was leaving. The parting was a very sad one.

Till their figures became blurred in the distance the merchant and his wife stood there looking after them and then returned home. The merchant's wife went in search of her daughter to tell her of the parting scene, but Rukmini was not on her bed. She called the maids and asked them where she had gone, but they said they did not know. A frantic search was made on all the floors but no trace of her could be found. Navakoti was informed and he too ran about the house hysterically and sent word to neighbouring houses for news of their daughter. He met with no success.

When they were making these frantic efforts to trace Rukmini, one of the maids brought a letter addressed to Navakoti as having been found on Rukmini's bed, which the merchant tore open and read: "Oh, my daughter, Oh Rukmini!" were the only words that escaped his lips before he fell down in a faint.

20

The Tragic Quartet

"DEAR FATHER," ran the letter which Rukmini left, "Please forgive me for leaving you in this way. I am going to a far distant country to marry a prince. Please don't have any fears on my account. Bhairava is more than a brother to me. He will conduct me safely to my destination.

"I owe you an explanation. It was I that acted the part of Bhairava's wife, for fear that you would stop my going away. I had access to his palace through a secret tunnel built underground. You will find its door just beneath my cot. When you threw *attar* on my sari, Bhairava noticed it and advised me to change my sari so as to put you off the scent. Beyond this there is no sinister plot on our part. It will be impossible for you to trace us, for by the time you read this letter, we will be flying over the seas. One of these days we will come and see you. Please comfort mother. Adieu."

Tantraloka and Rukmini literally ran to the seashore. On reaching it, the former fumigated the roc's feather which he had preserved and the birds appeared. Tantraloka and his companion climbed on to the back of a roc each and set off on their flight.

Crossing the seven seas the party finally arrived at Mandakini, the home of the rocs. Alighting there and thanking the rocs for their help, Tantraloka went to the village where he had left his steed. Riding on it he returned to Rukmini and both of them rode on the steed making their way to the forest-temple where Prince Madanmohan was languishing in his fond hopes.

On the way Tantraloka picked some flowers and making a bouquet of them, gave it to Rukmini to hold in the same manner as the statue, so that the Prince could recognize her quickly.

Soon they reached the forest-temple. Tantraloka said, "Madam, you enter by the southern entrance holding the bouquet in this wise. On the northern side you will see the Prince. He will immediately recognize you. I am staying out here."

"Why?" asked Rukmini.

"There is a reason for my action. I want to find out if the Prince has an abiding affection for me, particularly after all the trouble I have taken," replied Tantraloka.

"No, no", protested Rukmini. "I am sure he still loves you."

"Please do as I tell you. If he asks about me, tell him that I died on the way."

"No, I cannot say that!"

"Please for my sake tell him as I ask you, no harm will come out of it", pleaded Tantraloka.

Rukmini reluctantly agreed to do as she was told.

She met the Prince at the northern *prakara* before her statue. When she quietly went over and gave the bouquet he surveyed her from head to foot and after satisfying himself that she was the girl he was pining after, heaved a big sigh and smiled with satisfaction.

He looked around and not finding Tantraloka anywhere near, asked her, "Where is Tantraloka?"

"He died on the way."

Saying this she bent her head, watching him at the same time out of the corner of her eye.

On hearing her reply Prince Madanmohan was horrified

and drawing his sword plunged it into his heart, dying instantaneously.

His action was too sudden and unexpected for Rukmini to raise the alarm or otherwise prevent him. Now, remorse choked her: if only she had been truthful!

Feeling that she alone was responsible for the Prince's death she pulled out the sword from his heart and killed herself with it as she found no reason whatever for prolonging her own life.

Tantraloka waited a considerable time for the couple to come out of the temple; but when they did not appear he went inside and found to his horror the double tragedy.

He immediately realized that his innocent joke had taken two precious lives and so, convinced that he alone was responsible for their death, also took his life with that fatal sword.

In the afternoon, the temple manager who came round on his routine visit came across their three bodies. He recognized the Prince and the Minister's son. Sorrow overwhelmed him. Thinking that his own life was not more precious than the lives of those lying before him he too killed himself with the same sword.

In the evening, devotees thronged the temple, as usual, to offer prayers. While going round the *prakara* they noticed this tragic quartet.

News of this event spread like wild fire and the crowd of devotees swelled. All of them, not knowing the causes of the deaths, thought the deity responsible for taking the lives of four innocent people. Finally they decided that if the deity did not restore all four lives in response to their collective prayer, all of them should lay down their lives before the atrocious deity.

All those assembled prayed long and deep before the deity to restore the lives of the four dead persons. God was pleased with their prayer and appearing before them said: "I am greatly pleased with your collective prayer and the motive for it. The four dead persons will soon come back to life. Bless you all," and disappeared.

Just as he said, the Prince, Tantraloka, Rukmini and the temple-manager sat up rubbing their eyes as though they had awakened from a deep sleep. There was not a soul that did not feel thankful to the Almighty for the answer to their prayer.

The assembled devotees helped the Prince and his bride along with Tantraloka to return to Mandakini. The King and Queen were the happiest beings when they saw their son return with a bride who had no parallel in any of the world. Then Mandanmohan related the great part played by Tantraloka in bringing him his bride.

The Prince married Rukmini and at the same time Tantraloka too was married to another girl who was a suitable partner for him. And soon Prince Madanmohan ascended the throne and on doing so he made Tantraloka his Chief Minister.

At this stage the Curtain asked Vikramaditya: "Now, sir, who do you think out of the four who voluntarily took their lives out, made the greatest sacrifice?"

Vikramaditya replied with a twinkle in his eyes: "Of course, Tantraloka!"

The Princess-that-would-not-speak involuntarily retorted: "What a poor judgment! The Prince died because of Tantraloka's joke. The girl died because the Prince died. Tantraloka died because his Prince and his fiancee died. But the temple manager had nothing to do with those people and yet he died. Therefore his death constitutes the greatest sacrifice?"

By that time Vikramaditya had reclined on the pillow with success writ large on his face. The Princess too, realizing her big mistake in speaking, became dumb once again.

21

Man who Became an Ox

ALTHOUGH King Vikramaditya had won the first round, he felt from the look of the Princess who continued to throw a challenge, that he could afford to give her one more opportunity to keep her resolve.

He, therefore, invoked his faithful ghoul on the silken shawl which the Princess was wrapping around herself. He addressed the shawl, "Oh Shawl, your Princess refuses to accept defeat at my hands, nor does sleep come to either of us. There is still time before daybreak. May I, therefore, request you to tell me a pleasant story, so that I can spend the rest of the night listening to it?"

The Shawl replied: Sir, what story shall I tell except my own? I was born a silkworm. People spun my silk into thread, and wove me into silk-cloth which men from this palace purchased and gave to the tailor. The tailor cut me into pieces, stitched me, embroidered me and gave the finished work to the Princess. She, to cover her shyness, is wrapping me so tightly in folds that I almost gasp for breath. When I am in such a predicament how do you expect me to tell any story?"

On hearing the Shawl speak in clear human tones the Princess was greatly embarrassed. She immediately took the Shawl off and threw it down between her and King Vikramaditya.

King Vikramaditya smiled quietly at the Princess's reaction and felt encouraged. He addressed the Shawl which was lying on the cot, with the following words: "Oh Shawl, you can well see that the Princess is very considerable and understanding towards you. That is why she has freed you from her close embrace. Would you mind telling me a good story to while away my time?"

The Shawl began its tale:

There is a city called Ranganathapur where King Viravarman ruled. He had a daughter named Mohana and his Minister had a son by name Mativallabha. Being almost the same age Mativallabha and Mohana studied together and in course of time their companionship ripened into love.

One day, after Princess Mohana had come of age, she called one of her attendants and said: "My dear, I would like to meet my lover, Mativallabha, here tonight. Would you please arrange to bring him to my apartment without anybody else knowing it?"

Her confidante agreed and under cover of the darkness she managed to bring Mativallabha to the Princess's apartment the same night. The young lovers spent the night together. After that, it became a regular practice for them to meet together every night, without anybody, either in the palace or elsewhere, knowing of it.

As the days rolled by, the Princess realized that she had become pregnant. When she was past the fifth month, she felt she could no longer hide her condition from people like her mother. She told this to her lover and together they thought things over; they came to the conclusion that if the King came to know of their secret meetings and the consequences, he would not only not approve of the alliance but would definitely order their banishment if not the killing of the minister's son. So they decided that the best course of action would be to leave the country together for good.

One night according to their plan, they took some money and secretly escaped from the country. They walked for many miles and after reassuring themselves that they could no longer be pursued, they came to a stop at a choultry at the outskirts of a large city. They lived there as husband and wife.

Five months later, the Princess felt that the time had come for her delivery and so she asked her husband to bring a midwife from the city to attend on her.

Mativallabha who had had no experience of family life, much less an experience of this nature, felt rather overwhelmed. Then, however, out of necessity he went into the heart of the city seeking the help of a midwife. It was the custom in those days for midwives to live in the households of courtesans. Therefore, Mativallabha, hearing this, went to that part of the city in which the courtesans lived and waited hopefully outside one of the houses.

After a while, the mistress of the house came out and when she saw Mativallabha, she was much attracted by the appearance of this stranger. She immediately took a fancy for him, and felt that she must have his company. So she invited him to come into her house and give him fruits and drink. These preliminaries over, Mativallabha asked her: "Madam, I have come here on an urgent mission. My wife who is at the choultry, is about to deliver and so I have come here to fetch a midwife. I would be grateful to you if you would kindly lend me the services of one of your people. I shall, of course, reward her and bring her back safely."

On hearing his request, the mistress of the house thought for a moment and then replied: "My women have gone out to the bazaar and are expected back here very soon. As soon as they return, I will certainly send one of them along with you to help your wife. In the meantime, please partake of this *pan* and relax."

Mativallabha felt grateful for the lay's offer of help, accepted the *pan* she offered and chewed it. Immediately, he found himself transformed into an ox.

The lady of the house brought an iron chain from within

and tying it round the neck of the ox, led it to the shed where she tethered it and provided it with water and hay.

At nightfall she went to the cow-shed, brought the animal into her room and by giving it an antidote, she converted it back to a man, the minister's son. During this transformation process Mativallabha lost his memory completely, with the result that he forgot who he was and how he came to be there. He became her plaything and did all that she asked him to do. Several days passed in this manner, i.e., during the day-time he was an ox chewing the cud and, at night, the courtesan's paramour.

In the meantime, Mohana in the choultry was greatly agitated by the non-return of her husband. Hour after hour her pain increased. Tears flowed freely from her eyes. She wept her heart out at the thought that though born a Princess she had to suffer like a vagrant in this manner. She would have thought it paradise had her husband been with her. Many uncharitable thoughts crossed her mind, but she refused to entertain them and waited for the arrival of her husband with each advancing minute.

When at last her pain increased and became unbearable she started to cry which attracted the attention of passers-by who immediately rushed to her aid. Some women of the neighbourhood too came hurrying to her side to give whatever help was in their power.

By God's grace a son was born to her with no great difficulty. The neighbours were greatly moved by the story Mohana told them of her confinement and how she appeared to have been forsaken by her husband at the very important hour of her child's birth. At the same time she refuted the suggestion that her husband would have left her of his own volition.

After the first few days of the child's life, the people of the locality put their heads together and advised Mohana to file a petition before the King of the city, stating her case and requesting him to help her in tracing her husband.

Accordingly, Mohana went to the palace with the infant in her arms and sought an audience with the King. Dharmangada, the King, summoned his Minister and ordered him to render whatever help the lady needed. But, Mohana insisted on presenting her case before the King personally to which the King agreed.

She said, "Oh, Gracious King, my husband came into this city some days back for the purpose of seeking a midwife's help for my childbirth, but he has not returned since. I have had no occasion to complain against my husband and I am sure that he would not have left me like this of his own accord. My efforts to trace him have failed and I fell, under the circumstances, there is no purpose in my continuing to live without him. Please help me to set up a large fire in which I can immolate myself along with my child."

The King on hearing this strange request felt greatly embarrassed. He asked his Minister: "How is it, in our city, a thing like this can happen?" and he ordered that searchers be sent out immediate and that her husband be restored to her before nightfall.

The Minister, in his turn issued orders to the authorities responsible for carrying out the King's instructions. The whole machinery of the King's police force moved in this search for the missing Mativallabha, but only to return empty-handed. Whoever would suspect that he would be an ox by day and man by night? The result was communicated to the King, whereupon he invited Mohana to his palace and said, "Great Lady, I have tried my best to trace your husband, but I have not been able to find him. But something tells me that you should not lose hope. If you will but wait for sometime, I shall have further enquiries made."

Mohana was adamant. She would not listen to the King. So he said: "I shall place at your disposal enough money and convenience for you and for your child. You can live as long as you wish here, or in any part of the world. I beseech you to abandon your intention of entering the fire."

But Mohana felt that the King had an ulterior motive in offering to help. So she started insinuating against him.

The King quickly perceived her line of thought and finding no other way out of the situation, he ordered his followers to raise the fire and allow the lady to fulfil her wish.

It was dusk. According to the orders of the King a huge fire was lit. Mohana went to a nearby pool and having bathed herself and the child, came to the place. After going round the fire thrice, she was just about to enter it.

It so happened that, at that precise moment, her husband, Mativallabha, in his human form, was wandering along that thoroughfare in the company of his courtesan. On seeing the crowd and the raging fire his curiosity was aroused, so he made his way to the front of the group. There he saw Mohana and his child standing at the edge of the flames. Instantaneously his mind flew back and memory rushed forward. He recognized his wife and guessed her intention. Throwing aside the woman's hand he was holding, he rushed towards the fire crying "Mohana! Mohana!" and tried to pull her out of the flames that by then had started licking around her. He was just loo late. Mohana and her child were swallowed up in the merciless flames. Mativallabha stood looking at this tragedy shocked but soon realizing that he was responsible for the death of his innocent wife and child, did not lose time in entering the fire himself.

The courtesan saw her paramour entering the fire and as she could not bear the thought of separation from him, she too, entered the fire.

By this time a hue and cry had arisen which attracted the attention of the King and his Minister who were standing a few yards away in a pensive mood.

When the news was conveyed to them that along with the lady and child, her husband and his mistress had also entered the fire, they came to the front. It then struck the Minister that the tragedy was due to the inefficiency of his ministry. He felt himself to be personally responsible for the loss of these precious lives and decided that its expiation lay only in offering his own body to the fire. Bidding farewell to his Master and King, the Minister calmly entered the fire while King Dharmangada stood back petrified at the sight.

It did not take long for the King to realize that despsite the Minister's admission of his inefficiency, the responsibility for the entire episode lay on his own shoulders. But he thought of a better means for making amends for the tragedy. He, therefore, whipped out his sword from its sheath and hastened to the temple of Mother Goddess in the palace.

Sword in hand, he prayed to the Goddess; "Mother, what fault have I perpetrated to witness this unholy tragedy and who is responsible for the loss of five innocent lives? If You will but care for me and my kingdom I pray that you should restore these lives which have been consumed in the flames, or else, please accept this head of mine which I shall place before Your feet, as my last offering." And he raised the sword.

Immediately the Mother Goddess appeared before him and prevented him from using the sword against his head. She said, "My son, I am greatly pleased with your prayer. Here, take this *bhasama* and throw it into the fire and all the five of them will emerge out of it safely. Bless you."

The King fell on his knees before Mother Goddess and praised her heartily. Having donc this, he ran to the scene of the tragedy.

As instructed by his family deity, he threw the *bhasma* on the flames, when true to Her word, Mohana, her child, Mativallabha, the courtesan and the Minister walked out of the fire as though they were coming out of a shower of milk.

The King, and the people gathered there, were greatly overjoyed at this happy ending of what had threatened to become an ugly tragedy. The King greeted them warmly, invited the couple to his palace and entertained them to a sumptuous dinner. During the course of dinner, the King learnt all the antecedents about Mativallabha. Being greatly pleased with him, King Dharmangada appointed Mativallabha as his Finance Minister. The courtesan, whom the King honoured by rich presents, was happy to return to her home.

At that stage, the Shawl asked Vikramaditya, "Sir, you have heard the story. Tell me now correctly, of all the five persons who fell into the fire, whom do you applaud most?"

King Vikramaditya, smiling mischievously, replied, "of course the courtesan's action is most commendable."

The Princess-who-would-not-speak could not contain her ire on hearing this outrageous reply. So she retorted: "Mohana fell into the fire because her husband could not be traced. Mativallabha fell into it because he was ashamed of his past. The courtesan entered the fire because of her infatuation for her lover. The Minister who had nothing to gain by falling into the fire did so and he personifies the true spirit of a noble man. Hence, the Minister's action alone is to be commended."

Hearing this, King Vikramaditya remarked: "What a fool have I been? I am ignorant of something that is known to the Princess even though she is a woman."

But the consciousness of her interjection into the dispute made the Princess dumb once again. Her eyes nevertheless threw sparks of challenge.

22

The Resourceful Thieves

THINKING intently as to how he could break the silence which had for the third time taken possession of the Princess, Vikramaditya once again invoked the invisible ghoul in the bed-spread covering the Princess and entreated it to narrate another story. Particularly as daybreak was still far off.

Feeling at once elated at Vikrama's request and expressing grief at the insignificant role assigned to it as the Princess's bed-spread, it asked: "What story shall I tell in my present grief-stricken state?"

The Princess threw the bed-spread with trepidation between the cots occupied by her and Vikrama, astounded that it possessed the magical power of human speech. At Vikrama's sustained request, the bed-spread related as follows:

There lived in the town of Madakipur, in the kingdom of Kundala, a thief named Kartikeya. He had mastered his art so well that he was known as the "perfect thief". He had likewise trained his four sons whose names indicative of their proficiency in the art of thieving, were Full-thief, Three-quarter-thief, Half-thief and Quarter-thief.

Wishing to put to the test the prowess and skill of his four thieving sons, the father, "perfect thief", sent for his last son and addressed him, "Oh, Quarter-thief, you must proceed to Kundala immediately and bring back the spoils of your profession before nightfall."

In obedience to his father's command, Quarter-thief set out on his mission armed with a piece of broken mud pot shaped like a rupee coin and tied conspicuously to the corner of a shawl hanging over his shoulder.

On the way, he encountered a barber who was half-way through serving a peasant customer. He enticed the barber by promising double wages provided he would stop work on the peasant and attend on him immediately.

Attracted by the offer of a higher price for his services, the barber implored the peasant to wait and gave Quarter-thief a clean shave. Quarter-thief then asked for change for a rupee holding in his hand the coin-shaped mud-piece wrapped in his shawl. The poor barber was in no position to give change, whereupon Quarter-thief asked him to accompany him (Quarter-thief) to a nearby shop where change could be had.

As the barber started to leave, the peasant who was half-shaven protested. Quarter-thief thereupon suggested that the barber's five-year-old son should go with him. The latter entered one of the leading cloth shops, seated himself before the proprietor with the barber's son on his lap and asked to see the goods.

Being carried away by Quarter-thief's well-groomed appearance, the proprietor showed him costly silks and saris.

Quarter-thief pretended to examine the quality of the goods as a connoisseur, rejected a few items and finally selected goods worth some ten-thousand rupees. Getting ready to leave the shop, he blatantly bluffed the proprietor. "My wife and her relatives are waiting in my cart in a park close by. I wish to take the goods to them and get their approval. Could you therefore send along an attendant with me?"

Unfortunately for the proprietor, none of his attendants could be spared. So he was rather in a dilemma.

Taking advantage of the proprietor's unwillingness to let go the customer, Quarter-thief cleverly suggested that he would leave his young boy in the shop and take the goods.

Believing the boy to be the customer's son and proper security for the goods, the proprietor allowed Quarter-thief to leave his shop with the goods.

Once out of the shop, Quarter-thief lost no time in returning to his father who showered praises on his son for his worthy performance.

While the thieves were gloating over their ill-gotten gains, the proprietor of the shop grew apprehensive as time passed and the customer failed to reappear before him. At last, his patience exhausted, he asked the boy angrily: Where is your father? Sufficient time has elapsed to enable him to make three trips each way to the park."

The boy replied: "My father is shaving his customers."

The boy's reply not only puzzled the proprietor but annoyed him as well, as he thought the boy was being funny. As a precautionary measure, he tied the boy to a pillar lest he should run away; the boy frightened out of his wits, started crying and attracted the attention of passers-by. In the meantime, the barber went in search of his son whom he found in a sorry state in the shop. His son's plight infuriated the barber and he quarrelled so violently with the shopkeeper that the King's men had to intervene and take them before their King, Gopal, who conducted a proper inquiry into their dispute.

When he learnt what had happened during the hours of daylight in his kingdom, the King felt ashamed and warned the officers responsible for law and order thus: "I am sure that this thief, who has tasted without any effort the fruits of his nefarious activities, will return tonight in search of pastures anew. Hence I want you all to be very vigilant and catch the thief. Should you fail, punishment to you will be very severe."

The King and his Minister then conferred between themselves on the course of action to be adopted in the future.

While the King and his officers were taking stringent security measures, Perfect-thief Kartikeya called his third son, Half-thief, and expressed the desire that he should prove his skill at thieving that very night.

Accordingly, Half-thief made his way to the city of Kundala with some funds in his hands. While reconnoitering in the city, he heard of the exploits of his brother and about the King's order to the headman of the city that he should capture the night prowler without fail. He also gathered the information that the headman had a daughter who had married very early in life and whose husband had not visited her since their marriage. He was further informed that the headman's daughter had attained puberty and that his son-in-law had reportedly gone to far-off lands across the seas. Having found out all that was to be gathered about the headman's family, Half-thief bought himself appropriate dress so as to give the impression that he had just returned from a trading trip overseas with all presents that would gladden the heart of every member of the headman's family including his married daughter.

Announcing himself as the headman's son-in-law, just disembarked from the ship, Half-thief entered the headman's house at night just when the latter was having a hurried meal, entirely pre-occupied with thoughts of capturing the thief. Half-thief, however, in order to distract attention from himself cleverly paid his respects to the headman and his wife and gave them the valuable presents which he had brought with him. Needless to say everyone was pleased including the daughter who put on her best clothes and all her jewels with a view to receiving her supposed husband and pleasing him.

As the headman prepared to leave his house, Half-thief expressed a desire to accompany him and see the city; the former agreed to this request. On their way, they came across a pillory which had been put up prominently in a public place. Half-thief with feigned innocence inquired of the headman: "Uncle! What tree is this?"

"This is no tree but a pillory used to punish wrong-doers," replied the headman, whereupon Half-thief expressed interest in understanding how it operated and offered himself for the purpose of demonstration. Would any one, however agree to experiment on his son-in-law and incur his displeasure? So he himself got into the pillory to demonstrate how it worked. Seizing this opportunity, Half-thief fixed the headman in such a way that he could not get out of the pillory without the help of another person. Half-thief then hastened to the headman's house and frightened everyone there saying: "The headman has incurred the wrath of the King and has been pilloried. I am apprehensive that the King will confiscate the headman's properties." So saying he collected all the cash and jewels in the house pretending that he was going to secrete them in a place beyond the King's reach. Not merely that, he spent the early part of the night with the daughter and left the house with the valuables as they began to sleep as a result of mental strain and overtiredness. On reaching home, Half-thief earned his father's praises for his daring exploits.

At dawn, when his co-officers made a final round of the city, they found their headman in the pillory overcome with shame. They released him and took him before the King to whom he related his previous night's experiences. The King disgraced the headman for his foolishness, whereupon the Minister issued a boastful challenge that he would catch the thief that night.

It was now the turn of the second son of Kartikeya, Three quarter-thief, to prove his mettle. With his father's approval, Three-quarter-thief made his way to Capital Kundala. He heard of the Minister's vow to catch him and being very intelligent he also found out that the minister frequented a danseuse called Meena who lived in Kundala.

When he learnt of this side of the Minister's life, Three-quarter-thief got a splendid idea which he proceeded to put into effect. He went straight to the market, bought dress materials and other accoutrements which would enable him to dress exactly like the Minister. With meticulous care, he dressed himself so as to resemble the Minister even to the smallest detail.

At twilight when quick identification of persons is rather difficult, he went to the danseuse Meena's house and called her by her name. She was completely taken in by the fake Minister. As it was never the custom of the real Minister ever to call on her so early in the night she inquired: "How is it that you have come here long before the King's Council is over?"

"An important mission has brought me here so early tonight", he said and continued: "The thief, about whose recent exploits we all know, has planned to dress up like me, the Minister, and to commit theft in your house. So I have come to warn you. Please find a baton and a piece of rope so that we may trap the thief when he actually makes his appearance here tonight.

Meena complied with the fake Minister's instructions.

To while away the time, began to entertain each other.

At the appointed hour, the real Minister entered Meena's house, having dispatched his guards to strategic points in the city, with instructions to be alert and not to let the thief escape under any circumstances.

On spotting the real Minister enter Meena's house, Three-quarter-thief shouted, "Thief, Thief!" and running towards him belaboured him so severely that he fell down unconscious. Three-quarter-thief then removed the Minister's valuable dress including his marks of authority, re-dressed him shabbily and tied him to a pillar in the courtyard with the rope supplied by Meena.

After re-assuring Meena, Three-quarter-thief excited her avarice with an offer to re-make her old jewels in bigger and newer designs. She succumbed to the temptation and handed him all her valuables.

After staying there for the rest of the night, Three-quarter-thief gave her the slip, carrying with him all her valuables together with the Minister's personal effects. As he left, he jeered at the bound Minister for allowing himself to be trapped so foolishly.

As in the previous instances, the King came to know of his Minister's shameful plight through his subjects. He was beside himself with rage and not realizing what was in store for him the King vowed that he would catch the thief that night single-handed.

Kartikeya's joy knew no bounds when he saw that three of his sons had acquitted themselves creditably and had emerged unscathed from the ordeals set for them.

Priding himself on their training he finally put his eldest son, Full-thief, through his paces. At his father's bidding, Full-thief reached Kundala as expeditiously as he could and was told of the King's vow to capture him at any cost. Determined to put the King to shame, he thought of a plan. He bought materials necessary to set up a *pan* and cookies shop and at midnight, spread his wares on the side of the road which led from the city of Kundala to his hometown of Madakipur.

In order not to be outwitted by the thief whom he expected that night, the King made fool-proof arrangements designed to catch him; and so was having a final checkup going round and inspecting every nook and corner of the city. Satisfied that every arrangement was as perfect as possible, he was about to return to his palace when he noticed a small light gleaming in the distance. He proceeded to investigate it and encountered Full-thief in the garb of a petty road-side hawker. He inquired what the hawker was doing there at dead of night.

Respectfully getting up from his place and feigning nervousness, he replied: "I keep shop here daily at this time. Some thieves frequent my shop every night. The last two nights, a thief, came to me and said he had committed theft in the headman's house and robbed the Minister. I expect him to come tonight. He rewards me richly for *pan* and eatables supplied to him by me.

The King thought to himself: "Here is my chance to catch the thief through this hawker. I must befriend him." He made a cautious approach to the hawker, letting him into his plans with the promise of a rich award. Pretending to succumb to the King's temptation, the hawker impressed on him the necessity for absolute secrecy on their part and said: "you must disperse your men in different directions and must be alone with me."

The King agreed and did as he was told.

After a while the hawker suggested: "If you are seen with me, the thief will make a detour. You had better remove your valuables and clothing and hand them to me. You may also get into this bag so that you will not be seen. As soon as the thief approaches, I will let you out of the bag and you can immediately catch hold of him."

Even though the hawker's suggestion was ridiculous, the King did not stop to weigh its pros and cons in his anxiety to outwit the thief. So, the King played completely into the hawker's hands.

Immediately the King did as requested by the hawker; the latter made a bundle of the valuables, put out the light and raising a hue and cry quit the spot with alacrity. In the melee that ensued, all the guards beat one another in the dark and trampled on the bag which contained the King. It took them quite some time to realise the joke perpetrated on them and they began to look for their King. He was found crestfallen in the bag, while the five accomplished thieves were celebrating their success.

When the bed-spread finished its story, the Princess' Shawl asked Vikrama: "Oh, King of Kings! Who is clever, the four thieves or King Gopal and his men?"

Vikrama in order to provoke the Princess replied: "Of course, the King and his men."

Hearing this verdict, the Princess asked angrily: "Have you been sleeping all the while so that you have completely misunderstood the story?"

Expressing regret for his 'hasty' verdict, Vikrama made the Princess feel that he purposely did so in order to make the Princess-who-would-not-speak speak to him.

At this juncture, the Shawl explained that as Vikrama was the King of Kings the Curtain and Bed-spread wanted the Princess to realize Vikrama's worth. That was why they had narrated three stories and requested Vikrama's verdict on them. With the intention of making the Princess speak, Vikrama had deliberately given the wrong verdict, and as a result the Princess had failed to maintain silence. Now that she had broken her vow of silence, Vikrama could take her for his wife and together they could lead a happy life.

The conclusion of the Shawl Immersed the Princess in deep thought.

23

The Princess Marries Vikrama

WHILE the Princess was ruminating over defeat at King Vikramaditya's hands the latter addressed her: "Oh, Princess-who-would-not-speak! I accepted your challenge, entered your heavily guarded palace without being detected and had the Curtain, Shawl and Bed-spread narrate respectively three very interesting stories. I deliberately gave wrong opinions regarding the moral of each of those stories in order to provoke you to speech. You still object to my taking you as my wife?"

The Princess did not reply but reflected to herself: "However clever woman might be, a woman is ever foolish!"

Without waiting further for an answer from the Princess, Vikrama went over to the former's cot, took her hands in his and embraced her. Realizing the futility of further resistance on her part, and succumbing to Vikrama's caresses, the Princess replied: "My love and saviour! I am your slave. Therefore please marry me according to custom and Vedic rites."

Vikrama conceded to the Princess's fair request.

Overjoyed that such a fine person as Vikrama was her husband-to-be, the Princess immediately sent word to her mother, Amritamohini, through her confidante, of the events which had occurred in her chamber. She also sent a request to her mother that she send for the family's high-priest and make all necessary arrangements for her marriage with King Vikrama.

What more pleasurable duty could there be for Amritamohini than to arrange for her beloved daughter's marriage! Needless to say, King Vikrama's marriage with the Princess was conducted under the most auspicious signs possible and many were the happy recipients of alms on that occasion. Amidst great rejoicing and feasting, the newly wed couple went for a seven-day honeymoon. Honeymooning over, Vikram bade Amritamohini farewell, and accompanied by the Princess, his minister Bhatti and the invisible ghoul, he made his way to Bhimapuri. They camped in a park on the outskirts of the city. Vikrama then entrusted his dress and other belongings to the ghoul, and assumed his original garb of a mendicant.

Leaving the Princess and Bhatti in the park, Vikrama repaired to the inn of Bhimapuri where he had previously asked his attendants to remain until his return. Collecting his men, he returned to the park. From there, they all made their way to the city of Alakapuri.

On the outskirts of this city, Vikrama made his men collect the twigs of the banyan tree and eight other trees considered sacred by the Hindus. The twigs were gathered to be offered subsequently to the sacred fire, *Agni*, as the *Shastras* enjoined upon newly-weds to perform *homa*.

Tying the twigs into a bundle, the fakemendicant placed it on his shoulder, and asked his Minister to get his (the king's) palanquin. Carrying the bundle of twigs the King got ready to walk into the city accompanied by his retinue.

The Princess could no longer endure the sight of the King with the load of twigs. As a loyal and faithful wife, and passing Vikrama's test of her dutifulness, the Princess remonstrated with her husband and adroitly transferred the load on to her head.

In this manner, they reached the *durbar* of King Alakesa who was then holding council with his two courtesans, Dhanavati and Gunavati, and his Ministers. They were all amazed to see the Princess married to a mendicant and dutifully carrying the bundle of twigs. Gunavati seized this opportunity to belittle Dhanavati, particularly as she had goaded Vikrama earlier to go and challenge the Princess-who-would-not-speak, with the evil thought that, he would be disgraced. Gunavati now commanded Dhanavati thus: "Are you not ashamed to sit in the King's *durbar* while the Princess stands before us with a heavy load on her head?"

So saying, she sought the King's permission to leave the *durbar* went across to Vikrama in the mendicant's garb, and paid her respects to him.

With profound apologies to the Princess, she lightened her burden and took Vikrama's entire party to her palace. She gave them a good feast and made them rest in her palace for the night. Throughout the night, Dhanavati was beside herself with rage because she had been insulted by Gunavati. She did not realize, however, that the morning had still further humiliation in store for her.

Soon after sunrise, her master and King Alakesa sent for her and said: "The wandering mendicant not only accepted your challenge but has successfully vanquished the Princess-who-would-not-speak and has brought her before you just as you wished. Therefore, as agreed previously, you forfeit all your properties and belonging to Gunavati. You also become her slave.

Hearing the King's stern verdict, Gunavati was visibly moved as she was tender-hearted. She was full of pity for Dhanavati and interceded with the King thus: "I do not want Dhanavati to be my slave nor do I want her property.

Everyone present praised her for her noble and superior qualities. Gunavati hastened to her palace to narrate to the fake mendicant what had transpired at King Alakesa's palace.

Upon hearing the morning's developments, Vikrama asked Bhatti whether his six-month period of voluntary exile was over. Bhatti replied: "Yes, my lord! With last night that time has come to an end.

On hearing these words Vikrama took his original kingly form. Gunavati was enchanted with his magnificent personality and was supremely happy.

Vikrama, the Princess, Gunavati and Bhatti slowly wended their way to Ujjain. On the way, they prayed at the temple of Mahakali.

Vikrama once again assumed the reins of government of his kingdom and learnt from his Ministers of the welfare of his subjects during his voluntary exile. After meeting their needs, he continued to rule justly.

The statuette supporting the fifth step of the throne discovered by King Bhoja asked: "You have heard of the exploits of this dauntless, brave and just King Vikrama. Even if you have an iota of the qualities of the head and heart of Vikrama, you can ascend this throne. If not, you must retrace your steps and return to your palace."

King Bhoja and his minister Nitivakya were stupefied, hearing the words of the statuette.

In the meantime, the sun had set. They both descended from the throne, and returned to the palace. After evening prayers and supper they retired to sleep, wondering what story the sixth statuette would reveal.

24

Vikrama and the Merchant's Daughter

ON the sixth morning, King Bhoja and his Minister Nitivakya, got up with the rising sun as usual and finished their routine ablutions. After distributing largesse among the poor, King Bhoja entered the *durbar* hall followed by his retinue of Minister, prominent citizens and others. He burnt insense before King Vikramaditya's throne placed there, and reverentially ascended its steps one by one until he reached the sixth step. As he was about to place his progress thus: Whither King Bhoja? You act as if you know nothing about this throne. Have you forgotten so soon what the fifth statuette related to you yesterday?

Thus obstructed Bhoja replied: "Oh, statuette! Then tell me what you know of Vikrama". Thereupon, the statuette began as follows:

As the six-month rule of Vikrama came to an end, he and Bhatti started for the forests having said their prayers before their family deity, Mahakali, who blessed them. The faithful ghoul was, of course, their inseparable companion on this trip, as on previous occasions.

In the course of their wanderings, during which their daring and just exploits were many, they came to an attractive lake which was set amongst tall and luscious trees and shrubs. After quenching their thirst at this lake, Vikrama reclined on its bank with his head resting on Bhatti's lap. Since he was not quite sleepy, Vikrama was daydreaming, his eyes half-closed. Just then, an exceedingly beautiful and attractive girl, together with her companions, alighted on the lake side from a palanquin, entered the waters of the lake and began swimming around and playing with her friends.

The girl by chance caught sight of the handsome, graceful and stately form of Vikrama and immediately fell a victim to cupid's arrows. She was possessed of a burning passion to get Vikrama to play with her, but realized at once that the time was inopportune for the fulfilment of her wish. In order to set Vikrama on her trail, she adopted a clever ruse. She picked a Kalinga flower, placed it on her breast *(Stana)* and then put it over her footprint on the sand. Further, she made a sand mound, placed a tile on its crest and a lock of her hair over the tile. Her bathing over, she looked longingly at Vikrama out of the corner of her eyes and at the mound, and left in her palanquin surrounded by her companions. Before leaving the spot, she further encouraged Vikrama by signs to follow her.

Thereupon, Vikrama got up and wondering what the girl's signs signified, asked Bhatti: "Is she a human being or an angel descended from heaven? I have fallen madly in love with her and you must help me to attain her."

Vikrama's desire perturbed Bhatti, for he did not know where to find the girl. He had to devise a way out inasmuch as Vikrama would not stop short of finding her. With weary hearts, they neared the spot where the girl had bathed. Espying the sand mound, Vikrama questioned: "What is the mound supposed to convey?" Intelligent as he was in addition to being a gifted seer, Bhatti carefully looked over the mound, pondered deeply on its different aspects and was soon able to unravel its mystery. His interpretation was that the Kalinga flower on the girl's footprint revealed that she belonged to Kalingapur. The fact that she placed the flower on her breast indicated that her name was Dhana Amaravati. The lock of hair on the tile gave a clue as to her father's name, viz., Manickam. The tile on top of the mound meant to convey to them that Amaravati's mansion was located in front of a mud hut.

Bearing these clues in mind, Vikrama and Bhatti reached the outskirts of Kalingapur, following in the footsteps of the girls. Entrusting their clothing and possessions to the ghoul, they disguised themselves as aged brahmin and so entered the city. As they wandered through its streets, they passed Manickam's shop. Noticing the venerable gentlemen, Manickam invited them into his shop and paid them respects. He then inquired: "Whence do you come? What is the purpose of your mission? To which country do you belong?"

The fake brahmins replied: We belong to North India. We left our home with our families on a pilgrimage. We have visited Banaras and are now bound for Rameswaram. On the way, we have been separated from our families. As we have had no food for the last three days, we are weak and hungry and beg of you to give us provisions, so we may cook something to eat. Citizens of this town directed us to you as a generous and benevolent person." Manickam was flattered and ordered one of his servants to take the old men to his home and have his daughter give them alms.

Guided by the servant, they reached the merchant's mansion and were immediately recognized by Amaravati. She gave them a big basketful of provisions. Carrying the basket to a secluded spot, they assumed their real forms and examined its contents. As anticipated, they found a message among the provisions. The message directed them to a dancing girl's house in the city, where they were to wait for Amaravati. Accordingly, they proceeded to the dancing girl's house where they were treated to a sumptuous feast as she was one of Amaravati's friends. They also pumped information out of her that Amaravati was married when she was five years old and that the whereabouts of her husband, who had gone overseas soon after his marriage, were unknown. The girl, who had come of age, was pining for her spouse.

On hearing Amaravati's pitiable plight, Vikrama assumed the form of a pretty, youthful girl and Bhatti that of her beloved father and both of them reached a shop adjoining that of Manickam. The father discreetly inquired of the shopkeeper: "Is there anyone in this city belonging to our community?" Thereupon, the shopkeeper directed them to Manickam who was glad to meet people of his own caste.

To Manickam's questions about them, Bhatti in the father's garb, replied in plaintive tones: "We belong to Parampur. I have immense wealth and head our community there. This girl is my daughter. I gave her in marriage to my sister's son, who has gone abroad for trade. My daughter attained puberty two years ago and my son-in-law is yet to return. She is very impatient to join her husband and threatens to commit suicide if I do not find him soon. Therefore, in the course of a tour of the country in search of my missing son-in-law, I have come here and now intend to sail across the seven seas on my mission."

Manickam was moved by his compatriot's tale of woe, for was not he in similar tragic circumstances. The former took them to his home, fed them well and asked them to rest for a while. The guest took advantage of the innate goodness of his host and made this proposal: "My good friend! I am about to leave the shores of this country with a view to locating my son-in-law. Until my return, I would like to leave my daughter in your care. What do you say to this?" Manickam fell a victim to his guest's wiles and readily agreed as he thought a suitable companion would help his daughter considerably to forget her grief. Cautioning his daughter, the guest took leave of his host and left. Once out of sight of his host, Bhatti assumed his natural form and hastened to the danseuse's house for an enjoyable companionship.

As soon as Bhatti left, Manickam sent for his daughter, Dhana Amaravati, and said: "Beloved daughter! The husband of the girl, who stands before you, has gone the way of your husband. Her poor father has gone to search for his son-in-law, and has entrusted his daughter to my care until his return. So it is your duty to keep her as cheerful as you can until then."

Needless to say Dhana Amaravati was overjoyed at her

father's suggestion to which she readily agreed. Fondly, she caught hold of her new friend's hand and led her to her private chamber. She had her servant cook the choicest dishes and placed them before the fake girl. Both of them ate out of the same plate. During daylight hours, they went about the house as girl companions and amused themselves by playing at dice, swimming and roaming in the garden. At night, supper over, they allowed enough time to permit every member of the house to sleep soundly. Bolting the lock of Dhana Amaravati's bedroom, the fake girl turned back into King Vikramaditya and they both spent the night pleasantly. At daybreak, Vikrama once again became a girl! In this way they spent their time together.

Soon, however, an incident occurred to mar their happiness and to justify the age-old proverb that the course of true love is a bed of thorns. One day, the King of Kalingapur, Rajakesari, went in procession on a weekly round of the city, accompanied by his royal retinue. He was seated in a howdah on a richly caparisoned elephant. The blare of trumpets from bodyguards gaily dressed in flamboyant colours announced the King's arrival to the citizens. Attracted by the splendour and fanfare of the show, people came out of their houses into the street or stood on balconies and terraces of buildings to get a good view of the King.

Dhana Amaravati and her companion, however, were unconcerned about the events around them. They were lost in the admiration of their reflections in man-size mirrors before them and beautifying themselves. The King by chance noticed the two girls from his position on the elephant, and felt that the girls' behaviour was odd. He stopped his elephant for a while in front of their house and waited to see whether they would take any notice of him. To his bitter disappointment, they not only ignored him but went into the garden quite oblivious to their surroundings.

The King was infuriated at the way in which he had been ignored. He knew their background, and so their light-heartedness aroused his suspicions. Their cheerfulness was contrary to the attitude of married girls separated from their husbands. Thinking in this vein, he decided to investigate the matter.

Returning to his palace, he sent for the merchant, Manickam, and asked him: "Your son-in-law has still not returned. Will you, therefore, give your daughter in marriage to me?" Manickam replied: "It is not the custom in our community to remarry daughters," and added: "I entreat you to forget her." The King thereupon became very angry and accused Dhana Amaravati of having a paramour. Her father vehemently denied this accusation and said girls with paramours in his caste would be excommunicated. The King ridiculed Manickam for his stupidity and vowed to expose his daughter's secret lover in forty days.

Manickam was, however, upset at what the King had told him. He tried to console himself that everything was all right, but still he was disturbed in his mind. He, therefore, decided to go straight to his daughter's bedroom and surprise her. This he did and was very pleased to see that the two girls were fast asleep on different cots. Dhana Amaravati woke up with a start as her father sat on her cot, and felt perplexed by the unannounced visit of her father. He was satisfied and by way of explanation said: "I was seized of a desire to learn how you were and as I could not get to sleep, came to see you."

Bearing in mind his vow, the King called his headmen together and explained to them that they had to find Dhana Amaravati's paramour within forty days. If they succeeded, he promised them a reward of ten thousand guineas. Should they fail, he threatened that their eyes would be gouged and they would be banished to the forests.

Forty of the King's headmen were frightened at their King's orders, and decided to surround Manickam's house by night and keep a strict vigil on everyone entering it. Poor fellows! How could they know that the thief was within and not without? Thirty-nine nights passed without their getting any clue and the fortieth night had arrived. They had almost despaired of catching the secret lover, when dame luck smiled on them.

That night was a particularly sultry one. Dhana Amaravati and her companion were unaware that they were being watched.

They went into the garden at midnight and were enjoying the coolness of the night, seated on a cot, there. Gradually, they fell asleep together with a sheet drawn upon over them. In the meantime, the headmen were terribly downcast and were cursing their fate. One of them, however, decided to take a last look in the garden and was rewarded. He detected the cot, and lifting the sheet in a corner saw the young couple lost in deep slumber. He was overjoyed but restrained himself. He cautiously beckoned to his companions. Four of them gently lifted the cot and started to take it to the King's palace, surrounded by the other headmen. On the way, they had to pass through a Kali temple.

As it was still night they decided to rest there until dawn. Further, they took the cot into the sanctum sanctorum, left it there and locked the temple door outside.

As he was a seer, Bhatti already knew of the argument between King Rajakesari and Manickam. He, however, had not given much thought to the incident. However, that night a lizard chirred at his bedside and Bhatti understood its purport. He could see it flashed before his mind's eyes, just as one sees on a cine-screen, what had happened to the young lovers and where they were.

Immediately, he thought of a plan to rescue them. He sent the danseuse to the house of the priest of the Kali temple, had her bribe him ten guineas and fetch from him saffron robes for both of them and other paraphernalia needed to perform *puja* to Kali. The danseuse did as she was told and returned with those things.

Bhatti and the danseuse now changed into saffron robes to ressemble *sannyasins* and reached Kali's temple with the *puja* materials in their hands. The headmen resented this unwelcome intrusion and asked them why they had come there at dead of night.

They replied: "It is your Queen's order that we should perform *puja* to Kali at this hour unseen by any human beings."

Some of the headmen who smelt a rat objected and asked the fake *sannyasins* to get away. With an air of injured innocence, the *sannyasins* said: "Very well! We shall return without doing *puja*. We shall tell your Queen that you obstructed us." So saying, they pretended to retrace their steps. The headmen were in a fix – they were between the devil and the deep sea.

A fresh fear took hold of the headmen - that of incurring the Queen's wrath, the effect of which was more devastating than that of the King. They recalled the *sannyasins* and told them that they could finish their *puja* quickly and come out without probing into any other matter inside. On this specific undertaking they were admitted into the temple.

Once inside, Bhatti bolted the door and lost no time in waking up Vikrama and his girl friend and putting them wise regarding the danger confronting them. He bade them change clothing with himself and the danseuse. Then they all performed *puja*, with much blowing of the conch and ringing of the bell. They burnt incense too. Prayer over, Bhatti and the danseuse got into the cot and pulled the sheet over them with such meticulous care that none could say that the cot had been tampered with.

Vikrama and his girl friend resembling the *sannyasins* who had gone into the temple, now came out and distributed plantains and coconuts to the guards cautioning them to maintain strict silence about their visit; they hurried to Manickam's house feeling grateful in their heart of hearts to Goddess Kali for saving them from disgrace. Without further untoward incidents, they safely reached their abode and assumed their normal forms.

In the meantime, the guards were becoming impatient to go before the King. No sooner was it daybreak then they entered the temple and went straight to the cot. They found the couple snoring loudly beneath the sheet and made fun of them among themselves. Four of them lifted the cot and started for the King's *durbar.* The others followed gleefully, congratulating themselves on their success.

The King was mightily pleased when they placed the cot before him and explained how they found it. Haughtily he had a messenger go and fetch Manickam. The latter's heart leapt to his mouth when he took in the situation at the *durbar.*

With a flourish, the King had the sheet removed when lo! the sight froze him in his seat. Instead of Dhana Amaravati and her paramour, the danseuse and old Bhatti appeared from under the sheet. The King was shame-faced and did not know what to say. Manickam's joy knew no bounds when he emerged unscathed from the ordeal. The guards were crestfallen. What the King did in the circumstances is best left to the imagination of the readers.

While events were thus moving, Manickam's son-in-law returned to his native land with lot of wealth and invaluable presents for his wife and relatives. The advent of her husband was most distasteful to Dhana Amaravati, who used all her ingenuity to keep him at a distance from her.

Whenever Amaravati and her husband were alone, Vikrama, in the girl's garb, invented excuses to intrude into their privacy. The latter's calculated activities prevented the husband from consummating his marriage with Amaravati. In order to wean him away from Amaravati, she (Vikrama) acted as a decoy deliberately creating the impression that she was a flirt. The husband began to notice and evince interest in her. He learnt from Amaravati about her companion and soon realized that she was forlorn. In addition, she was far more beautiful than Amaravati.

All those factors goaded him to nurse evil intentions towards Amaravati's friend and he fell a prey to her flirtatious ways. One night, they met clandestinely and, getting the opportunity she (Vikrama) cut off the tip of his nose with a knife hidden in the folds of her saree. Thus disgraced, he fled from the country and was heard of no more.

Triumphantly the fake girl went over to Amaravati and related to her what she had done to the latter's husband and then they celebrated the event. The fake girl then told Amaravati that she would go and meet Bhatti that night. She advised Amaravati to raise a hue and cry the next morning that her husband had eloped with her companion. This she did and her father was apprised of this unforeseen development. He was worried as to what he should tell the girl's father when he returned and asked for her.

A few days later, just as he had feared, Bhatti-in-the-garb-of-the-girl's-father and Vikrama, in his natural form called at Manickam's house. Bhatti introduced Vikrama as his son-in-law and said he had found him in one of the islands abounding in the Indian Ocean. He further said they were in a hurry to return to their city and asked to see his daughter. Seeing Manickam silent, the fake guest sensed that something was wrong. The former discreetly told the latter that his daughter had eloped. The guest refused to believe the story about his daughter and threatened to complain to the King.

Manickam and his friends pacified the guest and his son-in-law and suggested a compromise designed to save the face of everyone involved in the affair. It was that Amaravati should marry the fake son-in-law and thus save both families from disgrace. Bhatti and his son-in-law pretended to consent with great reluctance. Manickam, who had cause to feel grateful because the King had not come to know of the ignominy which had befallen him, gave the couple a lot of money, valuable jewels and apparel and had them escorted to Ujjain. Bhatti did not forsake the danseuse but took her with him to Ujjain, accompanied by Vikrama, his wife and the ghoul. On the way, they prayed at Mahakali's temple, obtained Her blessings and then reached Vikrama's palace.

Vikrama prepared himself for the six-month rule of his kingdom.

Having ended its narrative, the sixth statuette challenged Bhoja thus: "Having heard of Vikrama's exploits, how do you compare with him?"

Bhoja did not reply, but descended the steps of the throne. He had enough food for thought.

25
Vikrama and Shani Bhagawan

ON the seventh day, King Bhoja and his Minister Nitivakya awoke with the sun and having completed their morning ablutions they performed the thirty-two *Dharmas* and took that meal.

Followed by courtiers they proceeded to the throne-room where they propitiated the divine throne, finally prostrating themselves before it. After showing all respects, King Bhoja started to ascend the steps thinking that the worst was over.

But immediately as he set his foot on the seventh step, the statuette supporting it burst into uproarious laughter exclaiming "Ho, ho! King Bhoja, you thought you were eminently qualified to ascend this throne by using incense before it! Not so, as you will realize when you hear how King Vikramaditya who ruled from this throne acquitted himself when he was in the clutches of Shani Bhagawan for seven-and-a-half years!"

King Bhoja on hearing this stopped and requested the statuette: "Would you be good enough to tell me how King Vikramaditya tackled Lord Shani?"

The statuette began:

During one of his self-imposed half-yearly exiles King Vikrama entrusted the rule of his kingdom to Bhatti, his Minister and went out into the forest alone. On the way he went to the temple of Kali-mata, his favourite deity and gone round Her thrice, prostrated before Her and prayed: "Kali-mata, please look after my kingdom during my absence."

Kali appeared before him and said "Vikrama, all will be well with your kingdom but I fear for you, as you have just started the *sade-sati* and soon you will meet Shani Bhagawan. You will have to spend the coming seven-and-a-half-years under his regime. I don't know how you are going to come out of this trial, but I advise you to prostrate yourself before him and supplicate that he should not put you to difficulties all of a sudden but to spread them out. He will be pleased with you."

"Yes, mother, I will follow your advice," replied King Vikrama. Kali-mata disappeared and King Vikrama went on his way to the forest.

Not long after, Shani Bhagawan appeared before him limping for one of his legs is shorter than the other. On recognizing him, King Vikrama fell prostrate before him and said "I am twice blessed by your honour's visit. If there is anything I can do for your honour, I shall so it with a greatest of pleasure."

Shani Bhagawan was immensely pleased with the behaviour of his quarry and said sternly: "I have come to direct your life for the coming seven-and-a-half years."

King Vikrama bowed submissively and replied. "As your honour wishes. Please have pity on me by not subjecting me to trials all at once, but to space them out over the coming years."

"Agreed," replied Shani Bhagawan and continued: "Now you are to go to Mathura and become the servant of its King Mathurendra for seven-and-a-half years."

"As your honour wishes," replied King Vikrama and handing over his insignia of royalty of Shani Bhagawan as an earnest gesture, he continued: "During my absence of seven-and-a-half years, I entrust my country to your care."

Returning to Ujjain, King Vikrama narrated the incident of his meeting with Shani Bhagawan to Bhatti and having instructed him fully as to the manner in which affairs of state had to be conducted under the rule of Shani Bhagawan, he departed to the forest accompanied by the inseparable ghoul.

After travelling throughout the day he reached the slopes of a mountain at sunset, where wild animals abounded. He selected a huge banyan tree under whose roof he took shelter for the night after partaking of the food brought to him by the ghoul.

Indra, in heaven, had two attendants, Ratnamala and Suktimala. They were lovely girls. Once while King Vikramaditya was a guest of Indra, Ratnamala happened to meet Vikrama and she was so taken in by his regal bearing and appearance that she immediately fell in love with him. After King Vikrama's departure she disclosed to Indra her love for Vikrama and her desire to join him. But Indra had asked her to wait and said: "If you go to Ujjain now, he will never care for you, for there are prettier girls in his harem; a time will come when he will take you and I will tell you then."

Devendra remembered his promise to Ratnamala on the day Shani Bhagawan caught Vikrama and learning by his divine powers that King Vikrama would be lonely and away from his country, he called Ratnamala to him and said, "I have good news for you. King Vikramaditya will be away from his country for seven-and-a-half-years from today and being under the influence of *sade-sati* he will be in need of feminine help. You therefore go straightaway to join him as he shelters under the banyan tree.

You may live with him for these seven-and-a-half-years and return here when he returns to Ujjain. Listen, I am giving you this boon: You will assume an ugly and distasteful appearance during daytime and at night you can assume your comely features with which you can live with Vikrama."

Bidding adieu to Indra, Ratnamala flew to where King Vikrama was resting. On nearing him she assumed her ugly appearance and approached him.

King Vikrama noticed her from afar and asked the ghoul: "How is it in this lonely forest infested by wild beasts I see a woman coming towards me? I am inclined to wonder whether she is a demoness or a goddess!"

The all-knowing ghoul replied: "Sir, she is from Indraloka. Indra has set her to you because of her love for you."

"You don't mean to say that she is an *apsaras*, for she is anything but beautiful!" said Vikrama.

Then the ghoul explained how she could be beautiful at night and ugly by day. She had reached them by then.

King Vikrama addressed the woman who stood before him in supplication: "Who may you be, madam, and what can I do for you?"

"Sir, I am Devendra's attendant. When you were his guest in heaven, I happened to see you and I fell in love with your good self. At my request, Devendra has ordered me to serve you for seven-and-a-half years from today."

"But I don't think I recognize you!" replied King Vikrama. Thereupon Ratnamala assumed her true appearance whereon King Vikrama felt greatly pleased. He accepted her to live with him on the conditions imposed by Indra.

During the daytime she took charge of the kitchen as a maid-servant in her ugly form and at night, she assumed her real form and slept with King Vikrama as his queen while the ghoul stood guard over them.

The next day King Vikrama armed himself to the teeth as a warrior and with the help of the ghoul wore all the paraphernalia such as bow, javelin, etc., customary for a warrior. Ratnamala in the shape of an ugly duckling constituted his maidservant.

Together they journeyed for the day and at nightfall reached a dilapidated *mutt* on whose side was a lake. They slept in that *mutt* during the night and early in the morning King Vikrama went down to the lake to wash himself. As he stood near the water brushing his teeth, he overheard an interesting conversation under water between a frog and a snake which had started to devour the former.

As we have already pointed out, King Vikrama knew the languages of all creatures.

Cried the frog: "If King Vikramaditya who is lord of this region comes to know of your high-handedness, he will certainly punish you."

Replied the snake: "I don't want to kill you for the sake of killing; but my hunger is such that unless I have something to eat immediately, I cannot survive."

King Vikrama who heard this conversation drew out his knife and cutting a large slice of flesh from his thigh, threw it to the snake which jumped at it, leaving the frog which ran for its life.

King Vikrama returned to his camp after bathing and performing his usual ablutions. Breakfast over, the party resumed journey.

After a short distance, Vikrama saw the snake and the frog hurrying towards them. Showing surprise he stopped.

The strange visitors too stopped before them and said: "Hear, King Vikramaditya! After you went, we thought who could that generous soul be except King Vikrama to throw his own flesh, and immediately we regained consciousness of our previous birth. We were both kings in our last birth, but Sage Narada cursed us to assume these forms. When we prayed for redemptions from the curse, he said "On the day you meet King Vikramaditya your salvation will commence. Serve him for seven and a half years, and after that, the curse will be removed. So have we come to serve you. You must accept us."

Kind-hearted man that he was, King Vikrama replied: "We shall be reaching Mathura next week and we shall stay in the choultry to the north of the city. You may therefore await us there." They bowed and disappeared.

King Vikrama and his party reached Mathura on the eighth day and they were received at the choultry by the snake and frog in human forms – they called themselves Ananta and Jalandhara. With their help King Vikrama settled his belongings comfortably and donning his accouterments started off towards the palace to serve the King.

Warrior Vikrama sought an audience with the King which was immediately granted. King Mathurendra was favourably impressed by the imposing appearance of the warrior and so asked him: "What can I do for you?"

Replied the warrior: "I hail from the north and am a warrior by profession, as you can see. I have seen many a war and have won praise from Kings like Vikramaditya – here is his testimonial." He produced one.

Said King Mathurendra: "I can well see that."

"I have come here to seek service under your Majesty. I can be your aide and protect your person well.

"Agreed; but what do you expect to be paid?"

"A thousand gold coins a day," replied the warrior.

The King turned askance at his Minister who was as shrewd as Bhatti.

The Minister too was greatly impressed by warrior's appearance and bearing and so gave his consent to the terms and then and there the warrior was appointed as the chief aide to the King of Mathura. Every morning and evening, his work was to attend the King's *durbar* and keep guard on the King's person and at the day's end to collect his fee from the treasury before returning to his lodgings which the King had arranged for him.

The fake warrior moved into his new lodgings the next day. He gave his earnings to Ratnamala whose business it was to run the house for him. She on her part sent Ananta and Jalandhara on errands to buy things needed for the household. After the day's work was over, the warrior would return home and partake of the excellent food prepared by Ratnamala together with Ananta and Jalandhara and keep chatting till late at night when the latter returned. Vikrama and Ratnamala in her *apsara* form, slept together in an apartment and the house was closely guarded by Ananta who kept his jaws open for any intruder to slip in and Jalandhara protected it from atop where he spread himself over house as an impregnable umbrella.

In Mathurendra's service were two other aides by name Karkotaka and Kotika who became jealous of the deferential treatment meted out to Vikrama. They decided to harm him. In the first instance they ingratiated themselves into the good books of the new warrior and became such fast friends that they started visiting Vikrama at his home, partaking of his hospitality and even staying late with him. While they paid frequent visits on Vikrama at his home, they caught a glimpse of Ratnamala in her real form and that excited them greatly. They struck upon a plan.

Next morning they approached the King and represented: "Your Majesty, the new aide has a woman leaving in his house whose likeness cannot be seen in this world. It is our considered opinion that she looks like an *apsaras.....*"

"So, what?"

"A more appropriate place for her we cannot think of than Your Majesty's harem", they replied.

The King knit his brows and said "Can I see her?"

"Of course, yes: we have a plan," and they secretly revealed it.

Accordingly that night the King disguised himself as Kotika and followed Karkotaka to Vikrama's lodgings and both of them dined with the latter. Bidding good night, they walked towards the door, while Vikrama closed the door of his apartment behind him.

Down the corridor, Karkotaka hid the King in a place of vantage and walked ahead alone. At the gate, he told Ananta

"Your master has asked Kotika to stay with him for more time. I will come and fetch him."

Little suspecting, Ananta let him out and closed the door behind Karkotaka.

The King in disguise, after waiting for some time, peeped into Vikrama's bedroom through a ventilator and received a great shock, for the beauty of the woman inside the room was really immortal. As he came down from his perch, he could not, for the life of him, resist the one thought of taking this woman to his harem. Her extraordinary loveliness went to his head like old wine.

26

Vikrama and the Pearl Princess

THE fake warrior little suspected that the King was spying on him and so he fell asleep.

At midnight Karkotaka returned to the warrior's lodging and asked Ananta permission to go inside to fetch his brother Kotika. It was given. When Karkotaka saw the King huddled in a corner he roused him and together they left for the palace after bidding goodnight to Ananta.

The King could not command sleep as he was greatly agitated by his love for the *apsaras* and so spent the rest of the night uncomfortably.

When the court assembled next morning the King anxiously awaited his Minister who arrived at the appointed hour. The Minister stood before the King having divined the state of the King's mind.

Mathurendra related to his Minister his nocturnal adventure and asked his advice as to how he could get hold of the *apsaras*.

The Minister replied: "Your Majesty! The warrior in whose possession is the *apsaras*, is the mightiest ever, as far as I can judge. It is my conviction that it is unwise to court his enmity, for it is very doubtful if all the might of our army will be equal to his. Further, what will other kings think when they hear that Your Majesty is after the spouse of a servant? Under the circumstances, I would meekly submit that his idea had better be dropped completely."

Replied Mathurendra: "I quite see your point, but without her, my life will pass away."

The Minister knitted his brows and thought furiously. He said at last: "If Your Majesty must get the woman, there is only one way. There is a city called Jeevitpura at a distance of three hundred *yojanas* from here. King Varanakesari rules it. He has a daughter by name Hasamukhi. Whenever she laughs, pearls drop from her mouth. The King then collects them and sends them to a pearl-merchant, Goraksha, in the neighbouring city of Mundaka who sells them for fantastic prices and remits them to the King. Thus the King has amassed huge wealth.

"But a *sadhu,* who happened to see Hasamukhi, fell violently in love with her and in order to possess her, he cursed the King, the queen, the army and the entire town to become lifeless, of that the town is now completely inactive except for the *sadhu* and Hasamukhi with whom he lives. Whenever he goes outside, the *sadhu* makes her a corpse by his powers and revives her on his return. As a result the princess has become very sad and never laughs.

"Now, if we commission the new warrior to bring the pearls produced by the princess laughing, within a certain date, he will have to encounter the *sadhu* who will most certainly curse the warrior and he will not return. Then Your Majesty can obtain possession of the *apsaras* he keeps."

King Mathurendra felt extremely glad that his Minister had devised an effective plan to fulfil his wishes. So when the warrior came at the appointed hour, he addressed him in the midst of all those assembled:

"Aditya! We desire to get a pair of ear-rings made for ourselves. We want for that a particular quality of pearls and they are sold by a merchant by name Goraksha at Mundaka. They cost a lakh of gold coins which we shall give you."

"Your orders", replied the warrior.

"How long do you think it will take for you to go and return with the pearls?" asked the King.

"Forty days," replied the warrior.

The King agreed and ordered that a lakh of gold coins, along with the warrior's forty days' wages be paid immediately and had him sent on the errand with due escort.

The fake warrior returned home and narrated to Ratnamala, Ananta and Jalandhara, of the King's commission. He, asked: "As it will take forty days, how do you propose to look after yourselves in my absence?"

Ananta replied: "Don't you fear, King Vikrama; even if the entire army of the King comes, I shall tear them to pieces."

Jalandhara replied, "I can throw the entire army into the sea!"

Said Ratnamala: "Any one attempting mischief against my wishes will be burnt by my powers."

Thus assured, King Vikrama wended his way to Mundaka. Riding on the shoulders of the ghoul, he crossed mountains, rivers and deserts till at last he reached Mundakapura. He enquired about the jeweller Goraksha and went to his house. Finding him there, Vikrama asked him: "O, Jeweller, I understand that you have the best pearls and that a set of them for ear-rings will cost a lakh of gold coins. I want one set and here is your money."

"I don't have stock of them now," replied the jewller. "I used to get supplies from King Varanakesari of Jeevitpura. When his daughter Hasamukhi laughed, those pearls used to fall from her mouth. But now a *sadhu* who fell in love with her has cursed the King, his wife and all his army and people, and lives with her against her will. Consequently the princess is very sad and hardly, if ever, laughs. Hence the scarcity of these pearls."

On hearing it, Vikrama started towards Jeevitpura. On the way, he discarded the warrior's accouterments and put on his customary regal apparel and meditating upon his favourite deity, Maha-Kali, he travelled in the direction of Jeevitpura.

When he reached the city, he entered it looking for some guidance; but to his consternation he saw the entire population standing, sitting or lying, lifeless like statues. It appeared that at a certain stage of their activity their *chaitanya* had been suddenly withdrawn by some invisible force. Things were half-finished. He then entered the palace. There too, he saw from the King down to the sentries, all lifeless.

He immediately recollected what the jeweller had told about the curse of a *sadhu*. So he called his faithful ghoul and asked: O ghoul, can you tell me where that *sadhu* is? Or the princess? Please go and find out for me."

The ghoul went and returned in a trice and reported: "The *sadhu* is engaged in a sacrifice and the head of the princess, severed from the body, is placed on the steps of the harem."

Expressing horror, Vikrama asked to be conducted to where the princess's head was placed. As soon as he reached the harem, he saw the gruesome spectacle of the beautiful head of the princess. He asked the ghoul again: "Where is the trunk of the girl, and how to revive her?"

The ghoul replied: "Her trunk is on the sofa inside the harem. Take this head and place it along with the trunk at the proper place. You will notice a wand nearby. Unscrew it at the top: you will find some oil oozing from its cavity. Smear that oil on the joint and the princess will come back to life."

King Vikrama hurriedly took the head inside and did as the ghoul asked him to do. Immediately the princess came back to life. But on opening her eyes, she expressed surprise at finding the charming Vikrama standing before her instead of the *sadhu.* She asked him:

"Who may be you, sir?"

"I am King Vikramaditya of Ujjain," replied the King. Thereupon the princess smiled and from that smile fell a bunch of pearls which King Vikrama carefully picked up and put aside safely in his pocket. He asked the princess: "What made you smile?"

The princess replied: The *sadhu* whose captive I happen to be, is mortally afraid of the same King Vikramaditya, that he would, if he sees me, take me away from his clutches. He is performing a sacrifice which will last for 40 days, at the successful end of which he will become the master of the three worlds. Today is the 37th day. Lest you should carry me away during his absence, he cuts my head, places it on the steps in this manner. When I learnt that you were the same Vikramaditya, the thought made me smile."

"I see!" replied King Vikramaditya. "Now, are you satisfied with the life you lead?" he asked.

"You don't mean to say that!" replied the princess with a look whose meaning could not be lost.

Thereupon King Vikrama said: "Dear lady, we have to deal with this man very cunningly. Can you help me?"

"With all my heart," replied the princess.

"So, when he returns this evening ask him (1) whether your father, mother and other people of this city will get back their lives and if so how? and (2) the secret of the *sadhu's* invincibility. For that, you must feign dejectedness when, out of his infatuation for you, he will importune you to tell the cause of it. If you tackle him well, he will come out with the full secret. You follow? Just now I shall sever your head from your body and place it on the step as before and retire to the Kali Temple where I shall stay for the night. I shall return to you at this hour tomorrow."

The princess smiled with consent, when another bunch of pearls fell from her mouth and the King picked them up carefully. After severing her head and placing it on the step, he went to the Kali Temple.

But at the same time he detailed his faithful ghoul to assume the shape of a lizard and overhear the talk between the *sadhu* and the princess when the former returned.

27

Vikrama Weds Hasamukhi

AFTER sunset, the *sadhu* came to the harem and brought the princess back to life as usual by placing her head along with the trunk and applying the oil from the wand. The princess stood up as from a sleep but unlike on other days, she leaned herself against a pillar and put on a long face.

"What makes you stand dejected that way?" asked the *sadhu.*

"Oh, nothing much," she replied.

The *sadhu* put his hands round her waist at which she quailed like the lily before a blast and with wide-open eyes blurted. "I was only bewailing my lot. Although born to a king, I stand alone today after being responsible for the death of all my near and dear ones. Am I at least happy? Everyday, I die and come back to life. Perhaps one of these days, in a mood of anger, you might choose not to revive me, then what happens to me? When I thought of that prospect, I became disgusted with myself."

"What a fool you are? Do you think I will take all this trouble to leave you dead? Look here, only three days remain for the fulfilment of the *yag* I am performing. When it is over, I shall be master of all the fourteen worlds and all the good things of life will be mine. I shall marry you then and you shall enjoy all!" replied the *sadhu.*

"May I ask you, sir, if my people who are dead now are dead for ever? For, you cannot expect me to be completely happy when all my people are dead."

"How silly of you? I have locked the lives of all the dead in a copper vessel which I have buried beneath the *bali-peetha* before Kali-Mata in the yonder temple. After the completion of this *yag* I shall sacrifice a live elephant to Kali-Mata in exchange for these lives and release them from that pot when they will enter into their respective bodies, thus coming back to life!" replied the *sadhu* with obvious gusto.

"I am satisfied," replied the princess and continued: "but I have another lurking fear whether there can be anybody who can harm *your* life, for in that case, it will be a great calamity to me."

"That is next to impossible. Listen I shall burn anyone whom I see by my sight. If I am to die, one must sever my head with one stroke; not a single drop of blood should be spilt: my head should be thrown into the sacrificial fire which I have raised and for 1½ hours my trunk should be kept tossing in the sky without touching the earth. A single drop of my blood on the earth will produce a thousand *sadhus* like me valorous and proficient. You will see now how difficult it is for anybody to accomplish this feat. So please take that fear off your head for ever," replied the *sadhu*.

"Ha! I am now happy!" said the princess beaming, and placing her hand on her breast, said: "I am convinced that nothing can kill you."

The ghoul, which in the shape of a lizard was commissioned by Vikramadiya to report this conversation, listened to it and ran to its master.

King Vikrama in the meantime had arrived at his destination, namely, the same Kali-Mata's temple. He bathed, went round the deity thrice and prayed for Her blessings. Kali-Mata appeared before him, gave him the sacred ash and a comfortable pillow to sleep on. But he waited for his faithful ghoul to return. Fatigue overcame his resolution and so he fell asleep. So when the ghoul roused him, he awoke with a start, but felt happy on hearing the full version of the conversation between the *sadhu* and the princess. As there was plenty of time for the day to break, the King fell asleep again only to be roused by the warm rays of the rising sun.

After going through the daily routine of bathing and prayer, King Vikrama armed himself with eighteen kinds of weapons and after falling on all fours before Kali-Mata, started to the palace, followed by the ghoul.

The *sadhu* too had risen early in the morning, and as was his wont, gone through the customary rites. Entering the harem, he roused the princess and after severing her head deposited it on the steps of the harem, and entered the *yagshala* for performing the rituals.

King Vikrama entered the palace and going into the *zenana*, first brought the princess back to life. Rising, she looked at King Vikrama with coy eyes and bowed.

Said King Vikrama: "I know all that happened between you and the *sadhu* last night. I know each and every word of what he said!"

On hearing it, the princess's eyes widened in wonder and a soft smile played on her lips, from which a bunch of pearls fell. King Vikrama picked them up carefully and said, "I shall first of all kill the *sadhu* and then come to you. Till then, be of good cheer!" Saying this he severed her head again and placed it on the steps as before.

On coming out of the harem, he asked the ghoul: "What is the best way of making an end of this *sadhu?*"

The ghoul replied: "I think the best way is this. He will return here this evening. I shall station myself at the first gate in the form of a lizard. You had better lay in wait in the shade at the second gate. On his approach I shall twitter. On hearing it, you be ready with your sword drawn out. As soon as he crosses the first gate I shall slam the gate behind him. He will turn back to see who did it. At that moment you cut off his head with one stroke of the sword. I shall hold the head and drink each and every drop of blood that falls from it and throw the head myself in his sacrificial fire.

On your side, you must throw the body up in the air and keep it floating like a ball for 1½ hours. Then he will automatically die."

King Vikrama hugged the ghoul for its excellent advice and said: "I don't know how I am going to repay my debt of gratitude to you." It became dusk and the ghoul addressed King Vikrama: "Sir, we can expect the *sadhu* to return now. You post yourself behind the second gate while I shall keep guard at the first as a lizard."

King Vikrama hastened to his post.

Soon the *sadhu* came, little suspecting what awaited him. As he crossed the first gate the ghoul gave the signal and the King was ready and his hand touched the sword's hilt. The ghoul slammed the door on his back. The *sadhu* turned back when King Vikrama's sword flashed across his neck from behind and in a moment it was being carried away to the sacrificial fire to be thrown in. King Vikrama tossed the body up and parried it in the air deftly like a volleyball for 1½ hours. When the period was over, the body fell down with a thud never to rise.

The ghoul too returned and said that the head was burnt to ashes and that the *sadhu* was dead. Thereupon King Vikrama ordered the ghoul to bring a live elephant from the adjoining forest and lead it to the temple of Kali-Mata where he went directly. On reaching the same he prayed soulfully before the deity for the accomplishment of his undertaking.

In the meantime the ghoul had tethered an elephant at the *bali-peetha* of Kali-Mata. Then King Vikrama killed the elephant as a sacrificial offering for Kali-Mata and broke open the *peetha* where he found the tell-tale copper-pot in which the *sadhu* had held all the lives of all the people of the kingdom captive. He broke the pot and released the lives which ran to their respective bodies.

Without wasting a second, King Vikrama ran to the palace and brought the princess back to life in the usual manner.

He told her: "I have killed the *sadhu* and in a short time all your people will regain their lives. If they ask you how it all happened, you are at liberty to disclose everything. I am hurrying to the temple of Kali-Mata."

On hearing it, the princess laughed in joy whereupon a bunch of pearls fell from her lips which the King carefully picked and pocketed. Bidding her adieu Vikrama hurried to the outskirts of the city where the Kali-Mata's temple was situated.

When the lives released by King Vikramaditya re-entered their respective bodies, the entire city came back to life. All of them said that they had a sort of swoon and pleaded ignorance as to how they regained consciousness. But they had a faint recollection of a *sadhu* who had won notoriety by his open avowal of love for the princess.

When King Varanakesari therefore asked his Ministers as to how it all happened, they said: "Perhaps if you ask your daughter she may be in a position to explain."

The King called princess Hasamukhi and asked her: "My dear, my Ministers say that you may be able to enlighten us as to how this swoon came upon all of us suddenly."

Princess Hasamukhi narrated all that happened from the advent of the *sadhu*, and how it was King Vikramaditya of Ujjain who saved them all.

The King embraced his daughter as tears of joy flowed from his eyes. He then asked her: "Where then is the great King Vikramaditya now, tell me!"

"At the Kali-Mata's temple," replied the princess.

King Varanakesari immediately arranged for a grand reception to King Vikramaditya and went to the Kali temple personally to invite him to his palace with all the respects due to a great monarch.

King Vikrama received King Varanakesari and seating him

by his side enquired after his health. He gave him light refreshments and after a short while, King Vikrama rode in state to the capital of King Varanakesari on a richly caparisoned elephant.

It became an open secret that the princess was to be given away in marriage to King Vikramaditya. Astrologers were called who selected an auspicious day for the celebration of the event which went off with all the *eclat* due to a royal household.

When the bride and the bridegroom were alone after a day full of fetes, King Vikrama placed his benign hands on the shoulders of his love whereupon she looked at him with eyes that looked like an ocean leaping with joy. A casual references to the unexpectedness of the event made her laugh which brought forth a bunch of pearls which King Vikramaditya carefully tucked away into his folds.

King Vikrama stayed with his father-in-law till the end of his furlough, but as its close drew near he confided to his wife as to how he happened to be there and asked for permission to rejoin duty at Mathura as Aditya. The princess informed her father who heard all about the circumstances and arranged for his departure along with his daughter. The customary gifts went with the party.

28

Vikrama on a New Mission

ON the way King Vikramaditya got down at Kali-Mata's temple and went into the sanctum along with his bride. They prostrated before Her and prayed. After going round the temple thrice, the party resumed its journey towards Mathura.

Returning to the city on the fortieth day, Vikramaditya drove straight to his lodgings where Ratnamala received them, embracing Hasamukhi fondly. She asked King Vikrama all about his quest when Jalandhara and Ananta stepped in, bowing devoutly.

Ratnamala soon set the table and entertained them to lavish food, after which they ate *tambul*. King Vikrama related his experiences. They were thus having a merry time at the joyous reunion, after which they went to sleep.

As the days given to Aditya for completing his mission drew to a close King Mathurendra became delirious in his infatuation. He had concluded that Aditya was gone for ever and Ratnamala was his for the asking. So, on the fortieth day, he called his Minister and told him to fetch Ratnamala.

Replied the Minister: "My Lord! It is unwise to be hasty. Aditya is a valorous and one cannot be too sure that he will not return. In any case we can take whatever action is necessary tomorrow."

The King reluctantly agreed and spent a sleepless night.

The day broke and the King was the earliest to announce himself in his *durbar* and hardly took any interest in the daily routine when Aditya stood before him to attention.

The King who never expected him to turn up much less on the appointed day and hour, received a shock, but still nursed the hope that after all, he might not have brought the pearls although he might have escaped death at the hands of the *sadhu*.

Feigning courage he addressed him, "Aditya, have you brought the pearls?"

"Yes, Your Majesty; here they are," said he and placed the bunches of pearls which the King examined. They flashed in their lustre.

The King concealed his bitter consternation and examining them asked his Minister: "How is it four different kinds are here?"

The Minister examined them carefully and replied: "They are quarter-grown, half-grown, three-fourth grown and full-grown. It must have happened like this full-throated laughter should have produced the full-grown pearl, the muffled laughter, smile and half-smile should have produced the others. But without doubt, they are the pearls from Hasamukhi's mouth."

On hearing this explanation, King Vikramaditya who was disguised as Aditya secretly admired the Minister who he thought was clever as his own Bhatti. But King Vikrama had little doubt that Minister would not be as long-lived as two thousand years as his own Bhatti.

The day's duties over, Aditya returned to his lodging, bathed, ate and slept soundly.

King Mathurendra too sent the precious pearls to his treasury and spent the night planning his next step.

As soon as day broke, Aditya completed his daily routine and was preparing to leave for the palace when Karkotaka and his brother Kotika dropped in for a chat after a long interval during which Aditya had been away.

While they were conversing, their roving eyes caught sight of Hasamukhi who happened to cross from one room to another. Suddenly their brows went up and they asked Aditya: "Brother! You are a wonderful man. Who is that new lady that went in just now?"

Aditya who had nothing to hide, told them the truth that she was princess Hasamukhi. They rolled their eyes in wonder and quickly slipped out.

Going direct to King Mathurendra, the Karkotaka brothers deposed: "Your Majesty! We made a great mistake!"

"What is that?" asked the King petulantly.

"Ratnamala of whom we had told you previously is nothing in front of another," said they.

"Where is she?" asked the King eagerly.

"Aditya has bought with him princess Hasamukhi herself. She is a hundred times more beautiful than Ratnamala."

"Is that so?"

"And we pity her that she has to live with Aditya."

"Yes?"

"She eminently deserves a place in Your Majesty's harem", said they in chorus.

The King could not conceal his eagerness to have a look at the new girl brought by Aditya.

So it was arranged between the Karkotaka brothers and the King that the same stratagem as they handled in the case of Ratnamala should be used, as Aditya had little suspected the King's infatuations or his efforts to dislodge him.

The same night with the aid of the Karkotaka brothers the King managed to see the two girls, who vied with each other in their beauty. The result was, as before, that the King became still more eager to possess both the girls.

As before, one of the brothers had to conduct the King home after his tantalizing experience.

As it was the early hours of the morning when the King reached the palace, he kept awake till the sun rose and after finishing his morning routine sent for his Minister – Diwakara was his name – and said:

"Aditya has now brought princess Hasamukhi. I happened to see the girl and what shall I say? Come to think of it, she is hundred times more beautiful than the first."

"Listen, Your Majesty," replied Diwakara. "Aditya is no ordinary sepoy. From the fact that he has brought you the impossible pearls, it appears to me very dangerous to antagonise him."

"You may be right," said the King. "But if I don't get the girl my life will ebb away!"

The Minister heaved a big sigh and said, "If that is the case, I shall propose a still more perilous adventure to Aditya from which he will never return."

"What is that?" asked the King.

"In *Nagaloka*, King Nagendra rules. He has a daughter. When she laughs, a *naga-ratna* falls. We shall ask Aditya to bring those gems. As you know, *Nagaloka* is to be reached after crossing several oceans. Even if he reaches, for miles around that region the land is saturated with snake poison so that if he touches the ground, he will become poisoned and die."

"That is the best plan. Send him immediately," urged the King.

The Minister sent for Aditya and in a few minutes he arrived in his uniform and stood to attention.

29

Achchyut Kanya

"ADITYA!" called Mathurendra and when he looked up, he said, "I am greatly pleased with your devotion to me and your prowess in fetching the pearls on which I had set my heart," and paused.

"I only did my duty, my lord," replied Aditya with great humility.

"I greatly appreciate your sense of duty and I am sure you will not hesitate to carry out my commands. I now want to make a grand necklace for my Queen. I have all the gems required for it except the *naga-ratna.* I wonder if you can help me to get one for me."

"As Your Majesty commands," replied Aditya.

"I am told," began the King, "that the *naga-ratna* I require is available at *Nagapura,* the capital of *Nagaloka.* I hope you know that *Nagaloka* is to be reached after crossing the seven oceans. King *Nagendra* who rules there has a daughter named Naga-Kanya. Whenever she laughs, a *naga-ratna* falls from her mouth. I want one of these *naga-ratnas* for the necklace. I cannot think of a better person than you to bring that."

For a moment Aditya looked up, for he could not help suspecting that a plot was being hatched against him. But to refuse the King on the spot would have been disastrous. So he said, "Yes, my lord, I will try to bring." "Ah!" exclaimed the King. "That is just like you, and once you decide on a thing, it is as good as achieved. I need have no further worries about it. My God, what sleepless nights have I not spent!" waxed the King.

Turning abruptly to Aditya, King Mathurendra asked: "How long, do you think, Aditya, it will take you to bring the *ratna*?"

"Sixty days," replied Aditya.

"Ah, that is but reasonable, considering the distance to be covered. But don't hesitate to ask for more, if you think it necessary."

"That is perfectly all right," replied Aditya.

The King thereupon orders sixty thousand gold coins to be paid to him, being his advance salary for the sixty days of his assignment and a further two lakhs of gold coins as the cost of the *naga-ratna*. These were loaded on mules and escorted to Aditya's lodging. The King bade Aditya bon-voyage.

Reaching home, Aditya called the members of his household to a conference and related to them the latest assignment of the King. "I am not quite satisfied with the *bona fides* of the King," he ended.

For a moment, his mind thought of rebelling, but he checked that impulse on moral grounds. "As long as I am in the service of another, I should carry out his behests, or it will be against *Dharma*," he concluded. With that decision he asked Ananta: "Now, Ananta, tell me how best I can cross the seven oceans."

"Sir, you need have no worry on that count. Just walk to the seashore and think of Jalandhara, my friend. He will be there instantaneously in his original shape of the frog on whom you can ride to the end of the journey. On reaching the other shore, think of me. I shall be there to carry out your orders!" replied Ananta.

Aditya turned in the direction of Ratnamala and addressed

her: "My dear, I know you can take good care of yourself, but what about Hasamukhi? She is young and quite new to this place."

"That you may leave to me. She will be like this," said Ratnamala, and taking a handful of water and uttering some *mantra* she splashed it on Hasamukhi's face when lo! the later became a wooden doll. She placed the doll in the corner of a cupboard and returned to Aditya with a triumphant smile.

"Keep her safely like that till I return," said Aditya approvingly.

Bidding them all adieu, Aditya came out of his lodging and riding on the invisible ghoul reached the seashore in a trice. There he thought of Jalandhara who appeared from the sea as a giant frog. Aditya stepped on to his back and crossed the seven seas at break-beck speed.

As Jalandhara could not actually touch the island of *Nagaloka*, Aditya had to disembark on another island called Achchyut Nagar in close proximity to *Nagaloka*. And Jalandhara, after depositing his precious cargo, returned to Mathura.

Aditya, accompanied by the ghoul entered the streets of Achchyut Nagar and went about sightseeing. At a certain stage he heard the heart-rending wails of a woman issuing from a house and being pith-hearted, he could not help stopping and offering a word of solace to her.

That house belonged to an old widow who eked her living by selling plantain leaves from her garden. Aditya on hearing her pitiable cry, consoled her saying, "Please, don't grieve like that. It pains me very much. If there is anything that I can do to alleviate your suffering, I shall be very happy to do that."

The old woman who had never in her life heard any words

of sympathy was greatly impressed by the earnestness of Aditya and stopping her weeping for a while said: "Listen, Sir, in this city rules a King by name Achchyuta. He has four daughters. He has been trying to marry his first daughter. But whoever marries her, dies the same night. Like this, hundreds of bridegrooms have died. The King, in his madness, is determined to find a living husband for that wretched daughter. So, each day he marries her to a son from each house and the same night that son dies. Today is my son's turn. I have to send my only son for whom I have taken infinite pains to bring up, being a poor and uncared-for woman. I know my son will not come back alive. I am therefore bewailing my lot. How can you help me?"

"Do not grieve, mother," said he. "I will be the eldest son to you today and do let me go and marry the King's daughter!"

"Oh, no! I am already suffering this terrible life for some sin committed by me in a previous birth. And I won't add to my bill by causing another woman's child to die in the place of mine. Let me wash off my sins for once!" cried the lady.

Aditya explained, "Mother, listen to me. What you say is correct only if you *force* me to take the place of your son. But here, it is I that offer myself, voluntarily, for this business. So, take that fear off your chest, and like a good mother, let me go in the place of your son."

Aditya's argument appeared to her to be reasonable and so she agreed to the proposal. She quickly set about preparing a nice meal for the kind soul who so generously offered to help her and she served him with infinite tenderness. Aditya was immensely pleased with the food offered, as he was very hungry.

As they were chatting merrily, came the royal procession with all its fanfare, for fetching the King's new son-in-law who, everybody knew, would not see the light of day or breathe the air on the next.

Aditya, as the eldest son of the lady, was garlanded, made to wear the bridegroom's clothes and ornaments. When ready, he was carried on the back of the state-elephant preceded by a large concourse of men, women and music. To a common observer it all appeared to be a great farce, but nonetheless real, because of the King's dead earnestness. The ghoul dressed like Aditya's bearer, also rode on the elephant alongside of the bridegroom.

There was the permanent marriage pandal whose green appearance was maintained. The King and other officials personally received the bridegroom and no sooner was the latter seated on the dais than the Princess, attired in glorious robes was brought to his side. The royal *purohits* uttered Vedic *mantras* and Aditya clasped the Princess's hand in holy wedlock.

The whole event went off with mechanical precision and when night came, the couple was ushered into the bridal chamber which was decorated gorgeously. There, the bride and bridegroom partook of the sweet things, ate *tambul* and played a couple of games of chess but during the third game, the Princess excused herself saying she felt like sleeping and lay down on her cushion losing consciousness.

This rather unceremonious act on the part of his newly wedded wife set Aditya thinking. He wondered if it was not all a deep-laid plot. Snapping his fingers, he conjured up his faithful ghoul, and asked it. "Tell me all about the mystery of this girl!"

The ghoul applied its superhuman talents and divined the story about her which it related as follows: "Listen, my lord! You will remember we came here on our way to *Nagapura* in *Nagaloka.* Now, Nagendra, the King of that city, has a son by name Adi Sesha. He is in love with this Princess. Everyday he visits her in this chamber in the form of a serpent. He comes through a tunnel, starting at the base of the

Vinayaka's temple at the outskirts of the city and ending up here at the corner. He manages to send her to a hypnotic sleep while he is half way through it. When she complained of sleep today, he was already on the way and will be up here any moment. On coming up, he bites the bridegroom who dies. After staying with the girl in her unconscious state for the rest of the night, he runs home back by the same way."

"Is that so?" exclaimed Aditya.

The ghoul continued:

"Presently, I shall put on the dress of the bridegroom and lie by the side of the Princess. Since I am impervious to all poisons, Adi Sesha's bite won't do me any harm. But as soon as he does so, you cut off the tip of his tail, when he will rush back thoroughly embarrassed since he will know that somebody has discovered his secret.

"It is easy for you to kill him, but as he is the brother of the *Naga Kanya,* to whom we are going, I do not want you to spoil your future relationship."

Aditya approved of the plan and drawing his sword waited in the shade thrown by the oil lamp. The ghoul dressed as the bridegroom immediately lay by the side of the unconscious Achchyut *Kanya.*

After a few seconds a slab from the corner of the room lifted itself automatically and from that orifice came out a ferocious looking serpent which proceeded with upraised hood straight to the bridal cot on which the couple lay. With deafening hiss it stung the bridegroom but the next moment, instead of the bridegroom, the snake writhed with pain, its tail having been cut off by Aditya from his concealment. The snake did not wait any more, but retreated hastily into the gaping floor and escaped. The ghoul and Aditya had a hearty laugh over the whole affair.

Aditya then changed into the bridegroom's robe after a few minutes when Princess Achchyut Kanya regained her consciousness. On seeing her husband in glorious form, she hugged him passionately when the ghoul discreetly slipped out.

Early in the morning when Aditya opened the door of his bridal chamber, he was shocked to see people waiting outside as usual with all the paraphernalia of a funeral procession! So he invoked the ghoul and thrusting a lathi into its hand, he ordered it to drive the mourners away. When the ghoul did so, the mourners fled in panic screaming. "The ghost that kills the King's son-in-law is after us-*hooey*!"

30

Naga-Kanya

THE mourners who ran helter-skelter did not stop to look back if anything was following them until a watchman standing on the way stopped them by force. When they saw that they were not pursued they heaved a big sigh of relief and adjusted their garments. To the annoyed watchman they could only blurt out their experience incoherently.

"You mean to say that King's son-in-law is not dead and that you saw him opening the door?"

"Yes; with our own eyes we saw," they replied in chorus.

"Come on, then, let us go and report to the King. He will be greatly pleased", and all of them went to the King's *durbar* and reported.

The King could hardly believe his ears that his son-in-law was alive and dragging his two Ministers by the hand, rushed to his daughter's apartment. To his astonishment he saw the bridegroom attired in royal robes looking radiant and mighty. It did not take long for the Ministers to recognize that the bridegroom was no other than the mighty monarch, Vikramaditya of Ujjain.

Great was the King's joy on learning this and with due deference he greeted Vikramaditya.

Preliminary enquiries over, King Achchyuta related to Vikramaditya of how his efforts to get his first daughter married brought about the systemic death of numberless bright young men. He ended with his request: "Mighty King, please tell us how you overcame the fate of the previous suitors."

King Vikramaditya related his own part in the drama when all those assembled were greatly delighted.

King Achchyuta got all his four daughters married to Vikramaditya and for some days the newly-weds had a fine time.

One day Vikramaditya thought it was time for him to get going. So he contemplated on Ananta. Ananta too appeared before him in a trice.

Vikrama first of all enquired of him about Mathura and then of how Ratnamala and Hasamukhi were doing. Ananta replied that everything at Mathura was satisfactory.

Then Vikramaditya said: "Ananta, you know why I called you. It is time I start for *Nagapura.*"

Replied Ananta: "Yes my lord; but the way to *Nagapura* as you know, is strewn with snake poison. For a mile on all sides no human can pass, as he is sure to be scorched. I shall first of all go to Nagendra and ask him to give his daughter in marriage to you. I think he will agree. To enable you to go there, I shall arrange to clear the way from poison for your safe transit."

"That will be excellent," agreed King.

Ananta resumed his original shape of the serpent and had no difficulty in getting Nagendra's audience where he stood bowing.

Nagendra asked him who he was and what he wanted.

Replied Ananta: "My name is Ananta and my master is King Vikramaditya of Ujjain who is at Achchyut Nagar presently and he asks the hand of your daughter."

"Is that so!" exclaimed Nagendra. "It is a privilege and pleasure for me to get that alliance. Do bring him along."

"Yes, Your Majesty," replied Ananta. "But he being a human cannot come over here and his passage will have to be immunized."

"Oh yes, I agree. I shall have his way down here cleared of poison," said Nagendra. He immediately issued orders for clearing the way of snake poison for a mile around. The King's messengers ran for carrying out the orders.

In the meantime, Nagendra addressed Ananta, "Within an hour the island will be made safe for King Vikramaditya. Kindly go and fetch him, if you please."

Bidding good-bye to Nagendra, Ananta crawled back to Achchyut Nagar where King Vikramaditya was staying.

On seeing Ananta come back so quickly, King Vikrama asked, "Ananta, did you have a safe journey? What did Nagendra say?"

"He felt greatly pleased with the alliance. He asked me to fetch you immediately. The island has been made safe for your arrival. The way has been cleared of snake poison for a mile around."

King Vikrama called on King Achchyuta and explained to him how urgently he had to leave for Nagapura in the last lap of his mission. He similarly convinced his four new wives about the urgency of his mission and promised to take them with him on his way back. With great reluctance King Achchyuta and his daughters bade him bon-voyage.

Riding on the ghoul and followed by Ananta, King Vikrama started for Nagapura which he reached in no time. Halting at a wayside near the capital, Vikrama sent word through Ananta to King Nagendra of his arrival. Nagendra on his part, on hearing of King Vikramaditya's arrival, sent his ministers with due respects to invite him. Accordingly they proceeded to the inn and after paying their respects, brought him in a procession to the palace on an elephant preceded by music and dance.

King Nagendra met King Vikramaditya at the palace gate and as the latter got down, he bowed, and arm-in-arm they proceeded to the *durbar* where King Vikrama was given an equal seat with King Nagendra. After preliminary enquiries they had a short lunch.

Ananta thereafter got leave of his master to proceed to Mathura. Reaching Mathura, he related to his companions his experiences up to Vikrama's arrival at Nagapura.

King Nagendra lost no time in calling the *purohits* and astrologers and fixing the date for the marriage of his daughter with Vikrama. The entire city and the palace were decorated gorgeously in an unprecedented manner and on the appointed day and hour, King Vikrama married Naga-Kanya amidst great pomp, Vedic chants and music.

At nightfall the newly-weds ate whatever was allowed for the first night and entered the bridal chamber which was decorated most artistically. The bridal cot was strewn with *parijata* flowers which did duty for the mattress and was decked with cherubic modes holding the lamp and incense sticks.

The couple settled themselves comfortably on the cot, ate *pan supari* and were chatting good-humouredly when a joke from Vikrama made Naga-Kanya burst into a laughter, when like the resplendent sun, a few *nagaratnas* fell from her mouth. King Vikrama collected them coolly and put them into his vest-pocket. They spent the night together as the god of love and his spouse.

King Vikrama lost count of the days at his disposal in his new-found joy till a day was left, when he went to Nagendra and sought his permission to leave immediately for Mathura along with Naga-Kanya. As all fathers Nagendra felt too very sad to part with his daughter and so said: "Sir, can't you leave her here till your half-yearly exile is complete upto the time of your returning to Ujjain?"

King Vikrama replied: "Nagendra, I am not here on my half yearly self-exile, I am under *sade sathi* and under the paramountly of Lord Saniswara. At his command I have chosen to serve the King of Mathura as his orderly. I came here only to fulfil his order to bring the *naga-ratnas* from your daughter's mouth and luckily, got her for my wife. If I do not report within twenty-four hours, my promise will have been broken."

King Nagendra could no further delay his departure and so he sent his daughters along with Vikrama with due honours.

After taking leave of him King Vikrama and Naga-Kanya climbed on the ghoul which brought them to Achchyuta-Nagar in a few minutes. He rode straight to King Achchyuta's palace along with Naga-Kanya and sought his permission to take his four daughters back with him.

King Achchyuta too pleaded with him not to take his daughters till completion of his half-yearly exile. But King explained the circumstances of his service under Mathurendra when King Achchyuta had nothing further to say. After embracing him and fondly smelling his daughters on the forehead King Achchyuta bade them farewell with due honours.

The six of them walked to the seashore when King Vikrama thought of his friend Jalandhara who immediately appeared before them from under the sea as a giant frog. All of them found comfortable seats on his broad back and Jalandhara safely carried them to the other shore.

Once ashore, King Vikrama and his five new wives rode again on the shoulders of the ghoul while Jalandra, in human form followed them and all of them reached the neighbourhood of Mathura. They stayed on the way till it was dark and at night fall entered the city and reached their residence.

Ratnamala was beside herself with joy and the first act she did on sighting Aditya was to revive Hasamukhi who was languishing in the cupboard as a wooden doll, by sprinkling water that was charged with a counter-spell. She pulled her out and brought her before Aditya and together with her stood before him bowing.

Aditya collected all his girls together. Seating himself on a well-laid cot, he drew Ratnamala towards him and after fondly caressing her, said: "My dear, all of us are hungry. Will you let us have quickly something to eat?"

Ratnamala jumped from the cot and ran like a deer in to the kitchen to prepare the food. After that, Aditya dispersed the other girls too to go inside and be of help to Ratnamala.

Since Ratnamala was in her disguise, her appearance was revolting, and Naga-Kanya immediately became allergic towards her. So she called her co-wives aside and said, "If our husband had uttered a word, any one of us would have brought a better looking housemaid from our palace! I don't know how he manages to eat the food prepared by such a foul-looking woman!"

The other girls too agreed.

The dining bell went and all the women, together with Aditya, Jalandhara and Ananta lined up for meals and sat down. Ratnamala went about running like a top and serving them enthusiastically.

Suddenly Naga-Kanya who was seated opposite to Aditya developed nausea and started vomiting.

Growing apprehensive, Aditya asked her, 'what is wrong with you? Is your health not all right?"

"My health is all right! It is the food that is revolting!" replied Naga-Kanya contemptuously.

"Oh! None of us find anything wrong about the food. On the contrary we have always found Ratnamala's hand endowed with special flavour!" said Aditya.

"Exactly. Her revolting look has endowed a *special* flavour to her cooking and that made me vomit," replied Naga-Kanya.

Aditya immediately recognized the trouble with Naga-Kanya as being psychological and immediately signalled to Ratnamala who went inside.

"Ratnamala!" called Aditya and the woman who returned was the celestial Ratnamala, in all her glory. Naga-Kanya's eyes opened wide with wonder on seeing her. Aditya watched them with a mischievous smile.

31

The Well of Mercury

WHILE Aditya was lost in the joy of the reunion, King Mathurendra was counting the hours of his non-return. He waited till nightfall, but not seeing Aditya return, sent for his Minister. When the latter came the King told him: "Today is the 60th day since Aditya went and so far he has not turned up. I am certain that he has fallen a victim to snake poison. Let us now decide on our next step." The Minister replied: "May it please your Majesty – haste makes for waste. No doubt his contract expires today, but only if he does not return before daybreak. If, however, he does not turn up by then we shall look to the next step tomorrow."

Even as they were conversing Aditya was heard approaching them by the sound of his high-heeled boots. They looked up and Mathurendra's face turned visibly pale. Aditya as usual stood to attention before the King and deposited at his feet the tell-tale *naga-ratnas*.

King Mathurendra took them in his trembling hands and had little difficulty in recognizing their genuineness. He passed them on to his Minister who too respectfully looked at them and applied them to his eyes, as a mark of esteem.

The King formally asked Aditya of how he fared in his adventure to which Aditya replied that all went well.

Handling over the valued gems to the comptroller, the King rose from the *durbar* after bidding goodnight to all the courtiers.

Aditya too retuned to his lodging to spend the night with his seven brides.

Aditya thus spent a few days happily with all his girls. As was the wont of the Karkotaka brothers, they too started visiting him.

During one of these visits, they happened to see Naga-Kanya. They also learned from Aditya about her identity. Straight they went to King Mathurendra and reported on the unparalleled beauty of Naga-Kanya.

The incorrigible King too expressed his desire to have a look at the new girl. It was agreed to handle the same strategy as was used on two former occasions and the brothers departed.

The following night, the Karkotaka brothers came in for a chat with Aditya. After a short stay, Karkotaka left his brother behind as usual, and went out to fetch the King. At the gate Ananta asked him if he was going home. Absent-mindedly Karkotaka replied in the affirmative.

When thus everybody had retired, Ananta as was the practice, built himself into an impregnable fort round Aditya's home while Jalandhara expanded himself into a strong upper cover. But for all outer appearances there was little change.

Karkotaka returned with his brother who was really King Mathurendra, as usual, but as they set foot at the gate, the sharp teeth of Ananta pierced their feet and the snake poison was deadly in effect. Both of them fell down senseless. Ananta immediately went and reported to Aditya of what had happened to Karkotaka and the King.

Aditya guessed the evil intentions behind the two. Yet he said: "However evil was Karkotaka, he had been my friend. So cure him completely of poison. The King was a victim of temptation held out by Karkotaka. Draw the poison from out of his head and senses, and concentrate it at his knees so that it may be sort of deterrent for him."

Accordingly Ananta did. Karkotaka recovered completely but when he saw Mathurendra struggling to stand up, he had no further option but to lift him bodily and carry him to the palace.

When the morrow came, King Mathurendra realized to his distress that his legs had been paralysed. Being at his wit's end, he sent for his Minister, Diwakara, to whom he related the incident of the previous night and asked: "Under my present state, how shall I proceed in my next step?"

The Minister replied: "What shall I say, Your Majesty? This man who has the power to bring the pearls and *naga-ratnas* should really be of extraordinary valour. It does not appear to me wise at all to antagonize him."

"But," replied the King, "the alternative to it is my certain death!"

The Minister drew a deep breath and replied, "Your Majesty, I have come to the conclusion that Aditya is so valorous that he will even win Indra. It is futile to send him on second-rate adventures. I have a last plan and that is this. You must proceed to the forest on the fastest steed and Aditya should accompany you ostensibly for having a look at the well of mercury. When both of you peep into it you must let slip into it your ring of insignia and exclaim that it had fallen accidentally and order Aditya to get it quickly back from the well. You must, without waiting race back to the palace. Aditya who will jump into the well will never come back alive. You can then have his women for yourself."

"An excellent idea," agreed the King and dispersed the Minister.

Next morning the King moved to the *durbar* on crutches pretty early and waited for Aditya who came exactly with the chime of the bell, and stood to attention.

Addressed the King: "Aditya, I have a fancy for having a

look at the well of mercury which is in the forest yonder. Will you accompany me?"

"As your Majesty orders," said Aditya and added: "Please permit me for leaving you for a few minutes so that I can come back properly changed for going out."

"By all means; please hurry up," commanded the King.

Aditya who could not make out the relevancy of the King's strange request invoked the ghoul as he reached his lodging. It appeared. Aditya asked: "Tell me now all about the King's new assignment to me."

The ghoul exercised its super-human powers and said: "King Vikrama, Mathurendra is making the last bid to make an end of you. It is his plan to deliberately drop his ring into the well and make you jump into it without ever coming out of it, because the liquid is very dense and poisonous."

"I see! Fool that he is," remarked he and beckoning to his friend Jalandhara, he said: "Go this instant and stay inside the well of mercury. Keep alert. Immediately when the King drops the ring, catch it and hand it over to me: you should not delay even by a second."

"Yes", said Jalandhara and withdrew.

Aditya replenished his *pan-supari* box for the journey and hurried back to the King whom he met half-way, ready for the journey. Another steed was there which was to carry him. The two of them spurred their steeds and made straight for the forest. The way had been made clear for them and guide-posts on the way led them easily to the well in the deep of the forest.

The King alighted first, followed by Aditya whose observant eyes roved round the hands of the King.

"How shining is the mercury here!" said the King looking beneath, but immediately followed: "What a fool have I been! I had been toying with the ring of insignia and the thing has fallen into the well! Will you kindly take the ring out and follow me?"

Without even waiting for an answer the King jumped on to the back of his steed and raced back, not once looking back.

As pre-planned, Jalandhara picked up the ring even before it fell and handed it back to Aditya who jumped on his steed and raced behind the King.

After about an hour the King became tired and got down near a grove but hardly had he settled when Aditya reached him on his steed. The King looked back and exclaimed: "Aditya! Did you get the ring back? I had an urgent matter to attend to, and so did not stop for you. Where is it?"

"Here, Your Majesty!" said Aditya handing the ring back. The King's surprise knew no bounds but he bit his lips to cover his anger. Most casually he asked for the *pan-supari* box which Aditya was holding and treated himself to a dose of it.

Resuming their journey both of them reached the palace. All along, the King had been wondering how Aditya had been able to recover the ring within the batting of an eyelid. Lest his plot should become clear, he did not speak about it.

The next day while the King was holding the *durbar*, with Aditya in attendance, Lord Saniswara came there diguised as an aged brahmin. He held in his hands a ripe lime in which was concealed Vikrama's ring of insignia. The old man walked up and presenting it to Aditya blessed him and together with him walked out. The seven-and-a-half-years of *sade sati* had ended and Saniswara's suzerainty ended with it. So he returned the insignia.

Saniswara took Aditya to a forsaken *mutt* and there explained to him the facts and requested him to go back to Ujjain to assume kingship.

In the meantime the King whose curiosity was roused by the unceremonious departure of Aditya with a brahmin sent his courtiers to report whither they were bound. On learning their destination, Mathurendra himself went along with his Minister to were Aditya and the aged brahmin had gone. On the way Mathurendra related to his Minister how Aditya had recovered the lost ring in practically no time.

To their astonishment instead of Aditya they found a King in all his glory in deep conversation with Lord Saniswara. The King hid himself at a distance and listened to the conversation.

Said Saniswara: "Vikrama, I know how cruelly Mathurendra treated you. I shall therefore catch hold of him."

King Vikrama replied: "Lord, please don't do that. Mathurendra only fell a victim to another man's temptation. Even then, whatever he did to me has ended to my benefit. I am not sorry for the trails. For that, I have made him a paralytic. So, kindly spare him, his Minister Diwakara and all his courtiers."

Mathurendra had no doubts about the identity of Aditya and so he lost no time in coming out and falling at King Vikrama's feet craving pardon for all the ills he had done him. His Minister and courtiers followed in supplication.

"I pardon you all," said Vikrama. Mathurendra again fell at his feet and prayed: "In your large heart there is no room at all for any ill-feeling. Please cure me of my paralysis too."

King Vikramaditya called Ananta and ordered him to take the poison away from Mathurendra's knees which he did immediately.

Mathurendra threw his crutches away and again fell at the feet of King Vikrama and Lord Saniswara who blessed him.

32

Ratnamala Escapes

AFTER Lord Saniswara left them, King Mathurendra arranged for a grand reception to King Vikramaditya. He took Vikrama on a richly caparisoned elephant in a huge procession round the city, himself walking on bare feet. Eighteen kinds of music played before the procession. The streets were gaily decorated with flags and festoons.

On reaching the palace, Mathurendra held out his hand and received King Vikrama solicitously and conducted him to his throne, seating him thereon, while he himself stood by him respectfully. The *durbar* was packed to capacity.

In pin-drop silence Mathurendra introduced Vikrama to his officials and the audience, and ended, saying, "Your Gracious Majesty should forgive me for the crime of treating you, although unknowingly, as a serf."

King Vikrama smiled graciously and replied, "On the contrary, I am going to present you with all the girls of mine whom you loved, excepting Ratnamala!"

Mathurendra felt as though he received an electric shock; but recovering himself, replied: "Your Majesty, if I had known your identity, I would not even have dreamt of it. Please forgive me once again."

King Vikrama replied: "Mathurendra, you know that no one who comes to me with a request returns dissatisfied; I cannot make an exception of it with you. So, you must accept what I offer. If you refuse, it will prove to be a slur on my name!"

Continuing, King Vikrama said: "You have been paying me all these seven-and-a-half years all that I asked of you and treated me most conscientiously according to the nature of the post I sought and accepted. You may, therefore, treat this offer of mine as being in return for those kind acts."

Not waiting for any reply King Vikrama called Ananta and ordered him to fetch his women. When they arrived, Vikrama bade Ratnamala sit by his side on the throne, and after coaxing others into acceptance, gave over the rest of them to King Mathurendra with a spoonful of water.

Calling Minister Diwakara, Vikrama said: "I have always admired your intelligence and compared you to my Bhatti. Will you kindly arrange to bring from my home all the money that was paid to me as wages which I have kept?"

Diwakara sent messengers to bring them. When they came in with huge bags, King Vikrama thrust into the hands of Diwakara several bags of coins and distributed the rest among other kings and nobles present. He did not forget the poor and the needy to whom also he distributed gold with both hands.

Towards the end, he called Mathurendra aside and explained, Mathurendra, I was serving under you for seven and a half years at Lord Saniswara's behest, for I was doing his term. Now that he has relieved me, I want to hurry to Ujjain and look after my state affairs. I am most grateful for all the good things done by you. Please bid me farewell!"

Saying this, he started, taking Ratnamala with him. Once out of the city, he rode with her on the shoulder of the ghoul while Ananta and Jalandhara followed them.

The party first went to the lake on whose banks King Vikrama met Ananta and Jalandhara as the serpent and frog. There King Vikrama delivered them from their curse when they became Kings as before.

Resuming his journey he rode on the shoulders of the ghoul to Ujjain along with those two Kings and Ratnamala.

Before entering Ujjain, King Vikrama made for the temple of his family deity, Bhadrakali, went round her several times and offered prayers. Later, he entered the city and reached the palace. After sending Ratnamala away to the harem, Vikrama went to the state-room and occupied the celestial throne.

Vikrama liberally rewarded the two Kings who were delivered of their curse, and sent them home with blessings to resume their rule.

After bidding all adieu, Vikrama called his Minister Bhatti and ordered him, "Bhatti! Ratnamala and myself would like to go through the streets of Ujjain in procession. So get the state-elephant properly decorated for us to ride on."

Bhatti immediately issued instructions for a grand procession with the said elephant gorgeously decorated.

In the meantime, Ratnamala who went to Vikrama's harem, suddenly recollected that the seven-and-a-half-years of her term with Vikrama ordained by Devendra had come to an end. Fearing that further stay would enrage Devendra, she flew to heaven, without informing any one. She could do so because she was an *apsaras*.

Going straight to Devendra, she stood bowing before him.

"Ah!" exclaimed Indra, "There you are. I know you will be prompt in returning. But after the long years you have spent with Vikrama, do you think he will let you go away like this?

For aught I know of him, you can expect Vikrama here any moment. And, you know, being my very great friend, it will be difficult for me to say 'no' to him. So, will you do this? Go and hide yourself in any of those one thousand dark cells down here and let me see if he can spot you there."

Ratnamala accordingly went and hid herself in one of those places which it was humanly impossible to discover.

When the procession was ready to start, Bhatti informed Vikrama that Ratnamala could not be found anywhere in the harem. Bhatti reported that he had himself gone and made a thorough search without success.

King Vikrama on hearing it was a trifle disappointed at the beginning, but being a man of strong will, decided to find her out wherever she might be. His first thought went to heaven as being the most natural place she might have gone to. So, riding on the ghoul, he made straight to heaven, and stood before Indra.

Indra received him with great affection and asked of him, "I hope Lord Saniswara did not trouble you too much, did he?"

"Oh, no! But I came here on an important work," replied Vikrama.

"What is it? Tell me just now if it is so very urgent."

"Ratnamala, whom you sent to me, has just disappeared. I wonder whether she came over here by any chance."

"Ratnamala? Not to my knowledge," said Indra

"No, no, please don't joke, I am dead earnest; I am positive she came here," protested Vikrama.

"If you are so sure, you are welcome to find her and take her!" replied Indra with mischievous smile.

King Vikrama then called the ubiquitous ghoul and ordered it to find out where Ratnamala was. It had no difficulty in entering the dark cells in one of which it found Ratnamala huddled and so returned and informed Vikrama. With its aid King Vikrama penetrated the dark cell and found her out. Dragging her by the hand he stood before Indra who laughed in great mirth.

In the end, Indra gave away Ratnamala along with six more *apsaras* to King Vikrama and after honouring him suitably, bade him good luck.

King Vikrama together with the seven women, rode on the

ghoul, reaching Ujjain quickly. The procession then started, thus fulfilling the schedule.

It so happened that those *apsaras* were the disciples of Sage Narada and other *rishis* who taught them dance and music. When they therefore came to know that their *chelas* had gone away to the earth, they felt sadly disappointed as they had great expectations of them. So they went to Devendra and complained.

Devendra felt sorry for them, but he said, "It is impossible for me to get back what has been gifted away to King Vikramaditya. But if you think you can, I have no objection to your trying to get them back."

"We shall try."

Saying this, the *rishis* came to Ujjain and disguising themselves as aged brahmins, stood at the palace-gate awaiting the arrival of King Vikrama who had gone out in procession along with the *apsaras*.

The procession returned and along with it King Vikrama and his *apsaras*. When they came past them, the *rishis* shouted loudly, "May God bless Vikrama."

This caught the attention of King Vikrama who got down and bowed before them. The *rishis* who had been waiting for this occasion said in one voice: "We have heard it said that no one who comes to you returns empty-handed. We have no one to attend to us and we want those *apsaras* for that purpose!" pointing out to the seven women seated on the elephant.

Without a word King Vikrama ordered for a tumbler of water and pouring a spoon of water on the hand of each *rishi*, he gave away all the seven *apsaras*. King Vikrama was the happiest man when he had done so.

Receiving them, the seven *rishis* hastened to heaven and stood before Devendra who was wonderstruck at the sight of the *apsaras* come back.

"How did you manage to get them?" asked he.

The *rishis* reported what actually happened and praised the utter detachment and grace with which King Vikrama parted with the girls.

Devendra then moralized: "Whether in the earth or heaven I have not come across a King or man or *deva* who can be as great and noble as a thousandth part of King Vikrama." All the *devas* and *rishis* present praised King Vikrama.

At Ujjain, at the conclusion of the procession, King Vikrama sat down at some leisure and related to Bhatti all his experiences during the last seven-and-a-half years till his return to Ujjain. On his part, Bhatti too narrated the important events that had taken place at Ujjain during Vikrama's absence. After thanking all the nobles and citizens present, King Vikrama retired.

After bath and evening prayer, King Vikrama had a hearty meal consisting of thirty-two dishes, ate *tambul*, wore fragrant flowers and entered his bed-chamber where his one thousand and eight *devis* received him with open arms. In this manner King Vikramaditya ruled over Ujjain from the divine throne for a long time, living in voluntary exile every alternate six months.

At this stage the statuette holding the seventh step addressed King Bhoja, "Do you think, Bhoja that you can accomplish as much as a billionth part of what he did. If not, get down and walk home!"

King Bhoja and Nitivakya who had completely forgotten their mission listening to the absorbing story told by that statuette, came back to their senses, and being asked by the statuette to return, did so sadly, fully realizing the greatness of King Vikramaditya.

As though sympathising with King Bhoja's plight, the sun hid himself beneath the western ocean. King Bhoja and Nitivakya wended their way back to their apartments and retired for the night.

33

Danseuse Aparanji

ON the morning of the eighth day, King Bhoja and his Minister awoke with the sun and went through the morning ablutions. After *puja*, they performed the thirty-two daily *dharmas* enjoined on kings. Finishing breakfast they entered the *durbar* where all nobles and the citizens had assembled.

Walking straight towards the celestial throne once occupied by King Vikramaditya, King Bhoja had a full-length *puja* performed to it by priests. He himself prostrated before it at the conclusion of the *puja* and ascended the steps with trepidation.

Nothing happened till he reached the eighth step when he heard a sudden clap of hands followed by the exclamation: "Hey, Bhoja! After all, the expostulations of my seven sisters appear to have fallen on deaf ears; for, you do not seem to have become any the wiser for them. Let me ask: in what way do you think you are qualified to sit on this throne belonging to Vikramaditya the Great? Can you boast at least of a thousandth part of his valour?" This challenge came from the statuette supporting the eighth step, which had suddenly become animated.

Although King Bhoja had become accustomed to this sort of pulling up each day, the manner of the present challenge was something uncanny and he became nervous. So he cupped his hands before the statuette and begged, "Oh statuette, could you further enlighten me with the great exploits of King Vikramaditya? I shall be greatly indebted to you!"

"Hear, then, of the episode of Aparanji!" said the statuette and narrated the following story:

During one of his half-yearly self-imposed exiles, King Vikrama took Bhatti also with him after entrusting the task of running the government of his state to Vibhoga, Bhatti's son, and his other Ministers.

As usual the King and his Minister went to the temple of Bhadrakali before leaving and offered prayers to Her. Kali appeared in front of them and blessed them for a safe journey.

Carried by the ghoul, Vikrama and Bhatti crossed many a river and forest and, on the way, punished men or beasts when they were unlawful. Thus they reached the Vindhya hills. At a certain place of that range, flowed the river Jallari and on its bank was situated the city of Rajapuri. That city was ruled by a King named Rajasingh. He was famed for his justness of rule.

In that city lived a courtesan by name Aparanji. She was beautiful and wealthy. She had a lover who went by the name of Appaji to whom she was greatly attached. It was said that they had grown together in love from their cradle.

One day, Appaji, like all mortals, fell dead. But Aparanji was so infatuated with love for him that she would not admit of his death. She decided therefore to move even the heavens for Appaji's revival.

Accordingly she took the corpse to the temple of Kali-Mata at the outskirts of the city. After distributing food, clothes, money, etc., to the poor, she prayed and prayed before deity that the Mother-Goddess could not help appearing before her.

When she did so, Aparanji took hold of Kali-Mata's feet and washed them with the stream of her tears, entreating Her to give back her lover. Mother-Goddess felt pity on her and observed:

"Aparanji, within a week from now King Vikramaditya with his Minister Bhatti will come to this city in the guise of a jewel-merchant. If you win his unqualified love, he can revive your lover. I may tell you this: whatever he asks you, including your self-immolation in the fire, you must carry out willingly. He will save you and you can in turn save your lover by the same power." After saying this, Mother-Goddess disappeared.

Aparanji returned home with the corpse which she embalmed and carefully preserved in a box, eagerly awaiting the arrival of Vikramaditya.

In the meantime, Vikrama and Bhatti disguised themselves as jewellery merchants. The former called himself Kanti Senior and the latter Kanti Junior. They spread their wares which consisted of huge quantities of all kinds of gems in the marketplace and started plying a brisk trade. The jewellers and connoisseurs of the city were amazed at the quality and variety of gems displayed by the Kanti brothers and liberally replenished their treasures with them. With sunset the brothers repaired to an old inn which they had made their temporary abode. A week was spent in this manner.

One evening, returning to the inn, Kanti Senior felt a longing to visit the street occupied by courtesans. So, leaving word with the Junior, he walked down to the bazaar where he treated himself liberally to fragrant ignites like musk and bought and put on gorgeous apparel suitable for the occasion. As he went about the particular street, scanning the balconies, a particularly fascinating courtesan caught his attention and he found himself ascending one soon. On its spacious verandah were laid luxurious couches on one of which he reclined comfortably and waited for its owner to turn up.

That house happened to be the one occupied by Aparanji who by chance came out. On seeing a visitor poised on the cushion with expectancy she plied a scrutinizing glance which revealed the high nobility of the visitor not usually met with. She advanced towards him elegantly and from her knowledge of physiognomy, it was small guess for her to divine that the visitor could be no other than Vikramaditya of whom Mother-Goddess had spoken. His apparel fitted well with the description of a well-to-do jewel merchant.

She put on her best smile and stood before him solicitously but meekly. Kanti Senior was instantaneously taken up with her form and demeanour and allowed himself to be conducted inside and seated on her bed. She treated him to excellent food and drink, and behaved as though she was being honoured by Kanti's company unlike the ordinary courtesan who generally started with business. King Vikrama wondered at his luck. He felt there was divine flavour in the *tambul* she gave him!

Kanti Senior spent the night with her like the God of Love with Rati. Aparanji captivated his heart by displaying her consummate skill in the art of love as described by ancient writers on the subject and also entertained him with dance and music. Before the small hours of the morning Vikrama was like the fly in a bottle of honey.

King Vikrama in his nocturnal adventures, never used to stay beyond sunrise; he was invariably back before daybreak. But in this particular instance, he had overstayed and even then, could return to his inn with the greatest reluctance. This struck Kanti Junior as particularly odd and set him thinking and working on it.

Said the Junior to the Senior when the latter returned: "Your Majesty, does it look proper to return late thus with all the marks of a nocturnal revelry?"

"You are right, Bhatti!", replied Senior, "but this lady is completely different. I have never in my experience come across a woman, so selfless, so devoted and so very likeable.

With great difficulty I tore my mind away from her for the day!"

"Your Majesty!" said Bhatti, "Can a courtesan, by her very nature ever be faithful or love one without expectation?"

"No; but not Aparanji!"

"I beg to differ; more I venture to suggest that this lady hasn't got an iota of love for you!"

"Can you prove?" challenged Senior.

"Yes; tonight when you go to her house, as I am sure you will, please do as I ask. At the time of returning, ask her to cut off her braided hair and give it to you, if you can."

"I promise," replied Vikrama, and after bath and food both went about their profession of vending jewels. Kanti Senior had little mind in his sales; but for the Junior's sharp eyes, many clever buyers would have knocked a huge bargain.

The day's work over, Kanti Senior's legs dragged him to the apartments of Aparanji. He dressed himself more gorgeously and found himself climbing the steps of Aparanji's place. Aparanji too appeared to have waited for him, for she suddenly appeared, slid her hands into his and danced her way into her bed-chamber which was decorated like the nuptial chamber of an *apsaras*, and from where celestial incense was floating bewitchingly into the nostrils of even passersby!

When night was drawing to a close, Kanti Senior was so overwhelmed by her attentions that he felt it a sacrilege to suspect her of infidelity, more so to ask her to part with her braid. But inasmuch as he had accepted the challenge thrown by Bhatti, he was put in an awkward position. As he felt uneasy, Aparanji put him at ease. "Beloved! You seem to feel embarrassed over something. I beg to be pardoned, if I have offended you in any way," said she.

"Oh, no!" protested Kanti profusely and said, "er-er, I want that braid of hair of yours, for some important purpose and I don't know if I am within my rights in asking it of you... absurd though it is...."

Aparanji did not wait for any explanation, but proceeded straight to bring a pair of scissors with which she cut her wealth of hair which she had so beautifully done Ajanta-wise and handed it to Kanti with a smiling face.

Kanti was stupefied at her readiness, for he anticipated at least a few moments of reflection on her part, especially since women of old held their braid of hair as a symbol of beauty. On one side, his compassion for the devoted Aparanji welled up in him and on the other, he bit his lips at the absent Bhatti for his calculated outrage on the lady of his love.

Without looking back at Aparanji for shame, Kanti walked out in a huff to demonstrate that for once Bhatti was wrong.

Back at the inn, he roused Bhatti and threw the lump of hair which had so charmingly adorned her and was so willingly given away by Aparanji, and flung the question: "Now, what do you say?"

"I am not surprised: I am all the more convinced that Aparanji is anything but devoted to you," replied Kanti Junior with a sneer.

"How do you say that?"

"Your Majesty will know that soon. If I may take the liberty, I would request you to do this when you visit her tonight. Kindly ask her to cut off the tip of her nose and give it to you."

"I am sure she will! If I bring it, will you concede that she is devoted to me?" asked the King.

"I shall tell that at that time. Please bring it," replied Bhatti.

Kanti Senior waited for the sun to set to proceed to Aparanji's house. When he went, he found Aparanji more than ever eager to receive him. There was not a flicker of anger on her face on what he did the previous night. She conducted him to her bed-chamber where she treated him to light refreshment. They spent the night in a manner which made Kanti feel proud of her.

As he was preparing to depart, Bhatti's challenge came to his mind and he fumbled for words, whereupon Aparanji put him at ease by offering, "Sir, please do not hesitate to tell me anything, if you feel like it."

Afraid of looking at her, he told her, "I am sorry to have to ask you to do a difficult job for me."

"Please ask,' encouraged Aparanji.

"I want the tip of your nose for some important purpose," Kanti blurted out.

"Here, you can have it," replied Aparanji who took out a knife from the cupboard and cut off her nose neatly and gave it to him.

Kanti was astounded at her act and felt guilty. His anger against his Minister mounted as he started realizing that his request was diabolical. He ran home to tell Bhatti to stop this nonsense.

Seeing Bhatti at the inn, Kanti Senior threw the nose-tip before him and interjected: "What do you say now?"

Junior shook his head and said gravely, "I still maintain that the woman has not an iota of love for you."

Vikrama thumped his foot in rage.

34

Aparanji Shuts Out Vikrama

"I am sorry to have to contradict Your Majesty's opinion," continued Bhatti, "and truth is always unpalatable I hope to establish my theory today."

"How? asked Senior.

"Tonight while returning kindly ask her to cut off her breast and give it to you," said Bhatti with a stern countenance. Kanti Senior biting his lips thought furiously.

Looking at the way Aparanji behaved, he could not believe even a wedded wife would love him in such a manner and put up with all the humiliations he had been inflicting. If her heart was not set on him, why should she behave that way, he wondered. Or was it the intention of Bhatti to drive a wedge between him and the lady by inciting her on the one hand by humiliations and disfiguring her at the same time?

Kanti Senior wanted to find out once and for all the truth about the matter and so he went that night to Aparanji's house. She was her old self, and showed little repugnance towards him. Steeling his heart, he got from her willing hands, what his outrageous Minister had wanted and ran to the inn.

Finding Kanti Junior, the Senior flung what she gave, at his face, and asked: "What do you say now?"

"I have no reason to change my opinion now. Give me eight days' time to prove her hypocrisy to the hilt, replied Junior.

"Oh, you have still not changed your mind! However, I agree to you on this condition if you now fail to prove your contention, you will be subjected to those very humiliations which you so callously prescribed for her."

"Yes; I too have one condition: you should stop visiting her for eight days from now", replied Junior.

"I promise," agreed Senior and retired.

For eight days thereafter the Kanti brothers concentrated on their business, namely selling gems. Beyond a certain reticence on the Senior's part there was no difference in the relationship between the two.

Early on the ninth day Kanti Junior said: "Your Majesty, I am going to demonstrate to you that my opinion of Aparanji is the correct one. May I therefore request you to follow me without asking any questions?"

"Yes," replied Senior demurely and did as he asked. The two merchants collected all their belongings, swung their wares on their shoulders, paid all their dues and called on some important people to bid them good bye. All of them were surprised at their sudden departure, but Junior explained that they had some pressing work at home.

After leaving the environs of the city, the merchant brothers walked for about four miles and entered a forest path. After going a few yards, Kanti Junior selected a clean patch of ground adjoining the pathway and addressed Senior: "May I now request you to lie hidden behind the thick bush yonder and keep watching what I do, without coming out?"

"Yes", agreed Senior, wondering what else he had up his sleeve.

Kanti Junior collected some dry fuel and carrying them together to that spot started to make a fire. When the fire grew big, he fed it with more fuel and leaves. The fire began to rage. Suddenly Junior began to beat his breast, pull at his hair and loudly lament.

Some passersby who noticed it came near him and asked:

"Why are you weeping?"

"My brother Kanti Senior and I were returning. A deadly cobra which crossed our way bit my brother who fell dead instantaneously. I am doing his last rites by burning his body here - *Oom* - *Oom* -"

The travellers expressed their sympathies and started resuming their journey. The Junior beckoned to them and asked: "Are you going to Rajpuri?"

"Yes", they replied.

"Will you do me a favour?" requested Junior. "At Rajpuri, there is a famous danseuse by name Aparanji. My late brother was her favourite lover. Will you kindly convey to her that Kanti Senior died by snake-bite and that his brother is doing the last obsequious by burning him here and that he will soon depart?"

"Surely we will," they replied and departed.

When Aparanji heard that Kanti Senior had died and his body was being burnt near the forest path, she immediately put on her best dress, applied oil to her head, wore red-flowers, and sought audience before the King who granted it immediately.

Represented she: "Your Majesty, my favourite lover Kanti Senior had died of snake-bite in the forest yonder at the fourth mile. I am going to enter his pyre as his faithful spouse; please permit me to do so."

The King guffawed hilariously and said: "If that man is gone, there are umpteen paramours to wait on you. If you people start behaving like this, what is the world coming to?"

"You must forgive me; but I have made up my mind," replied Aparanji and with the King's consent started walking briskly towards the forest.

Kanti Senior who had been watching the drama enacted by Junior suddenly saw at the far distance, the silhouette of Aparanji hurrying towards them. He had no further doubt of Aparanji's intention to immolate herself at his supposed pyre. So, he came out of his hiding and accosted Junior, "What more trouble are you going to put me and the lady to? Look! She will be here in a few minutes. Do you still doubt her love for me? And now I must warn you; if anything amiss happens to her – I suspect she will most certainly fall into this fire – I will hold you fully responsible for the crime. Do you hear?"

"I do; but why don't you wait and find everything for yourself?" replied Junior, losing his patience.

"That means you still hold on to your opinion? You must have been a stone in your last birth!" exclaimed Senior digusted.

Kanti Junior laughingly replied, "I am sorry to tell you I am more than ever convinced that Aparanji has the least little love for you!"

"You are monster in human form!" retorted Senior.

"Please wait and see; she will be here now and so, kindly hide yourself," entreated Junior.

When Aparanji came near him, Junior re-enacted the drama about his brother's death so well that she did not even wait for its confirmation. Aparanji had remembered Mother Kali's tip even to immolate herself in the fire if need be.

She contemplated therefore for a few moments on her beloved Appaji and closing her hands in prayer, entered the raging fire coolly.

Kanti Senior who was watching her intently rushed to save her, but Junior put out his strong hands and forbade him from doing so. In a second, her whole figure was enveloped in the flames and she was no more to be seen.

Kanti Senior stood stupefied. For a moment the whole world became extinct for him. But Junior shook him from his stupor and said, "Your Majesty! Now let us push ahead. Please invoke your family deity Bhadrakali and bring back Aparanji to life."

At this Kanti Senior became animated and prayed fervently to Bhadrakali for Aparanji's restoration. Kali appeared before him and gave him a pot of holy water, a holy wand and sacred ashes with which she said he could revive her.

Kanti Senior accordingly sprinkled the sacred water on the huge fire before him which died down immediately. There inside was the body of Aparanji fresh and charming. When he smeared the ash all over her body and touched her with the sacred wand, she sat up lovely, all her blemishes having evaporated.

Standing up, she asked Kanti Senior without even looking at him: "May I request you to give me more of these sacred things?"

Kanti senior instinctively handed over to her the pot of water, the wand and the sacred ash left over. On receiving them, Aparanji walked home briskly without once looking back while the Kanti brothers looked on her receding form, petrified.

Reaching home, Aparanji broke open the door of her bedroom where she had deposited the embalmed body of her late paramour Appaji. She opened the box reverentially, and with trepidation, sprinkled the holy water on the body, smeared the holy ash and touched it with the wand. As if by a miracle, Appaji sat up several years younger. When he looked up, he was immediately locked up in the fervent embrace of Aparanji from whose eyes flowed tears of joy.

For a time Kanti Junior, that is, Bhatti was standing silent at the forest, but King Vikrama shook him from it with the question: "And now what do you propose? The bird has flown!"

"Please follow me; we shall catch it," replied Bhatti and together they walked towards the city inn where they waited till dusk.

At nightfall Bhatti said: "I think you can take the night on from me and visit Aparanji if you feel like it."

"I would love to," replied King Vikrama eagerly.

In a few minutes Vikrama found himself racing along the steps leading to Aparanji's balcony and tapping at the doors of her bedroom from which heavenly incense was issuing in profusion.

"Who is there?" asked Aparanji's voice and in a few second, the door was slightly opened and Aparanji herself stood at the door.

King Vikrama smiled eagerly at her, but Aparanji cut in short saying, "I can't see you now" and shut the door on his face.

35

The Treacherous Queen

FOR a moment King Vikrama felt dazed. Anger and contempt rose in his bosom in alternating currents at the audacity of the courtesan, but Bhatti's warning struck him as the silver lining in the picture and it lit his path as he smiled within his mind at his awkward predicament. He retraced his steps to the inn where Bhatti was anxiously waiting for him.

"How is it, Your Majesty, you have returned so early today?" asked Bhatti.

With a heaving bosom, King Vikramaditya replied, "Will you forgive me, Bhatti, for all the indignities I put you to on account of this vile woman?"

"What happened? Did she refuse to entertain you!" asked Bhatti, feigning surprise.

"Please don't ask me. It was all a mirage she did. I wish I listened to your wise words and had nothing to do with this woman," replied King Vikrama, thoroughly disillusioned.

"Please explain yourself," pleaded Bhatti, whereupon King Vikrama retold in detail what happened to him at Aparanji's place. Bhatti's eyes glinted with apprehension.

King Bhoja who was so absorbed in this story, asked the statuette: "O statuette, what I do not understand is that, while King Vikrama was unable to divine the true intentions of Aparanji, how could Bhatti find it out from the beginning?"

"Hear me, King Bhoja," said the statuette, "When Bhatti knew that his King was strongly attracted by this woman, he went one night to Bhadrakali's temple in that city and prayed before Her. She appeared before him and revealed the true intentions of that courtesan! She further ordered Bhatti to help the woman to carry out her intentions because of Her own promise to her!"

Bhoja thus cleared of his doubt, asked, "What happened to the princely merchants thereafter?

The statuette continued the story:

King Vikrama and Bhatti spent the night at the inn and at daybreak started trekking for the adjoining city. They were travelling through a forest path. On the way King Vikrama said to Bhatti, "One should never have faith in courtesans!"

As soon as he said it, they heard a peal of laughter mocking him emanating from the ground. When they looked in that direction, they witnessed a cast-off coating of a serpent producing the sound, immediately rising in the air with a swirl and finally disappearing high in the air!

King Vikrama who witnessed it asked Bhatti, "What is this phenomenon?"

Bhatti who too saw it, racked his brain and not finding any solution, replied: "I shall tell you after three days" to which the King agreed. They walked further, observing the peculiarities of the forest and reached the next city by nightfall.

They took shelter in a *mutt* for the night. Tired by the day's walk and his recent nerve-racking experience, King Vikrama fell into a sound sleep. But Bhatti could not get an ounce of sleep. Finding that the King was fast asleep, Bhatti walked out of the *mutt* and invoked the ghoul which promptly appeared.

He related to it his late experience of the laughing snake-coil and sought its help to transport him to the temple of Mahakali at Ujjain immediately. The ghoul obeyed and in a trice Bhatti stood at the gate of Mahakali.

At that dead of night, Mahakali was having a conference with her *ganas* or forces. But Bhatti, unmindful of it, went round the temple thrice and started praying.

Mahakali, on noticing him asked, "How is it Bhatti, that you are here at this time, when you should have been with your king who is far off?"

Bhatti replied: "Mother, what you say is true, but I came hurrying to you in a special circumstance. Having been disillusioned by the treachery of Aparanji, my king and myself were travelling along the forest when my lord happened to utter that all courtesans were unfaithful. Suddenly, the dead coil of a serpent became animated, laughed in derision at those words and flew into heaven. The King asked me to explain its significance. I tried my best, but being unable to do so, I promised to let him know of it in three days. In order to keep my promise I came to you posthaste seeking an explanation.

Mahakali had an indulgent laugh at his expense and said: "What derided you in the coil was really Mother Earth. She could not tolerate the sentiment expressed by the King which was manifestly partial. For, the courtesan is not alone in her unfaithfulness. There are black sheep everywhere. At the present moment, for instance, the King's own senior Queen is keeping the company of a *rakshasa* in her harem. She sports a parrot; it is not a real parrot; it is that *rakshasa*. When she places a special pearl-necklace round his neck he becomes the parrot. When she takes it off, he becomes his original self. She converts him into a parrot during day-time after keeping his company at nights."

Bhatti was thunderstruck at the revelation but was nevertheless cleared of his doubt. Falling at her feet once again, he left for the *mutt* on the shoulder of the ghoul where the King was sleeping like a log. He roused the King from his sleep.

When the King woke up, Bhatti put on a sorrowful face on seeing which King Vikrama asked the reason. Bhatti related his trip to Ujjain and what Mahakali told him. On hearing it, blood rushed to his temples and fire sparked through his eyes. Vikrama thundered: "Perfidy, thy name is woman!"

Bhatti put his hands on the King's shoulders and soothed him.

The King asked, "What shall we do about it now?"

"We must start immediately to Ujjain and kill the *rakshasa*," advised Bhatti.

Calling the ghoul, King Vikrama asked for all the weapons he had deposited with it and arming himself to the teeth, rushed to Ujjain on the ghoul's shoulder. Bhatti accompanied him.

When they descended straight into the Queen's room through the balcony, she was having a merry time with the *rakshasa*. The King's fury at the sight knew no bounds; he thundered at the intruder, "Who are you?"

The *rakshasa* trembled at being caught so unawares. He kept mum. But King Vikrama drew out his sword and splashed him into two. But no sooner did the two halves fall down, than they joined together and he started fighting! King Vikrama again cut him into two, the *rakshasa* again came back to life. This went on till daybreak when Vikrama out of sheer ennui, threw the trunk above the head once.

Thus placed, the two parts of his body did not come together, but lay inert, the *rakshasa* dying ultimately.

When they found that there was no spark of life left in the *rakshasa*, the King and Bhatti buried him and left the city. For some days they stayed in a forest adjoining Ujjain.

One day King Vikrama asked Bhatti, "How many days are there yet for the completion of this exile?"

"Twenty-five days more," replied Bhatti.

"Oh, is that all? Will you do one thing? You may now return to Ujjain and look after State affairs. I shall stay here for the 25 days alone and return at the appointed time."

"How shall I leave you alone even if it be for a few days?" asked Bhatti.

"Don't worry. I shall manage myself. Further, what can happen in 25 days?" replied the King laughingly.

Bhatti reluctantly retuned to Ujjain acting on the wishes of his King and looked after State matters.

King Bhoja who thought that the story was coming to a close asked the statuette: "You have not told us how King Vikrama spent the 25 days before returning to his headquarters?"

"Oh, you mean that? I shall tell you presently!" replied the statuette.

36

Vikrama Becomes a Parrot

SAID the statuette: In his younger days King Vikrama had a classmate by name Vijaya who was an iron-smith by birth. They were such fast friends that there was practically no secret which one knew and the other did not.

One day Vijaya asked Vikrama to teach him *indrajala* (magic arts) in which the latter had attained proficiency. When Bhatti who was a common friend, knew of it, dissuaded Vikrama from complying with that request; for instinctively he felt that Vikrama was looking for trouble. But Vikrama brushed aside Bhatti's fears and taught Vijaya the eight-fold *siddhis; anima, mahima, garima, laghima,* etc. By them one could even leave one's body and enter into another's dead body.

Vijaya became an adept in the new art and his initial successes went to his head like old wine and he there and then planned to become King Vikramaditya and sit on this throne one day or other.

While Vijaya was thus waiting for an opportunity news came to him that Bhatti had returned to the capital while King Vikramaditya stayed behind, Vijaya jumped at it and repaired to the forest searching for King Vikrama. He spotted him after a day's search.

King Vikrama was overjoyed at seeing his old friend and welcomed him saying: "Vijaya, how glad I am to see you! How are things? Your business is prospering?"

Vijaya folded his hands before his King and friend, and nodded his head in the affirmative.

After a few minutes' rest, they together went out hunting the wild animals of the forest. It was noon and they became thirsty on account of the morning's hard work. Sighting a pool, they got down and drank handfuls of the crystal water and rested below a huge banyan tree on the roadside.

That tree happened to be the favourite resort of the parrots of the region. King Vikrama lay down on the green with his head on the lap of his friend who was sitting. The cool breeze that was wafted on them induced the much-needed sleep to the pair and they felt drowsy. King Vikrama, however, could not sleep. His mind was wandering from one subject to another. At that time he noticed a pair of parrots engaged in amorous play in a secluded branch which was right above his head. As they were playing, the male parrot suddenly fell down dead. On seeing it, the female parrot became first desolate, then flew down and turned her dead partner with her wings and feet pathetically. King Vikramaditya was greatly moved by the sorrow of the bereaved parrot and suddenly he felt he should comfort the female parrot. So he called into action his magic powers and leaving his own human body entered that of the dead. In a second the dead parrot came back to life and on seeing that, the female one danced with joy and together they flew once again to the top of the tree where they chirped and played once again merrily. King Vikrama in his parrot body did all that was in his power to make the female partner feel wonderfully happy.

Vijaya was really awake at the time of the above occurrence, and noticed the drama of the parrot pair. But it did not strike him at first that Vikrama had entered its body. But when he chanced to look down, he found that Vikrama's body was lifeless and it struck him immediately that he must have entered the dead parrots body! Here was his golden chance, he thought. So he immediately exercised his own powers of magic and entered the body of King Vikramaditya.

Seeing that the two parrots were too engrossed to notice him, he put on the accouterments of King Vikramaditya which were lying aside and slipped away from the place. He made straight for Ujjain.

As soon as he was within sight of the city, he sent word through passersby to Bhatti that King Vikrama had returned and he was waiting at the outskirts to be received. When Bhatti heard this news he became sceptical, because he saw no reason why his lord should change his mind so suddenly. Further, there were several days more for the expiry of the exile period. He felt that some mischief was afoot and he blamed himself for leaving the King to fend for himself in the lonely forest. However, he arranged for a suitable reception and himself went ahead to receive the King.

"Hallo Bhatti, how do you do?" asked fake Vikrama. Bhatti replied suitably and finding that there was a little difference between his master and the new one, he resolved that he should find out the mystery behind the sudden re-appearance.

The new Vikramaditya was taken round the city in procession as usual on the royal elephant and as soon as he reached the palace, Bhatti sent word to the King's harem about the King's arrival. He also gave them to understand that he suspected some mischief in the sudden reappearance of the King and that somebody was possibly impersonating him. Consequently, the queens should not permit the new-comer to enter the *zenana* on the pretext that they are at the moment observing *Gouri Vrata* and it would last for ten more months. The news was duly conveyed and the queens had no difficulty in believing the story, because it came from Bhatti.

When as usual the new Vikrama entered the harem during the course of his visit, the chief servants informed him decorously of the *vrata* of the queens, adding that they would prefer the King not to enter the harem for ten months. The new Vikrama asked Bhatti, "Is that true, Bhatti?"

"Yes, my lord; because we were in the forest, we were not informed of it," replied he.

Subsequently, Bhatti introduced the new king to a few danseuses of the palace with whom the new Vikrama felt perfectly at home. He utilised every opportunity to enjoy the luxuries of the fabulous King of Ujjain. So much so, the affairs of the State came into the hands of Bhatti in their entirety.

Bhatti in the meantime was thinking of the way by which he could trace out his master. He was convinced that the real Vikrama was lost in the body of some beast or bird of the forest. While it was so difficult to trace even humans, it was much more so to trace the denizens of the forest. But he comforted himself at the thought that his master being what he was would certainly manifest himself in a way that was not common. Consequently, he was constantly on the hear-out for things of extraordinary happening all the world over from which he could make a beginning.

Really, Vikrama who transformed himself into a male parrot became so thoroughly engrossed in his new environment and experiences that he absolutely can forgot his past. Even in his bird-life he could carve himself out as a leader. In a very short time his outstanding abilities of leadership attracted the entire community of parrots of the region which started surrounding him day in and day out. If he sortied down to the banks of the lake to quench his thirst, the whole parrot community of the place followed him. If he slept all of them slept.

It was therefore not unnatural that a hunter of the place became fascinated with this community life of the parrots, not because of its rhythm, but because of its value in terms of money. So he was counting the days when he would be able to lay hands on them.

It so happened that one day he found himself just beneath the tree which the parrot group had made its temporary home. While they were out he spread out his huge net cunningly and gummed the branches and was waiting for the birds to return. The birds as usual following their leader returned and settled themselves on that tree the same evening when lo! all of them without exception found themselves trapped. They raised a hue and cry and accosted their leader with this question: "Sir, we have been your true followers all these days and now we find ourselves in trouble as a result. Now tell us the way to get out of it."

Vikrama the parrot replied: "Friends, don't get disheartened. There is only one way to get out of this difficulty. When the hunter pulls down the net, all of you should feign death and not until you hear a signal from me should you open your eyes or move your limbs. Thinking that all of us are dead he would assuredly leave us behind when we can make good our escape."

In the meantime the hunter who was witnessing this wholesale catch from a hiding place, was gloating over his good fortune in having such a huge haul and was imaginarily counting the coins he would get from buyers and the mansion he would build and the clothes he would buy for favourite deity!

When he felt sure that all the birds were securely caught in his net, he made his appearance visible and climbing the tree pulled out the net with the deftness of a skilled craftsman. Yards and yards of net came into his hands each with a crop of catch and not till he pulled out the last lap did he feel safe; but when he started examining them, he was startled to see the first one dead. He went on to the second parrot, and that too was dead.

"What a bad luck?" he exclaimed. The third, fourth and everyone of them was dead. His heart nearly broke and all his calculations tumbled down. Still he continued to examine the remaining parrots. Until the very last he was hopeful, but all of them were dead.

As he threw down the last dead parrot, the knife which he was holding accidentally fell down and that proved to be the signal on which all the 999 parrots flew into the sky. This alerted the hunter who suddenly closed down on the last parrot which was right below him. He caught it in his hands and shook it violently as it became suddenly clear to him that it was that leader-parrot which was responsible for the whole game which made a fool of him.

"I shall munch your head now," roared he.

The last parrot was none other than King Vikramaditya, who slowly opened his eyes and addressed the hunter: "O, hunter, what can I do if the other parrots flew away? Now that you have caught me, what will you gain by killing me? On the contrary, if you follow my advice you will gain a hundred times more than what you would have by the sale of those parrots. Will you listen?"

The hunter was astonished to hear a parrot speak human language.

He replied, "Yes, I am willing to listen".

Said the parrot: "Now you take me to the bazaar where the richest merchants are doing business and if you show me to them, I promise I will get you a real treasure."

The hunter was impressed by the request and accordingly he took the parrot to the bazaar and was soon offering it openly for sale.

A few of the passersby casually asked its price. He replied, at the instance of the parrot, a thousand gold coins. But those people did not even look at him for the second time thinking that he was mad.

As the day wore on, the hunter became disheartened. At that time a rich merchant-prince by name Soma passed that way. He was a young cub and his father was a gold merchant. Like others, he too sparingly had a look at the parrot which the hunter was offering for sale. Being struck with its beauty he casually asked for its price when the hunter replied as usual, a thousand gold coins.

"What?" retorted the young merchant. "One coin is the usual price, but because this is a little more beautiful you can legitimately ask for one more coin, but never this fantastic price. What do you say?"

On hearing this, the parrot itself replied: "Hullo merchant! Look here, you say I am very costly, but I give you a challenge. You buy me at that price and leave me at your shop and within one month, I shall get you ten thousand gold coins. Are you game?"

When the merchant prince heard that, he was not only astounded by the bird's performance, but was greatly convinced of its ability to do as it told.

Without speaking a word he wrote out a hundi for a thousand gold coins and gave it to the hunter who in return gratefully handed over the parrot to the merchant.

Soma took the parrot and walked straight to his father's shop. It so happened that at that very moment, his father was starting a new business for him. The arrival of the parrot at that moment augured well in the eyes of those assembled.

All the guests assembled were suitably served with *tambul*, fruits, drinks, etc.

Immediately after, Soma gave orders for making a golden cage inlaid with nine kinds of gems in which he put the parrot and hung the cage permanently before the counter. The parrot was given royal food at the appropriate hours.

After a few days, the parrot addressed Soma: "My dear sir, I want to advise you on one thing. If you listen to it, I am confident that you will be amassing huge wealth. All that you have to do is to put up luxurious cushions all round the place and ask your customers to be seated comfortably and leave the bargaining to me. Do you agree?"

"Right, go ahead," said Soma and he did as the parrot had asked him.

Within a very few days, Soma's shop was crowded with buyers and his profits were mounting everyday.

In a short time Soma completely left the management of the shop to the parrot, placing only a few assistants at its disposal and himself hardly attended the office.

The secret of the parrot's success was, of course, its clever banter, sense of humour and above all its extraordinary behaviour. People even came to it for adjudication of family disputes! They naturally did not demur even when the parrot demanded exorbitant prices. They willingly paid, because the parrot was the wonder of the age.

In a very short time Soma became ten times richer than his own father, who was reputed to be the richest merchant of the place.

37

The Parrot Escapes

IN the same city, Magadhapur, lived a danseuse by name Rupasundari. Only the richest people of the town could afford to make her acquaintance because she demanded one thousand gold coins for her company! Consequently, Surya Kesari, the heir apparent of the State, Matsya Vallabha, the Minister, Vijayaranga, the Commander-in-Chief's son and the Tahsildar's son, etc., were the only people who could frequent her house. Of course, Soma too belonged to that distinguished coterie.

On one day, two poor brahmins of the place were bathing in the local tank adjoining the temple. One was called Sastri and the other Dikshit. On that day while they were bathing early in the morning, Rupasundari's maidservant too happened to be washing her clothes by their side.

At that time Sastri confided to his friend Dikshit: "Dikshitji I had a strange dream last night, that I had the company of Rupasundari the danseuse!"

On hearing the confession, Rupasundari's maid pricked her ears up and ran to her mistress to whom she reported the conversation.

Rupasundari immediately hurried to the tank in the company of her maidservant who pointed to Sastri, who was performing *japa* in wet clothes, as the man who had confessed.

Rupasundari went directly to Sastri and pulled him by his waist-cloth.

Sastri who did *japa* with closed eyes was startled to find Rupasundari standing before him like Bhadrakali.

She roared: "You dreamt that you had my company last night, didn't you? Pay me my fees of one thousand gold coins right now."

Sastri who never had the good fortune of seeing even one hundred gold coins together in his whole life reeled back at the prospect of being hauled to the court, when his throat became parched and his tongue glued to the palate.

"I am a poor brahmin and where shall I go for the money?" pleaded Sastri imploringly.

"But you had the temerity to dream about me, eh? Shell out the money or come to the court," threatened the woman and hauled him before the court. A large crowd followed them.

The King gave them immediate audience. But when he heard the plaint and the defendant's reply, the King felt unable to decide the case and so sent the litigants to his Ministers. The Ministers too heard the statements of both parties and while they sympathised with both, they could not find a way of settling the dispute.

At that stage, one of the Ministers suggested: "How about sending this case for adjudication to that parrot owned by Soma? People say wonderful things about it."

"That is the best way," agreed all the Ministers and together with the disputants, they went to Soma's parrot for presenting the case.

In the meantime news about this sensational case got round and there was a big stampede before Soma's shop.

The parrot asked Rupasundari to state her case.

Rupasundari addressed the parrot: "Listen parrot, this

brahmin had the pleasure of my company, but refuses to pay my fee of a thousand gold coins."

The parrot then addressed Sastri: "You come from a learned family and yet why did you refuse to pay the woman her fee for her company?"

Sastri replied: "Hear, parrot, I never went to her house nor sought her company. I was sleeping in my own house. I only dreamt that I had the company of a woman who resembled the complainant. I was relating this dream to my friend this morning while bathing in the temple tank. Her servant who overheard our conversation reported it to her and she has now sued me for the fee. How can I pay her?"

The parrot then asked Rupasundari: "Woman, how do you feel justified in asking him to pay for an act he dreamt?"

Rupasundari replied: "I am fully justified in demanding my fee, because in that dream, my soul and his were at one."

On hearing this, the parrot smiled and asked all assembled to make room. It then asked the servant of the shop to bring a pole and a bag of one thousand gold coins. It erected the pole at the centre of the crowd, and, tied the bag of gold on top of it. Beneath that pole on the floor, it placed a large mirror where the reflection of the bag was seen.

The parrot then called Rupasundari near it and said: "You are a clever woman and your case is just. Now, do you see that bag of gold in the mirror? That should naturally belong to you. Take it!"

Rupasundari looked at it but stood idle, not knowing what to do.

"Why don't you take your fee?" asked the parrot.

"How can I take what is only a reflection?" replied she.

"I don't know. If you can take it, that will rightly be the fee for what occurred to that man in a dream!" replied the parrot.

All the people assembled laughed at the absurd situation created by the parrot. Rupasundari felt greatly humiliated.

Addressing the parrot, she said: "You wretched parrot, you, who do not even cost a single coin, how dare you humiliate me in this gathering? I shall no more bear my name, if I do not tear you into pieces and munch your head!"

"Don't be so hasty in pledging what you cannot do," replied the parrot. It continued: "I am a small thing, no doubt, but you will concede that, in judging your case, I have been fair to both of you. It was never my intention to humiliate you. It is you who have taken offence at my judgment. In doing so you are behaving like a cad. Yet, I am willing to take up your challenge. If you insist on yours, you shall not only fail in your boast, but I shall surely see that your head is shaved clean and you go round the local temple of Vishnu in sack-cloth and ashes thrice, uttering 'Govinda' 'Govinda'."

"All right," replied Rupasundari, and added, "within eight days from today, I shall fulfil my pledge," and returned home, followed by a jeering crowd.

For four days together Rupasundari had neither food nor sleep. She was busy planning as to how she should fulfil her vow to wreak vengeance on the parrot.

The fifth from that was the day when Soma used to visit her. So, she asked her servants to bolt the gate of her house from inside at the time of his arrival.

As usual, Soma who had been out of the city and just returned, arrived at the gate of Rupasundari's house, dressed luxuriously. He was surprised to find the gate locked. He knocked at it loud and long and a servant opened it and said, "You are not to be allowed: that is the order."

What have I done to merit this treatment?" he asked.

In the meantime, Rupasundari herself had walked down to the gate and replied: "You have not done me any harm. But I have a request to make, which you should grant."

"Make it, and you shall have it," replied the young merchant.

"You must permit me to keep the parrot which you sport in your shop," she replied.

"Oh! Is it for that you are making such a fuss? You shall have it!" he said.

"Right now?"

"Right now!" said he and within a few minutes, he returned with the parrot in its cage.

The parrot which found itself being thus transported guessed immediately the fate that awaited it. It saw no useful purpose in arguing with Soma in that state of his mind. Banking upon future developments, it resigned itself temporarily to fate.

"Here you are," said Soma, as he handed the cage over to Rupasundari, who after a malicious look at its content, took the cage and passed it on to her servant for safe custody.

The pair then walked to the luxurious bedroom where they spent the night in a manner Soma had never experienced before.

Soma left her with reluctance in the early hours of the morning.

As his form disappeared in the street, Rupasundari promptly ordered her servant to fetch the cage she had given the previous night. It was immediately brought.

Poking the parrot with a needle, she addressed it: "Let me see what happens to your vow. I shall fulfil mine right now!" and roared with a devilish laughter.

The parrot did not choose to reply, because it realized that it would only aggravate her feeling.

Calling her cook, Rupasundari ordered: "Today, cook this exclusively for me. Make a pudding of her body and a soup of her head. You hear?"

"Yes, madam!" replied the woman and took the cage away with her.

Rupasundari, with pride heaving her breast at the thought of her easy conquest over the legendary parrot, departed to the tank to have her bath.

The cook after completing routine work, took out the cage, opened the shutter and held the parrot for cooking it in the manner in which her mistress had ordered. She was of course handling it carefully. But a better opportunity would never recur; so the parrot thought and made a bold bid for escape by pecking at the cook all over her face and scratching her hands and breasts. The frightened woman let go her clutch when the bird flew into the sky!

For a moment the cook felt dazed. She immediately realized that her mistress would not leave her easily if she came to know that the parrot had escaped. So, she ran to the market and purchased a fowl more or less of the same size as the parrot and returned to the kitchen and before Rupasundari returned, she was ready with the "parrot dishes."

Rupasundari, after bath, went round the deity adjoining the temple thrice and returned home. She dressed herself and entered the dining hall. She called the cook and asked her if the "parrot dish" was ready. She said "yes" and so leaves were spread.

When the dishes were served Rupasundari spotted out a "parrot-part" and holding it by the hand, observed: "Where are you, parrot, and where is your *saval*?" and munched it between her teeth.

She took out another and holding it by the hand, asked "Did you not say you would shave my head and put me in sack cloth and ashes? And would make me go round the temple, disfigured, and utter "Govinda,' 'Govinda'? Oh, *Ustad* parrot, where are you now?" and she crunched it between her teeth. Thus she ate the whole dish with fiendish delight.

38

The Parrot Wins the Bet

IT is not uncommon to find people who love the flesh-pots of life also longing for spiritual accomplishments in their inner hearts. Apparently, they do so to counterbalance the exuberance of their outer life; they derive a sort of mental satisfaction in that double life. Danseuse Rupasundari was one such.

She had been nursing the idea of entering heaven with her body, in flesh and blood, and God knows for what. The idea had never occurred to her as naive or absurd, and she had blind faith in the local deity to help her gain her objective and so, despite all her preoccupations with this mundane world, she never failed to have *darshan* of the Lord in the local temple at nightfall, go round Him several times and pray soulfully for the success for her pet ambition.

Parrot Vikramaditya who had escaped from Rupasundari's maid, had in the meantime made the tower of that temple his headquarters where quite a number of his species lived. He started living among the new birds as successfully as he did at the tree.

Vikrama saw Rupasundari visiting the temple day after day at the appointed hour and praying. At first it aroused in him a smile and later sympathy. Finally curiosity made him find out what she was so keen about in securing from God when humanity was so blindly munificent on her.

So, one night he came and sat on a perch very near and overheard her prayer. She said, "Oh, Narayana, if you have any pity, please take me to heaven in this embodied form!"

On hearing it his curiosity turned into astonishment and finally subsided into a plan of action. He waited for the next night to turn up.

At the appointed hour, Vikrama the parrot, flew straight into the sanctum of the temple and hid itself behind the deity. The *pujari* had lowered down the lights and departed. Then came Rupasundari in her wonted manner and started her prayer without disagreement or ennui. She said, "O Lord! How long am I to wait like this? When will you condescend to hear my petition and take pity on me? Lord, Lord, Lord!"

"Rupasundari!" emanated a sound from behind the deity and continued: "We are greatly pleased with your devotion to us and we have decided to help you achieve your life's ambition!"

Rupasundari became flush with excitement on hearing those words as she wore the beatific look on her face. With hands set apart *a la* Meera, she became enthralled at the thought of literally having worked a miracle and so exclaimed: "Is that true, what you say, Lord! Lord! Am I to enter like this? When? Please say how and when? Lord... Lord..."

"Wait, Rupasundari!" said the voice from the sanctum and continued: "There is one more test we would prescribe and if you pass that too, the gates of heaven will open right before you!"

"What is that, Lord? I am prepared to undergo any test, please tell me, please, now... now..."

"Listen, Rupasundari. This is the final test and you might find it difficult..."

"No, no, nothing is too difficult for me... please say..."

"You will hear it. First of all you must dispossess yourself of all material belongings — your house, jewels, ornaments, everything — by giving them away to the poor and needy. After doing that, you must come to our temple with your head completely shaven, only the saffron clothes of the sadhu on, and the Vaishnava mark should shine all over your body. You know that persons with hair will not be admitted into heaven and only my *bhaktas* can have entry. In this Vaishnavite garb, you should go round our temple thrice reciting our name as loud as possible. After that you must come and stand beside the *dwaja-stambha* when the aerial chariot from heaven will descend before you. You can ascend on it and fly to heaven in flesh and blood. The coming Friday would be the most suitable day for your object, so be gone!"

Rupasundari could not contain her joy at the unique revelation in which the Lord had acquiesced to her request. It would be an unparalleled event in human history when she, a woman and a danseuse at that, would attain what was denied to even great *tapasvins* of the epics.

"Ha, ha....", she started laughing and dancing as if in delirium. Saying that she would do as bidden by the Lord, Rupasundari ran home.

Needless to say, Rupasundari had no sleep at all at night. She waited drearily for the day to break. Calling for her best palanquin, she dressed herself for an audience with the King and sent an urgent prior message of her arrival for a very important business.

Accordingly the King, his Ministers and high officials of State were ready to receive her. Formalities over, Rupasundari related to the King her prayer to the Lord of the temple and His benevolence in granting her wish.

All those assembled were greatly impressed with her statement and the King was the first to compliment her: "You are indeed lucky in being thus favoured by the Almighty. This is a rare privilege even for sages like Sanaka. We too are blessed in that such a saint as you happen to live in our kingdom."

Rupasundari gracefully acknowledged the King's compliments and replied: "There are barely seven days for the event. Such instances are rare even in *Puranas*. May

I respectfully submit that, at your instance, all the kings of the 56 kingdoms may have the benefit of this unique event and be blessed! If Your Majesty sends out invitations to them immediately, they can be here in time."

All the Ministers agreed to that suggestion, adding that it would considerably add to Magadha's reputation. Rupasundari then and there dictated the form and content of such an invitation and saw that they were sent out before she left the King's *durbar.* One such invitation was addressed to Ujjain too. The King duly honoured her and escorted her to the gate.

Rupasundari set out in a business like manner in conforming to the details of the Lord's commands. She first of all called all her relatives and friends to whom she gave liberal gifts and bade adieu. She then signed the documents for giving away all her properties. During the remaining days she was giving away all that was left of her in the shape of jewels, clothes, cash, etc.

As the day neared, kings and princes from far-off lands, not to speak of the masses, made a beeline for Magadha and before long, the city was overflowing with humanity to witness the miracle of embodied Rupasundari ascending heaven.

When Bhatti looked at the invitation, his brows went up with scepticism. He could not believe for a moment that anybody could ascend heaven in flesh and blood, much less a woman of Rupasundari's calibre. He felt it was a hoax and so he asked the messengers who brought the message in his usual inquisitive way "Are there any more wonders in your country?"

They scratched their heads and one bright member of the mission replied: "Yes, sir. A rich merchant by name Soma has a parrot. It speaks like a human and acts like a God. Many people go to it for advice, arbitration and what not. Everybody has nothing but praise for it!"

Another messenger said: "This very same Rupasundari

once brought a funny case before this parrot" and he narrated the case in detail, ending, "one doesn't know if the parrot will after all fail in its vow."

Bhatti, who heard the story, could not help linking the parrot with his master Vikrama and Rupasundari's proposal to leave this world for heaven would surely bring the parrot in the picture before she did so, if at all. So, collecting a proper retinue he left for Magadha immediately in response to the King's invitation.

On the appointed day, the temple of the city was overcrowded and despite traffic regulations there was jam at every street corner. Inside the temple, before the deity, was built a high rostrum on which the Kings of the different countries or their representatives sat eagerly looking forward to the event.

Rupasundari, true to her word, had dispossessed herself of all her belongings and like a true *sadhu*, bathed in the sacred tank, and, clad in saffron robes, the Vaishnavite marks gleaming from her forehead and arms, appeared on the scene, followed by a train of devotees singing in praise of the Lord. Rupasundari went round the temple thrice as commanded by the Lord and entered the temple uttering His name. The immense crowd clove into two to make way for her. Thus she reached *dhwajastambha*. The whole assembly became tense with excitement as she stood bowing before it expecting the divine chariot to descend.

A whiff of air from the sky made the people to look up but except for a bird, a parrot, which seated itself on the *stambha* nothing yet had happened, Pindrop silence reigned.

A sudden hoarse laughter from above tore through this solemnity and said: "Rupasundari! Now tell me, who has won the bet, you or I? You said you will wring my head and eat me. I said 'don't make wild promises', but you insisted and now you reap your reward!"

All eyes turned to the top of the *dhwajastambha* from

where this speech came. It was the parrot that broke the silence so unceremoniously.

The parrot then addressed those assembled: "Hear Kings and gentlemen! This Rupasundari came to me with a funny case and when I adjudged it most conscientiously, she challenged my integrity and swore to eat me up. I tried to wean her from her foolishness but she defied. So I accepted her challenge and vowed that I would see her dispossessed, shaved clean of her hair, disfigured and go round this temple thrice uttering the Lord's name. She got me from the merchant-prince who was her paramour and she would have done me just as she had threatened but for my luck I escaped from her cook. I call this providence and a reward for my fairness in dealing with her case. After escaping, I worked on her weakness, foolish as it is, and deputised for the Lord by speaking in His voice from behind the idol and made her work out her destiny by her own hands. Gentlemen, tell me, who has won the bet?"

On hearing these words, Rupasundari's discomfiture became so great, that ruined as she was, instantaneous death came to her as a solace. The entire assembly praised the parrot for its resourcefulness and spat on the woman who had so heartlessly tried to kill the parrot. Then everyone noticed the parrot flying and sitting on the shoulders of Bhatti, who clasped it to his bosom uttering, "Master! Where had you been languishing all these days? How many sleepless nights did I spend in tracing you? I knew when I heard about the legendary parrot dispensing justice that it must be you only and so I came running here and I have been rewarded by the Almighty."

It was not difficult for the Kings assembled to divine that since it went to Bhatti the parrot was no other than King Vikrama and all were full of praise for the powers of the great King.

Bhatti took the parrot away with him to Ujjain on the ghoul. Inside the strong room of the ministerial apartment at Ujjain, Bhatti reverentially asked the parrot: "My Lord, how after sending me, did you happen to enter this body?"

The parrot related how the treachery of Vijaya had deprived him of the means of entering his original body.

Bhatti replied: "I thought as much. But I shall soon set matters right."

Leaving the parrot in the strong room, Bhatti sent word to the harem that the queens should decalre their *Gouri Vrata* as ended that day. On hearing that message the queens at once understood that King Vikrama had come.

The harem attendant communicated the news of the end of the *vrata* to fake Vikramaditya. After hearing it, he was on tenterhooks to visit the *zenana.* So he sent for Bhatti and revealed his desire. Bhatti said he could, but reminded about the bullfight ceremony which usually marked the end of such *vratas*. He explained: "This afternoon there will be a bullfight in the palace arena which will be witnessed by the queens and Your Majesty should also be present."

"Oh, I see! I forgot. We shall do so with pleasure," replied fake Vikrama.

The women stood on one side of the arena and on the other, the men of the palace. The trainers introduced through subways two hefty bulls from opposite ends.

Bhatti explained to fake Vikrama: "The bull on that side is the King's bull. This one is the Queen's. In this fight the King's bull must win. Then only will the queens admit Your Majesty into the harem. If it fails, some other means have to be devised."

"That is all right!" replied fake Vikrama.

The fire-breathing bulls charged at each other furiously. Within a short time, the King's bull was badly mauled by the Queen's and soon died. All the women assembled, laughed and heckled the King.

Fake Vikrama found himself caught between the scorn of the women and the failure of his ticket to the harem by the undignified behaviour of his animal. The one thought uppermost in his mind was to avenge the insult by killing the Queen's bull.

He came to a quick decision. By retiring to his room, he left King Vikrama's body and entered the dead bull's body and started charging the Queen's bull.

That was precisely the moment for which Bhatti had been waiting. He ran up to his room, brought the parrot and signalled King Vikrama to enter his own body left vacant by the stupid Vijaya. Vikrama did so leaving the parrot-body. All this happened behind the scenes and nobody except the persons involved knew of the changes.

Now real Vikramaditya and Bhatti were standing as innocent onlookers but Bhatti's instructions had already gone out to the keeper of the bulls to slay the King's bull, fighting in the arena. Who can defy or delay Bhatti's orders? Poor Vijaya, in a bull's body, fell down dead cut into two halves.

King Vikrama and Bhatti went to Bhadrakali's temple for receiving her blessings first and later, had a fine dinner. At night he related to his queens his adventures during his exile.

The statuette asked Bhoja: "Bhoja, you have just been listening to the exploits of our great King Vikrama. If you think you can be as valiant as a thousandth part of them, you can ascend his throne."

On hearing it, King Bhoja returned home with Nitivakya, thinking all the way of the powers of the great Vikramaditya.

39

Vikrama Catches a Tartar

AT daybreak on the ninth day, King Bhoja and his Minister Nitivakya woke up and went through the morning routine, and after food, dressed themselves and followed by royal retinue, left for the durbar where the counsellors awaited them.

Bhoja, as usual, propitiated the divine throne in the prescribed manner and mounted the steps, thinking that the worst was over.

But as he set foot on the ninth step, the statuette holding it became animated and addressing Bhoja, said "King Bhoja! on this throne sat our great emperor Vikramaditya and with the help of the great Bhatti, his Minister, he ruled the kingdom in a manner that defies description. You ought not to have tried to sit on the same throne."

"May I request you, O statuette, to tell me why you make that statement? Will you tell me about the great exploits the great Vikramaditya performed, for my edification?" said Bhoja.

"Listen, Bhoja," said the statuette and narrated history.

Starting on one of his self-imposed half-yearly exiles, once King Vikrama with Bhatti went to the family deity Bhadrakali before whom they prostrated. The Mother-Goddess blessed them.

Riding on the shoulders of the dutiful ghoul, King Vikramaditya and Bhatti crossed several forests and rivers, admiring on the way the myriad pattern of creation.

On their way lay the banks of river Tungabhadra. On that bank stood a town called Ambapuri. At the outskirts of the town was a lake. As it was early morning, the royal pair got down from the ghoul with the intention of bathing in that lake.

While they were preparing to do so, they saw a party of men carrying the dead body of a woman which they threw right before the steps of the lake and returning after spitting at the corpse with obvious contempt.

Out of curiosity Bhatti called one of the men who did so and asked him: "Why is it that, instead of arranging for the funeral of this lady, you are throwing this body thus to be eaten by vultures?"

"That is a story", replied the man. Continuing he said: "This lady was unfaithful to her husband; she lived with her paramour. So we killed her as a punishment for her unchaste life and threw her body here so that it may be lesson to other women of the town who will be coming here for bathing."

The men went back.

While Bhatti was wondering at the ways of those men, he saw two women approaching the lake with water pots on their hips. He became curious and wanted to know the reactions of the first two women at the sight of the corpse of one of their own species so outrageously thrown by the opposite members of their society.

Of the two ladies one was older and she appeared to be married. The other who was younger was unmarried; Bhatti could find it from their dress. Both of them looked like coming from a rich family. From their looks, Bhatti guessed they were sisters.

On seeing the corpse, the older lady started weeping.

Not being able to divine the reason, the younger one asked: "Sister, why do you weep?"

"That woman, who lies dead there, is also a woman like us. When I thought of her fate, tears came to my eyes."

"What happened to her?"

"Oh, that is a story. It seems she was unchaste and people found her out. So they killed her and placed her body here for us to be warned."

"Poor woman, she was not clever enough, that is the difference!" replied the younger one with a twist of her lips and proceeded to the lake with no trace of emotion.

Bhatti who overheard this conversation became thoughtful. How could one who was yet unmarried make a statement such as the one made by the younger woman? So thinking, he went back to King Vikrama to whom he related all that he saw and heard.

The utterance of the younger lady at the sight of the dead woman stuck of King Vikrama's throat.

After a few moments he told Bhatti: "Bhatti, I am going to find out how clever is this young lady you told me of. Right now, I am asking her father to get her married to me. What do you say?"

"As Your Majesty wishes", replied Bhatti.

The King and Bhatti waited for the two to start back.

They followed them to their home which was a palatial building. After fixing it, they made enquiries of the neighbours and learnt that they were the daughters of a rich jeweller by name Praval; that the latter had large estates and only two daughters of whom the older was married.

Next morning King Vikramaditya and Bhatti disguised themselves as jewel merchants — their favourite game — come from foreign lands and with the aid of the resourceful ghoul, carried a cart-load of valuable gems to the market.

They spread their wares in the busy part of the city and started trading. Crowds of passersby were soon collecting around them and buying gems in huge quantities.

News of the arrival of the foreign merchants reached the ears of Praval who, armed with instruments for expert examination and money, appeared on the scene. He was fascinated by the heap spread before him, no single particle of which was a fake or even of lower quality.

During the conversation, Praval made enquiries about them. Bhatti replied: "We come from Kanchi. Our father's name is Dhanapala. We came here with a double purpose. One is of course merchandise. The other is to look for a suitable bride for my elder brother who is here."

"Oh, that is splendid. You come from a place well known to me. I have many relatives there. Will you be good enough to honour me with a visit to my house and partake of the humble food I give?

"With great pleasure," replied King Vikrama and Bhatti together.

So, collecting their wares, the royal pair followed merchant Praval to his house where they were entertained with lavish food and drinks.

When they were ready to return, Praval addressed Bhatti: "You said you were looking for a bride to your brother. I have a marriageable daughter who is very good-looking and well-read. This is her picture. If he is willing, I shall give her hand to him."

"I am greatly honoured," replied Bhatti looking at his master through the chink of his eyes, who signalled approbation.

On an auspicious day Vikrama, the fake merchant, and the younger daughter of the merchant of Ambapuri were married in a grand manner.

For about a month, Vikrama lived in his father-in-law's house. Each night, Bhatti on one side and Vikrama on the other side, used to keep a vigil on the girl. She was on parole for practical purposes.

After a month was over, the foreign merchants asked the permission of Praval to take his daughter away to Kanchi which was given. The merchant sent valuable presents along with them.

The party of three rode on a car improvised by the ingenious ghoul for some days when an old-looking fort came to their sight. The outer gate was locked and the lock which was giant in shape bore all the marks of resistance to heavy hammering.

They asked a passerby the story about that fort.

He said: "This fort encloses a town called Kalakanthapur. King Kartick was its ruler. He was childless. One day in a mad frenzy he drove all his subjects out of the town and locked this fort dying with this curse: this lock shall not open except by the touch of King Vikramaditya of Ujjain."

When the man was gone, King Vikramaditya touched the lock which instantaneously gave away, as the bow of Lord Siva at the touch of Sri Rama. The party entered the fort which was fully replenished. Except for human beings, the town looked rich.

King Vikrama and Bhatti went to the palace in the fort and occupied the cosy chambers of the late King. The palace stores were full of undecayed provisions and so Vikrama asked his bride to prepare food for them all, which she did admirably. Thus they lived in that deserted town for a month.

At night, the two men used to lock the lady in a room and the King on the one side and Bhatti on the opposite side of the room would keep vigil and eavesdrop through the ventilators.

Practically no one visited the fort. Even when they did, like the washerwoman who took their clothes away to wash, they came while the royal pair were present. While going out for, say, hunting, they locked the gates securely with giant locks. Life went on uneventually as the royal pair were straining themselves on their self-imposed check on how clever that girl was.

Their washerwoman had an unmarried son. While washing the clothes of those newcomers one day, the sari of the new lady attracted his attention. The perfume emanating from that sari was so enchanting that he started calculating, adolescent that he was, how attractive and desirable should its wearer be.

Young as he was, his blind love for the unknown woman started gnawing at his vitals. He spent sleepless nights and the washerwoman who noticed the decline in the health of her son got alarmed and so she asked him: "What ails you, my son?"

The young man who had not known the ways of the modern world and its civilization told the truth.

On hearing it, the old woman placed her finger on her nose and with a terrified look admonished him: "Foolish boy! Do you know that the woman is a queen and is protected by two kings day and night? Give up this mad idea: I shall get you married to a nice girl from our own people next month. Be a good boy, do you hear?"

The young washerman went back with downcast eyes and agitated look. Try however much, he could not erase the idea from his mind. On the contrary, it started ballooning in his simple mind with the result that he asked his mother one day: "Mother will you do me a favour? Will you tell her about me and what I feel? I don't mind about her reply. If you don't do that, I shall die."

He was the only son of the old woman and so reluctantly she agreed to convey his message to the lady.

When she went to the palace the next day to deliver washed clothes, she conveyed her son's message, fearing all the time that she would be handed over to the men. But instead, the lady laughed and replied "Tell your son that where there is a will there is a way" and went back.

Mystified, the old woman walked back after satisfying herself that none of the two hawk-like men had overheard their conversation. She faithfully reported to her eager son what had transpired between her and the new woman of the palace.

The young washerman jumped on hearing what the lady had said. He concluded that it was a positive encouragement and so was determined to meet her, come what might.

That night, he surveyed the fort for possible ways of entry. At last he came across a huge banyan tree near the fort several hundred years old spreading its rope-like tentacles down into the fort. Clapping his hands, he ascended the tree and soon found himself descending along one of them into the fort. In cautious footsteps he advanced and located a living room by the light. It was the palace room where the party lived and outside which Vikrama and Bhatti kept all-night vigil. The ghoul's post of duty was at the main gate outside with the giant lock on.

It was pitch dark outside and except for the rustle of leaves and the cackle of toads, the night was still. At a certain moment, the braying of a stray donkey outside the fort sent a shiver through his spine. But that did not deter him from his pursuit which became all-absorbing like that of a *yogi*.

Climbing over the adjacent building which was short, he made carefully for the terrace of the palace room and located the chimney through which he peeped. His object was there. The lady was really a marvel of creation. He did not mind even if he lost his life in trying to meet her.

He surveyed the scene once again like a general before a war. There was nobody else inside the room. They were outside, if any, he concluded.

He tied one end of an improvised coir ladder to a spoke of the chimney and threw the other down, which, naturally, attracted the attention of the lady.

She did not appear to be perturbed. On the contrary the sound appeared to stimulate her.

Emboldened by her behaviour the young washerman entered the opening to the chimney with cat-like agility and quickly descended down the ladder, only to find the lady ready to receive him with open arms!

40

Washerman Becomes King

ONCE the washerman's son and the merchant's daughter were together, they forgot all else; they had the night entirely for themselves. They sang and laughed and danced deliriously which the stone-walls of the fort echoed.

When Bhatti heard the sound of mirth, he thought that King Vikrama had entered the room. He reflected: "After all, our King has proved himself no better than the common man in the street! Of course he was every right to do what he likes with his wedded wife; but why should he put me in the wrong by doing things on the sly?" And so, he left his post and walked towards the steps of a lake outside the fort.

On the other side when King Vikrama heard the mirthful laughter inside the locked room, he thought: "I never thought Bhatti would prove so unfaithful to me! If only he had expressed his wish to marry the girl, I would be the last man to stand in his way. How true is it that appearances are deceptive!" Disgusted, he too left his post and walked towards the lake outside the fort.

Bhatti was sitting on the step leading down to the water. As it was pitch-dark, King Vikrama too sat a stone's throw away from him without knowing the other, with his palm locked at his chin. Thus they sat till daybreak each determined not to see the face of the other.

When the sun rose, the King happened to turn back when he noticed the sitting figure of Bhatti not far from him. Not willing to have any more truck with him he got down into the lake with a view to finishing his morning ablutions and walking away. Bhatti too happened to notice the King walking down to the lake. A trifle wondering, he followed him at a distance and while cleaning his teeth, uttered audibly: "If the King wanted to have his lawfully wedded wife, who am I to say no? Why should he do so on the sly?"

When the King heard this, he pricked his ears up and turning towards Bhatti asked: "So, it was not you inside the room with her? Is that correct?"

"I? I don't understand you at all! Do I take it that my Lord too was not inside the room with her?"

"Not I!"

"Not I!"

"But who?" uttered they in chorus.

"So, the girl has been as good as her word!" Thus thinking Bhatti walked briskly towards the fort determined to find out who the interloper was. Concluding that he must have entered from the roof, he winded his steps up the seventh floor of the palace.

Not being able to account for Bhatti's brusque departure, the King too returned to the fort and seated himself on the vacant throne immersed in deep thought.

As Bhatti was looking around for possible ways of entry for a third person, he saw two bearded and tufted semidivine beings shooting down from heaven and finally landing on a shrub of cactus not far from his watchpost. The *rishis* - let us call them so - untied their knotted mat of hair from each of which a woman came out. These two women walked a few yards and from their apron, released two men, their secret lovers. The *rishis*, their wives, and the two secret lovers of these women went in three groups presumably to answer the call of nature. After some time, they returned and wound themselves up in reverse order.

Bhatti who was witnessing this strange spectacle decided at once on a plan of action. Accordingly, he hastened down to where the *rishis* were collecting their things when they were about to take off. Falling at their feet, he prayed: "Holy *rishis*! Today is my father's *sraddha* and it is my custom to feed holy persons like you. I was looking all the time for such soul but now with the blessing of my ancestors I am glad to find you. Please deign to accede to my request!"

The *rishis* felt they could not brush aside Bhatti's request, for he had sighted them. So they agreed. Bhatti conducted them to the palace and offered them all the respect due to revered persons.

Calling the merchant's daughter, he asked "How much rice do you cook each day for us?"

"Three-quarters of a measure" she replied.

"Please take two-and-a-half measures of rice today and prepare dinner for some guests. Please be quick."

With the guests seated on golden seats, Bhatti was busy preparing the leaves for serving food.

King Vikramaditya who was a silent spectator to this drama was getting uneasy because Bhatti did not even appear to have taken notice of his presence, much less inform him of what he was doing. Yet he almed himself with a determination to see things through for once.

When food was ready, Bhatti spread ten large leaves with seats before them and signalled to the merchant's daughter to serve the dishes on all the ten leaves. When she did so, Bhatti prayed before the two *rishis* to be seated on the first two seats. They did so. Bhatti then requested King Vikramaditya to occupy one seat. He did so. Bhatti asked the merchant's daughter too to occupy one seat which she did. He too sat before a leaf. Thus five leaves had been occupied.

Then Bhatti addressed the sages: "Respected sires, on such occasions, it is our family custom to feed all the souls present in this house and not to feed a few only. May I request you to release the women up at your knots so that they too may partake of the humble food I offer?"

Embarrassed by this request, the *rishis* looked at each other; thinking that discretion was the better part of valour, they released the women from their matted hair. The two women sat before two more leaves. There were three leaves left.

At that time Bhatti addressed the wives of the *rishis*: "Holy women! It is unfair that while we have our food, other soul present here should starve. May I request you to release the men from your aprons so that they too may relish the meal so ably prepared by this lady?"

Alarmed at this revelation, the two *rishi*-women released their men without a word, fearing worse calamities if they lied. The two released lovers too took their seats. The *rishis*, on their part, were mortified with shame at the infidelity of their spouses. King Vikrama's eyes were widening with wonder at the series of revelations. Only one seat was vacant.

Then Bhatti addressed the merchant's daughter: "Madam, my requests to the *rishis* and their wives did not go in vain, as you can see. I hope my request to you too will likewise prove fruitful. When all of us are having our food, why should your lover alone starve? There is one more seat left. Please bring him, so that all of us can eat together!"

The merchant's daughter who had all along been apprehending danger from the dexterous moves of Bhatti, was stunned by Bhatti's request. She mechanically rose, walked up to the lumber room and brought the washerwoman's son from there, where he had been confined at daybreak.

King Vikrama could no more keep his silence. He rose and embraced Bhatti saying: "What a fool have I been in suspecting you of bad faith! Please forgive me! Will you?"

"My Lord, the whole credit for this episode should go to the merchant's daughter who had shown herself equal to her word," replied Bhatti.

All the ten of them had a fine dinner after which they ate *tambul*. Finally Bhatti requested the *rishis* that they might resume their journey.

Then the *rishis* said: "Since you have exposed our wives' infidelity to us, we have no use for them."

Looking around, King Vikrama said: "Bhatti, now that we know that the merchant's daughter loves the washerwoman's son I propose to unite them together and hand over the rule of this city to them after removing from it the curse of its last ruler. Similarly, I should like to unite the wives of the *rishis* with their lovers and make the latter Ministers of this State. What do you say?"

"As Your Majesty desire," replied Bhatti.

The *rishis* too gave their assent to the plan.

Accordingly, the washerwoman's son was installed on

the throne by King Vikrama himself with due pomp and ceremony. After the event, the *rishis* took off to their heavenly abode.

Leaving a grateful city, King Vikrama and Bhatti spent the remaining days of the six-monthly exile on the slopes of mountains and forest-ranges and when it was over, returned to Ujjain.

The statuette asked King Bhoja: "Do you think, Bhoja, you could be so magnanimous as all that? If you think you have a fraction of our Vikramaditya's greatness you can ascend this throne, or be gone!"

On hearing this enthralling story, King Bhoja walked down and returned home for the day followed by his royal retinue.

41

Swarnapuri

KING Bhoja woke up, as usual, in the early morning and after completing his morning ablutions, had his breakfast. By that time Nitivakya also came dressed for the *durbar.* Both of them followed by other courtiers proceeded to the *durbar* where the divine throne was placed.

After doing the customary propitiations for the throne, King Bhoja tried to ascend it. There was no trouble till the ninth step. But as he set foot on the tenth, the statuette holding it became suddenly animated and rolling its eyes in derision called out to King Bhoja: "I thought my sister had convinced you of your poor calibre compared to King Vikrama and dissuaded you from trying to occupy this throne. Apparently you are still unconvinced."

Said King Bhoja: "Can you tell me what you know of King Vikramaditya?"

"Yes, listen," replied the tenth statuette and narrated the following story:

In the island of Naga Loka on the slopes of Sveta Parvata, on the banks of Tamraparni was the city of Prathishta. A King by name Sadguna was ruling there. To his wife Sayujyavati was born a girl whom they named Sanchivi.

The King had a priest by name Kalakanta and to him was born a son whom he named Adimula.

The girl and this boy had been married in their previous birth, but were cursed by Rishi Vishwamitra for being late in receiving him. The lady however got a pardon from the venerable sage. According to it they were reborn in the world.

Now, when Sanchivi grew to be a woman, Sadguna wanted to celebrate her marriage suitably. When however she came to know of it, she called her father and said : "Father, I shall marry such a person who can give me an accurate account of Swarnapuri."

The father agreed and made a proclamation to the effect that suitors with such qualification might approach him.

When Adimula, the priest's son, heard that the princess was available for anyone, he wanted to try his chance. Fool that he was and considered as such by all the people of Prathishtha, he rang the palace bell and sought audience with the King.

The King called him in. Adimula said: "I want to marry your daughter."

"With pleasure," replied the King, 'but do you know the condition my daughter has set for her suitor?"

"I know that!"

"You know all about Swarnapuri?"

"Yes".

"Then, let us go to my daughter." So saying he took him to her. But when she started plying him with questions, he quailed before her. Ultimately, it turned out that he was trying to bluff her. But unfortunately she had been blessed with the faculty of remembering her past birth from which she knew all about Swarnapuri where she ruled with her husband.

In the end, Adimula was thoroughly exposed and put to shame. This, however, touched him to the quick. So he went all over the world to find that city of Swarnapuri without success. At last he returned to Prathishtha and sought the advice of his elders. They laughed at his foolhardy venture. However, they gave him a tip. "If you seek the help of King Vikramaditya of Ujjain, you may succeed."

Following that advice, Adimula went to Ujjain. He rang the palace bell and gained admission into it. Seeking an interview with the King, Adimula revealed his strange request.

King Vikrama too honestly did not know of this Swarnapuri. He promised Adimula to tell him all about that strange city soon.

So, handing over the reins of Government of Ujjain to Bhatti. King Vikrama started on his exile. He first went to Prathishtha after paying his respects to his family deity, Bhadrakali.

Reaching Prathishtha, he made exhaustive inquiries about the strange condition stipulated by princess Sanchivi for her marriage. Later he promised Adimula whom he left at his place.

"Look here, don't move out of this house till I see you later with all the details about Swarnapuri. I shall get you the hand of this princess."

So saying he got on to the shoulders of his dutiful ghoul which took him hundreds of miles away from Prathishtha. When he alighted for the day, it was in the midst of a deep forest.

42

Mystery Girl at Swarnapuri

NOT being able to find a single living soul round about the forest, King Vikrama surveyed the scene with a little dismay. He subsequently started searching the area for trace of living beings. As he did so, he came across a large plain at the centre of which was a lake studded with lotus flowers. By the side of the lake was a large iron cauldron which was being heated by an oven fed by logs of wood. He went near it and found to his surprise that the cauldron contained a large quantity of clarified butter which was literally boiling.

At the sight of this, King Vikrama asked the ghoul: "How is it that at a place where there is no sign of a living soul there is this pot of ghee which is kept boiling with no one about it?"

The ghoul exercised its supernatural powers and after learning all about it, replied: "O King! Seven *rishis* live at this spot. They practise very rigorous *tapas*. Each day one of them, after bathing in the lake, jumps into this boiling ghee and becomes roasted. The other six *rishis* come later, spread seven leaves and call out the dead *rishi*. Due to their yogi powers, the dead *rishi* returns from the cauldron in a new body while his old body remains in the cauldron as cooked meat which all the seven *rishis* share as their daily food. They live in this manner for a long time. Just now that *rishi* whose turn it is today to fall into the cauldron has gone to take his bath in the lake."

On hearing this strange episode, King Vikrama half wondered and half admired the ways of the *rishis* and came to the conclusion that he should seek the aid of these great *rishis* in knowing all about Swarnapuri of which even the ghoul appeared to be ignorant.

At that time he saw the *rishi* returning from the lake after his bath. He would fall into the cauldron. A brain wave flashed through Vikrama's mind. Accordingly, when the *rishi* was about to jump into the cauldron, he threw himself between him and cauldron and stopped him from doing so. Before the surprised *rishi* could ask him the meaning of his action, King Vikrama had jumped into the boiling ghee! The *rishi* stood petrified, apparently not knowing the next step.

In the meantime the other six *rishis* were returning to the spot after their ceremonial bath. They were surprised to see their seventh standing by the cauldron instead of being inside it, fit for their immediate food. As they were very hungry, they concluded that the other *rishi* had become a shirker. This made their eyes red with anger and as they were about to curse him, the seventh *rishi* fell at their feet and said: "Please don't curse me. I never wanted to fail in my duty. As I was about to fall into this cauldron as usual, a young man with all the thirty-two marks of a royal personage prevented me from doing so and before I could protest, he himself jumped into the boiling pot. I could only wring my hands in anguish."

On hearing it, the *rishis* knitted their brows and divined that the person who so daringly threw himself into the boiling ghee was none other than King Vikramaditya of Ujjain. So their lips broadened into a smile as they set about spreading leaves for sharing their wonted food.

"Vikrama!" they called, and from out of the boiling ghee rose King Vikrama in resplendent form quite unaffected by the boiling ghcc.

They called Vikrama too to partake of the fried flesh of his other body. All of them ate their meal and in that contented state, the *rishis* asked Vikrama: "Vikrama, what made you fall into the boiling pot?" King Vikrama replied: "To make this body of mine to be of some little use at least to Your Gracious Holiness!"

The *rishis* smiled complacently and said: "If you have anything in your mind that we can confer on you please ask."

King Vikrama asked: "May it please Your Holiness to let me know all about Swarnapuri."

The *rishis* replied: "Vikrama, little do we know of that great country. But we can direct you to a colleague of ours who practises *tapas* three hundred *yojanas* from here. He will be in a position to enlighten you."

Bidding good-bye to the seven *rishis*, King Vikrama rode on the ghoul to where the eighth *rishi* was practising penance. He stood before him bowing, in the twinkling of an eye.

The new *rishi* on opening his eyes divined the newcomer as King Vikramaditya of Ujjain and after blessing him asked: "Vikrama, what brought you here?"

King Vikrama replied: "Your Holiness! I have come to Your Holiness seeking knowledge of Swarnapuri!"

"Vikrama, I am sorry, I do not know anything of the great city, but I can direct you to a quarter from which you can gain knowledge of Swarnapuri."

"Please, direct me!"

"About a hundred *yojanas* to the north of this place is an island called Vincha. In that island is a giant banyan tree on whose lofty branches live the famous golden birds, rocs and other fabled birds. These birds roam about a thousand *yojanas* a day in their daily outings. So, you had better seek their aid. But I must warn you. As they are birds of prey, you must change your human form and listen to their talks for some time when you are likely to get a clue."

King Vikrama expressed his gratefulness to the new *rishi* and departed for the Vincha island on the shoulders of the ghoul.

He reached the island in a short time and with little difficulty found the giant banayan tree. On alighting at the island, he left his human body which he entrusted to the care of the ghoul and entered the body of a dead bee. With this new body he struck a hole high on the tree where he hid himself with the intention of listening to the talks of the fabled birds.

By sunset all the birds returned from their daily flight and settled themselves comfortably in their nests.

It was their custom to talk about their daily adventures, Accordingly, the golden birds asked the roc couple, "O rocs! which part of the world did you go to in search of food today?"

The male roc replied: "We crossed the seven seas and went a three hundred *yojanas* further when we sighted Swarnapuri."

At this, King Vikrama's heart missed a beat.

"What are the peculiarities you saw at that place?" asked the golden birds to the roc.

The male roc replied: "It is impossible to describe the great beauties of this place. But what struck us as odd was that there was not a single living being!"

Said the golden birds: "How funny! We too want to see that city. Will you take us along?"

"With pleasure," replied the roc.

It is unnecessary to add that King Vikrama danced with joy at the opportunity. He had little difficulty in finding a safe hiding place for himself in his bee form inside the giant wings of the fabled roc. When they were asleep, he stuck himself into the body of the roc unnoticed.

At daybreak, the birds started their daily amphibious flights. Followed by the golden brids and the invisible ghoul, King Vikrama in bee form flew in the direction of Swarnapuri sticking comfortably onto the folds of the great wings of the roc.

The entire group flew in formation. After crossing the seven seas and the three hundred *yojanas* of plains, the party crossed into the city of Swarnapuri. Greatly attracted by the luscious fruits of the city, they ate them with great relish till their bellies reached the breaking point.

While the birds were so engaged, Vikrama the bee disentangled himself from the folds of the roc and entered into the core of a tree where it rested in a contemplative mood. At that time the ghoul appeared before it along with King's human body. On seeing it, King Vikrama entered his human frame, leaving the bee frame and walked into the city.

In the meantime the birds after looking around the city returned to their abode in the Vincha island.

Followed by the ghoul, King Vikrama went round the city admiring its wonderful appearance. He mused: "I have seen many cities and towns, and even visited heaven; but nowhere have I seen such beautiful palaces, temples, thoroughfares and architectural beauties."

With the aid of the ghoul he procured some fruits and water with which he whetted his appetite.

Resuming his reconnoitering tour of the city, he came to a gorgeous building which was once the palace of Swarneswara. He went through the entire palace and wondered at its architectural excellence. Leaving it, he went along the streets. He saw the marvellous temples with their skyscraping towers dedicated to Brahma, Vishnu and Siva. The crest jewel among all of them was the temple dedicated to Lord Sundaramurti. Among the various marvels of the temple was its light which emanated solely from the very large number of gems mounted all over the place artistically. Its tower literally touched the sky. Being devout by nature, Vikrama entered the temple and went to the sanctum where he prayed before the Lord. After going round Him thrice, he walked into the thousand-pillared hall where he sat immersed in deep thought. It was about ten at night.

What was uppermost in his mind at that time was: "The city bears all the marks of great prosperity but what it lack is living beings. I have no doubt in my mind that it is due to some curse on the part of a great soul. What better purpose can there be in life than removing this curse! I must devote myself to that, although at the present moment, I am in the woods as to how to set about it. I trust God."

As he sat thinking in that strain, it was cut short by a lightning flash in the sky which revealed a female form rising on a flying horse, descending on the temple near the *dhwajastambha.* As he sat watching, the lady tied the horse on to the *stambha*, went into the temple tank, bathed in it, opened a cupboard from which she took out the paraphernalia for worship. His guess was right. She performed the *puja* of the Lord in the prescribed manner after which she again mounted the steed which started taking her into various mansions and buildings in the city. Within an hour and a half, she completed the round of visits and flew back on the steed in the same manner as she came.

King Vikrama who had been the solitary, unnoticed witness of the strange lady's movements at Swarnapuri, was musing within himself: "Could she be an *apsara, a naga kinnara* or a supernatural being? Tut! What a fool have I been not to have stopped and asked her who she was."

After repenting thus for his mistake, Vikrama spent the night investigating further into the mysteries of Swarnapuri.

Beyond what he had already seen, he could not discover anything new of value. At daybreak he was sadder but not a wiser man.

Finding that the birds which had carried him into the strange place had flown back, Vikrama availed himself to the shoulders of the ever ready ghoul which were available for him. The pair made straight for Adimula's house at

Prathishtha. The brahmin, on seeing King Vikrama back, blessed him gratefully.

"I have good news for you!" said King Vikrama.

Adimula stood to attention when King Vikrama said: "Adimula, you may go straight to the palace and ring the announcing bell. You will be conducted to King Sadguna's presence. Go there and tell him that you know all about Swarnapuri." And King Vikrama told him all that he saw at Swarnapuri, how its gorgeous palaces and temples were without a single living being and how a princess comes there every night on a divine steed and propitiates Lord Sundaramurti, etc.

In a greatly delighted mood Adimula dressed himself suitably for the occasion and rang the palace bell. The servants of the palace who came out were sceptical as the same lad had once before proved a fake suitor to the hands of the princess and consequently had to be driven out unceremoniously. They were about to bind him hand and foot and consign him to the lunatic asylum when some elders of the city intervened and said: "This man had been abroad recently and has, therefore, possibly seen Swarnapuri. Why not give him a chance to acquit himself?"

The sepoys thought there might be some truth in what the elders said. So they untied the chord round him and conducted him to the presence of Princess Sanchivi who, on seeing him, smiled pleasantly thinking it might be another hoax.

She asked, "I hope you have another yarn now to tell me as you did previously?"

"No, madam," replied Adimula and continued, "I have authentic news now. I have been abroad for quite a long time exploring all countries one of which was Swarnapuri and I speak now with first-hand knowledge!"

"I am very glad to hear that," replied Sanchivi. "Do tell me of what you saw."

"Listen," said Adimula. "The entire city of Swarnapuri is built of gold or at least it shines all over with the lustre of gold. It contains innumerable buildings and temples which vie with one another in artistic excellence. They are inlaid with costly and genuine gems. At the centre of that city is the majestic temple dedicated to Lord Sundara!"

At the mention of the temple, Princess Sanchivi's eyes widened and she moved closer to him so as not to miss any detail.

Adimula continued: "This temple is the highest ever, and wonderful as its tower appears, it is constructed in a way which has no parallel anywhere either in this world or even in heaven. To this temple comes a lady each night at 10 o'clock riding on a divine steed. She first of all worships Lord Sundara in due manner and afterwards visits the balcony of the palace. She stays there for some time where she plays on the *veena* in divine manner and returns on the steed before daybreak. The fort which encircles the city is itself surrounded by deep unpassable ditches. Lakes, fountains, large, well laid out gardens abound in the city. Even the trees are of golden hue, their leaves are emeralds and sapphires, their fruits are rubies. Great as that city is by all standards, it suffers from one disability, and that is, it has no living beings at all - not even an insect. Whatever being there was at a time stands there lifeless but without any deterioration. All this is true!"

Adimula's revelations had an electric effect on the princess who became suffused with love for the man; she took out a pearl necklace from her box and placed it round his neck. Folding her hands and bowing before him she said "My lord! I fully agree that what all you said about Swarnapuri is correct. May I tell you about one more thing? That lady whom you saw coming there each night to propitiate Lord Sundara is none but my humble self. I beseech you to come there within six months from today, seek me at the temple, bring all the dead back to life and marry me!'

Princess Sanchivi immediately sent for her parents and

courtiers. When they had assembled, she said, "Today my vow has been fulfilled. This brahmin had in his previous birth ruled over Swarnapuri. His name was Swarneswara. I was his queen, Kantarupi. When we were ruling the country with justice and fairness to the great happiness of all our subjects, Sage Vishwamitra came to our palace one day. A slight delay on our part in receiving him infuriated the great one who cursed that our city should instantaneously become void of living beings. Frightened at that curse, I fell at his feet for pardon. He modified the curse. He said I would be born as the daughter of King Sadguna of Prathishtha and I would be endowed with the faculty of knowing my previous birth and blessed me with the means of visiting Swarnapuri whenever I willed. He said I would join my husband by means of the vow I had made. Here, this gentleman has fulfilled my vow and being my husband Swarneswara, I have requested him to return to Swarnapuri and marry me to rule over our people as before. When my lord chooses to do so, I shall stay for ever at Swarnapuri!"

Turning to Adimula, Sanchivi said: "My lord, please do not make it long to return to Swarnapuri!"

A thousand thoughts assailed Adimula on his way home.

43

Swarnapuri Comes Back to Life

KING Vikrama who had been anxiously awaiting Adimula's return saw him comes back moodily. As he came near, Vikrama shook him by the shoulders and asked: "O brahmin, did you succeed?"

Replied Adimula: "Your Majesty, I told the princess all about Swarnapuri as taught by you. She agreed that they were all correct and calling her parents, she said she was my wife in my previous birth and that together we had ruled Swarnapuri. She said that we were cursed by Sage Vishwamitra because we were late in welcoming him. When she fell at his feet for pardon, the sage predicated that she would he born as Sadguna's daughter and myself as the priest's son. She has further asked me to return to Swarnapuri soon and meet her there so that we could be united and the sage's curse would be removed. I have now come to Your Majesty to help me go to Swarnapuri to marry Princess Sanchivi. I request your good self to personally see that we are installed in that kingdom."

King Vikramaditya who was never satisfied till his undertaking was complete immediately made preparations for taking Adimula to Swarnapuri. Bidding adieu to his parents, Adimula accompanied King Vikrama on his journey to Swarnapuri.

Together they sat upon the shoulders of the ghoul which tore through space along the now familiar route to Swarnapuri. On the way they had to cross the Himalaya mountains. While looking down on the wealth of the Himalayas, Vikrama noticed at a secluded spot Sage Vishwamitra himself engaged in *tapas*. Stopping the ghoul, the two of them got down and proceeded to where the sage was seated. They stood bowing before him silently till the sage opened his eyes.

When the sage opened his eyes, he immediately recognized King Vikramaditya and asked him: "Vikrama, what brought you here?"

Replied Vikrama: "O sage, please permit me to introduce my friend Adimula. Your Holiness will remember your visit to Swarnapuri and the curse to which King Swarneswara unfortunately became subject to. Your Holiness will also remember his queen interceding and begging your pardon. You were kind enough to predict their next birth at King Sadguna's kingdom and their reunion."

"I remember. What do you want about it?"

"My friend Adimula is King Swarneswara and I want Your Holiness to bless him."

"Adimula, be blessed. On reaching Swarnapuri, you will meet Princess Sanchivi. You shall be reunited and the entire kingdom shall become enlivened."

The King and Adimula fell on all fours before the great sage and after bidding him goodbye, the party resumed its journey to Swarnapuri on the shoulders of the ghoul with a merry heart.

After crossing the Himalayas they reached the said island and found the giant banyan tree in which the fabulous rocs lived. That was the last outpost. Satisfying themselves on the correctness of their route, they resumed their journey. They crossed the seven seas and three *yojanas* when they landed on Swarnapuri which, true to its name, was dazzling in the sunlight.

Alighting from the ghoul, they treated themselves to a sumptuous feast provided by the resourceful ghoul and afterwards King Vikrama took his friend along the streets of Swarnapuri showing him all its wonders. Adimula was simply overwhelmed by the sight of the city which remained intact expect for living beings. As they were looking on thus, the sun set for the day.

With the night setting on, Adimula had a dramatic metamorphosis. He immediately became King Swarneswara and regained consciousness of his past birth. Addressing Vikrama he said: "Mighty King, I now recollect that it is my good old kingdom. There is absolutely nothing that I do not know here."

King Vikrama nodded assent and by ten o'clock they reached the temple of Sundara before whom they fervently prayed.

At that time Princess Sanchivi, as was her wont, was seen entering the city through the sky on her divine steed. Coming down, she saw Adimula standing before the *dhwajastambha* whereupon she recognized her husband Swarneswara before whose feet she fell down prostrate, shedding tears of joy. The steed which usually waited for Sanchivi's return vanished into the sky and Sanchivi too became transformed into her old form of Kantarupi. Who can describe the joy of reunion?

Together the pair offered heartful prayers to Lord Sundara in an elaborate manner and accompanied by King Vikrama, the king and queen of Swarnapuri walked familiarly to their palace and occupied the throne.

There was a dramatic change in the entire city which became animated instantaneously. The ministers and courtiers who appeared just to have awakened from a sleep came in train and saluted the King. The city was humming with activity. The bazaar was buzzing. There was no indication that the life blood of the city organization had at any time stopped.

King Vikrama who was witnessing the change over was smiling broadly. In accordance with his promise to Adimula, however, he presided over the marriage of ex-Sanchivi with ex-Adimula.

To the immense gratification of both, King Vikrama stayed at Swarnapuri for a week after which he departed. He spent the remaining days of his six-monthly exile in the forest and at its completion, returned to Ujjain on the shoulders of the ghoul. He first of all went to the temple of Bhadrakali, his favourite deity, and prayed before Her for Her guidance and help at all stages of his life. Later he entered his throne room where he seated himself on the divine throne to the immense joy of his ministers and courtiers to whom he related the happenings of the last six months of his exile.

Later on he proceeded to the harem, ate the royal meal and enjoyed the company of his queen.

The statuette which was relating this story asked Bhoja:

"You have just heard that King Vikrama not only visited Swarnapuri, the most wonderful city in the world, but also got removed the curse on the King and Queen and on the entire life of the city. If you think that you can boast of even a small part of such heroism you are welcome to ascend this throne, but not otherwise."

On hearing this well-meant rebuke on the part of the statuette, King Bhoja retraced his steps down to the earth and along with his Minister Nitivakya returned to his palace for the day.

44
Princess Sadguna

AS usual, King Bhoja woke up with the rising sun on the morning of the eleventh day. He bathed in the sea, performed *puja* and offered *dana* and *dharma* in the prescribed manner. After taking his food, he started for the throne room followed by his ministers and courtiers at a respectable distance.

He offered prayers to Vikramaditya's divine throne and started ascending the steps. Till the tenth step he did not encounter any difficulty, but as he set foot on the eleventh, the statuette holding it suddenly became animated and exclaimed:

"If you are as valorous and chivalrous as our great emperor Vikramaditya you may ascend this throne, but not otherwise. Would you like to hear an instance of his greatness?"

"I shall be greatly indebted to you," replied King Bhoja.

Said the statuette:

While King Vikramaditya ruled from this celestial throne there was no limit to the *dana* and *dharma* he performed. The welfare of his subjects was his own welfare. Holding suzerainty over fifty-six countries, the great King ruled over Bharata justly and fairly.

A few days before starting on his half-yearly exile, King Vikrama ordered his faithful ghoul to go round the world and report to him any great difficulty in his dominion so that he could set it right.

The ghoul accordingly made a whirlwind tour of the continent and reported: "Your Majesty! King Swarupa is ruling over Varanasi. Although he was blessed in every respect for a long time he did not have children.

On the advice of the great *rishis*, he worshipped poor mothers and pious fathers and presented them with lands and wealth. He thus carried on *tapas* for a long time. By the grace of God a girl was born to him whom he named Sadguna. Unlike many princesses Sadguna learnt all the *Vedas, Shastras, Puranas* and had a rare intellectual attainment. She came of age and the God of Love made a permanent abode of his life in the person of Sadguna. As was the wont, the King arranged a safe residence for her at a balcony in one of his palaces and appointed suitable companions and aides for her safety.

It so happened that King Swarupa had been on a hunting expedition. Tired by the day's work, he got down the steps of a lonely lake to quench his thirst. On the steps of that tank he saw the wife of a *rishi* taking her bath.

She was young, extremely good-looking and in the environments he was, he found his mind falter on the *rishi's* wife. The more he tried to suppress his emotion, the greater it shot out and in a short time he became completely a slave of lust. To be short, he attempted to molest her. The *rishi's* wife being very powerful cursed him: "May you and your entire kingdom become devoid of life during daytime," and walked away briskly.

From that day Varanasi and her subjects including Princess Sadguna became corpses in daytime and became alive at night. Even so, she dressed herself suitably, wore attractive flowers and walked on the terrace enjoying the loveliness of the moon and the songs of night-birds.

As ill-luck would have it, Princess Sadguna came in for worse days. A *rakshasa* of very great proportions and prowess came into her life. He was a terror even to *devas, nagas* and *asuras*. He had many *apsara* women in his harem. There was practically no one, God or man, of whom he was afraid. Mountains were play-things for him; oceans were like soda-water for him. He tied all rogue elephants in a knot with a giant python garlandwise and threw round his neck. His laughter was louder than thunder and anger more dangerous than a volcano.

Happening to fly one night across this city which was gay like Indraloka, he put away his caravan down a mountain slope and hovered over the palace when he sighted the princess dancing to a tune. He lost his heart on this lady and by a whiff of air, he sucked her into his nostrils and took her to a cave in the Himalayas.

The *rakshasa* brought her the young ones of forest beasts to play; sweet fruits and beautiful flowers to please her. In his mighty, but simple way, he tried to win her heart. Sadguna, however, felt like a parrot at the jaws of a wild cat. She decided to outwit him; her wit was her only weapon against such great odds. So she said: "Oh great man! The moment you lifted me away from my palace, I have become yours. There is no doubt about that. Is there any escape for the sugar cane that enters an elephant's mouth? No, I am yours and you are mine. We are born for each other, Now, in order that our union might be happy, I have to undertake a *vrata* which will last three months. That has to be observed with very great austerity. You must help me end it successfully by not pressing for our marriage till then." The fool of the *rakshasa* agreed.

In the meantime, Sadguna's disappearance had put her parents to a further test. Throughout the night when they were alive, they wept and again became corpses by day. That was the position.

On hearing this strange recital, King Vikrama said: "Bhatti, you had better look after the country while I am away on my usual exile." He put on his full uniform, took the magic sword, prayed before Bhadrakali, and proceeded towards Varanasi.

King Vikrama soon reached the city of Varanasi on the shoulders of the redoubtable ghoul. He looked all over the place and became very sad at the sight of all living beings lying dead, at any rate for the day. He became all the more firm that he should deliver the city from its curse.

Assuming Padmasana pose, he concentrated on his favourite deity – Mahakali of Ujjain. She appeared before him immediately and asked him: "Child, what made you think of me now?"

"Mother, don't you see the state of this city and its occupants? I pray that they should be saved," replied Vikrama.

"Vikrama", said the Goddess, "haven't you read that the remedy for an illness lives in the source itself? I suppose you know that the King of this city invited the curse on himself and his people by his misbehaviour towards a *rishi.* She is the only person competent to remove it. You had better apply your mind in that direction." She gave Vikrama the sacred ashes and after blessing him vanished.

King Vikrama decided on a plan of action and according to it, assumed the form of a very old man of 120 and riding on the ghoul reached the forest where the great *rishi* lived.

With the aid of the ghoul he lighted a huge fire in the midst of the forest and started walking towards it uttering the holy names of the Lord. It appeared that the old man was going to fall in that fire. He was walking towards it slowly with faltering steps.

The *rishi* woman who cursed Varanasi happened to notice the old man's intention. She shuddered at the thought of the good old man immolating himself in the raging fire and with the kindness of a mother, ran towards him to find out if she could be of any help to him.

Bowing before him devoutly she asked him: "O, venerable sire, may I know what is the cause of your great sorrow that has made you decide on this step?"

The old man let flow a torrent of tears and replied: "O great lady, how shall I express the calamity that has overtaken me at this age? Please leave me alone, for I am the most accursed being in this world and I don't want to bother others with my woeful tale, for it is not in their power to redress. I must work out my own fate."

He started moving onwards the fire. But the lady stopped

his further move and expostulated: "Venerable sire, don't say like that. Even the ant can be of some use. Do tell me of your sorrow and it may be that I can do something to alleviate it. Please do."

"O lady, you seem to be a great *rishi* and I hope you are as good as your word. I belong to the city of Saraswati and my name is Ganga Bhatt. I have studied all the *Vedas* and *Shastras* and had been following the path laid down for me by God. Till I was a hundred years old, I had no children. But after propitiating the Lord in the prescribed manner at Varanasi, I got a son whom I educated in the *Vedic* lore with great enthusiasm. He also proved to be very smart and became a scholar very soon. I got him married in a good family at Varanasi. My daughter-in-law after spending some time with us returned to her parent's home at Varanasi and the story my son has brought about her, breaks my heart. She is a corpse by day and alive at night!

"My son could not bear the sight of his beloved wife and her relations literally webbing away and deciding that what was good for them was good enough for him too, departed to Varanasi with the intention of settling there.

"I however went to Varanasi to fetch my boy for Dipavali, but lo, the people of the whole town surrounded me and accused me: 'The day your son married in our city, the calamity has overtaken us. And we have little doubt that your son who is a great friend of our King is the prime culprit for the King's misbehaviour, for before he came, our king was a very good man. They heaped all dirty abuses on my son's head who, mortified by shame, ran to the Kali temple and severed his own head. My daughter-in-law who came to know of this tragedy, likewise, took her life. This was followed by other members of the family and thus the entire family has been wiped off. Tell me now, when my dear son and all these people have gone, what remains for me in this world?"

Saying this the old man almost faltered to the ground. The *rishi* woman ran to his rescue and holding his body like a mother, gently laid him on a heap of grass and wafted a light breeze with her apron. The old man protested vehemently saying: "Great lady, won't you leave me to my fate? There is nothing in this world to shed a tear for this wretched life of mine."

"Don't say so, sire. I shall indicate a way out of your predicament which will lead to the removal of your sorrow. Listen, that King of Varanasi invited this curse upon his head and those of his subjects by his misbehaviour towards me. I too was a little too harsh upon him because in the condition I was, I could not think of an easier way of escape from his wicked clutches. I now find that your son and daughter-in-law are unnecessarily put to death. I shall revive them. I now revoke that curse and bless that your family should prosper."

The fake Vikrama on hearing this, fell prostrate before that august lady and praised her: "The power of chastity is indescribable; even the Trinity of Gods has to bow before its might. Your grace has now spared millions of innocent lives. May your *tapas* prosper."

Saying this, Vikrama literally flew to Varanasi on the shoulders of the ghoul. He was happy to find that all the people and living beings had started living as of yore and the line of sorrow had disappeared from all eyes, except one and that was of the King, for he could yet have no trace of his daughter's whereabouts.

King Vikrama was not satisfied till the last vestige of sorrow was wiped out from the city. So he prayed to his favourite deity Kalimata who immediately appeared before him, and blessed him in his new enterprise.

Riding on his ubiquitous ghoul, Vikrama went after the *rakshasa* like a police dog. He succeeded in tracing his hideout and the place where Sadguna was kept captive.

While the *rakshasa* was away, Vikrama contacted Sadguna and asked her: "Who are you, lady, and what makes you live in the den of the *rakshasa*?"

Sadguna was too frightened to tell the truth for she was afraid it might be one of the tricks of her captor.

King Vikrama who understood her hesitation revealed himself and established his identity by means of his magic sword which was then world famous. Thereupon Sadguna disclosed herself as the Princess of Varanasi and narrated the danger she was in.

King Vikramaditya replied: "My dear lady, your father and mother are quite well now. I have removed the curse on your city and parents. It is now my duty to rescue you from this accursed demon and I promise I will do it."

"I am grateful to you, but I must warn you that it is now time for him to return. Please take me away before he does."

"No, my lady; if I do so it will not merely detract from my merits, but he will continue to trouble you, for the fellow will be after you. I must fight him now."

"O no, sir, please don't do that, for he has been blessed by the gods that he would not be killed by any human."

"That is all right. When he comes today, try to be nice to him and find out the secret of his life. I shall return to you tomorrow and do the needful. Cheerio!" And in the twinkling of an eye, he disappeared.

As usual the *rakshasa* returned with a cartload of fine flowers, fruits and honey thinking they would please his latest find – Sadguna. Laughing and singing uproariously he approached his lady love. Sadguna who had been treating him as contemptuously as Sita did Ravana, raised her eyes to look at him, which made the *rakshasa's* heart race like the war horse. All his teeth shone resplendently before her in a plaintive mood. When she started conquetting, he simply lost his balance and behaved as though he was off his senses.

Said she: "Sir you will be glad to hear that my *vrata* is now almost over. Perhaps tomorrow itself I shall have to marry you. But before I do that, I have one doubt which I want you to remove."

"Why one, ask a hundred, my love!' encouraged the *rakshasa.*

"You see it concerns us both. I would like to know your longevity, for I want to live with you for a very long time."

"Ha, ha, ha," roared the *rakshasa* and said: "As long as the sun and moon are alive you shall live with me?"

"I am quite happy to hear that, but suppose somebody wants to do you harm?"

"To me? Not even God Almighty dare think of harming me, you hear?"

"Please explain yourself."

"My life principle is beyond all human reach."

"That is to say?"

"I can't say any further."

"Is that the measure of your love towards me?"

"O no, I have kept it secret even from my limbs. But I consider you greater than even my eyes. Listen: Very far from here is a mountain by name Mallikarjuna. At the base of that mountain is the temple of Ganapati. If you lift him, you will find an underground passage leading to the heart of the mountain. There is a lake. In that lake lives a tortoise. In the bosom of that tortoise lives a vermin whose head constitutes my life-principle. You see now how difficult it is to reach that and until that is not done I am perfectly safe from all hands, be it man or God! So don't worry, my sweet!"

"Now I am satisfied. We shall set about living together from tomorrow. Goodbye."

The *rakshasa* returned to his lair with a tune in his mouth.

In the morning after the *rakshasa* had left for his daily

outing, King Vikrama entered the princess's hideout. Sadguna welcomed him and reported the conversation of the previous evening with the *rakshasa.*

King Vikrama bade adieu of Sadguna promising to kill the demon and to rescue her before the day was out.

Calling out his ghoul he rode posthaste to the mount of Mallikarjuna. He found the Ganapati idol which he lifted and with his magic sword in hand entered the cavity. It led him to a lake at whose banks lay the enormous tortoise. It appeared to him that Lord Ganapati being the prime remover of obstacles was directly helping him to remove the greatest menace of the world in the person of the *rakshasa.* He prayed to Him and to Mahakali for success.

Swishing his immortal sword he cut the giant tortoise asunder and from its bosom removed the vermin which was the life-principle of the *rakshasa.* It looked like a small snake and bluish in colour. Cutting it into two halves, Vikrama carried the head part to the mountain lair of the *rakshasa.* He waited for the latter to return and in his presence crushed the head of the life-principle whereupon the *rakshasa* fell down in excruciating pain and died. His body devoid of life was another mountain by itself.

His task over, King Vikrama took Sadguna too on the shoulders of the ghoul to Varanasi at her request. On reaching the outskirts of the city, Vikrama alighted on the banks of Ganga to have a wash and drink the heavenly waters. He left the princess at a short distance from there so that he could pick her up.

It so happened that a poor brahmin boy who was passing by looked at Sadguna and at that very moment was struck with love of her. The attack was so sudden and intense that he fell down in a swoon. King Vikrama who had been noticing the strange behaviour of the youngster ran up to him and gave him first aid. When he recovered his senses, he asked: "What ails you, my son?"

The youth laughed sheepishly and pointed to Sadguna.

It was not difficult for Vikrama to understand the youngster's requirements and so replied: "O, is that all? You shall have her. Come with me."

Taking the two along with him Vikrama reached the palace of Varanasi and he announced himself. Great was the stir at the news of the return of Sadguna and her rescue by King Vikramaditya of Ujjain.

It is difficult to describe the joy of reunion, more so that between children and parents. The King of Varanasi shed tears of joy on seeing his beloved daughter back. He literally prostrated before King Vikramaditya for bringing back his daughter. The entire assembly paid tributes to the ability of Vikrama and all the respects due to a distinguished monarch were paid to him.

When the functions were over, King Vikrama told the King of Varanasi: "Brother, I have not only brought your daughter back, but have brought you a son-in-law too."

"I am very glad to hear it. Whoever Your Majesty has selected shall marry my daughter!"

Whereupon the brahmin youth was produced before him and he was immediately accepted as the bridegroom. An auspicious *muhoorta* was selected and the pair was united in holy wedlock. King Vikrama presided over the occasion.

Handing over the rein of Varanasi to his son-in-law the aged King retired. King Vikrama himself taught the youngster the principles of State craft and took leave of them all returning to Ujjain at the expiry of six months.

"Do you think, Bhoja, you have the valour and generosity of the great King Vikrama? If you think you have, you can ascend this throne," said the statuette.

Whereupon King Bhoja and his Minister Nitivakya, followed by other courtiers, returned to the palace.

45

The Three *Apsaras*

ON the twelfth day King Bhoja woke up as usual before the sun rose, and after completing his daily routine, went through the royal formalities like awarding gifts, etc. Breakfast over, he started for the throneroom followed by his Minister Nitivakya.

Smilingly he ascended the steps after worship. He could do so up to eleven steps. When he set foot on the twelfth step, the statuette holding it addressed him: "Bhoja, you have so far been listening to the exploits of our great King Vikramaditya during his six-monthly exiles. Listen to the one which he did when he was ruling." And it related this story.

There was a city by name Vishnupuri whose ruler was Dharmaraja. He had three sons and one daughter. They were happily married and had many children. Thus the King had a very happy time. As time passed on, he had to answer his Creator and so he left the world. So did his wife. Loud were the laments raised by the royal children, ministers and subjects. But in course of time the sorrow having healed, the three sons assumed royal responsibilities.

As was the wont, the princes set about in all directions to see for themselves how other States functioned or how they could cultivate the friendship of kings. East, South and West did not bring much of a result worth recording, but when they went North, something extraordinary took place. After a few miles they came to a place which at first sight appeared to be only a grove. But as they went inside it, they found three sets of resorts – summer resorts with bowers, ponds, rest houses, etc. This increased their curiosity and they began to search the entire colony, but they could find no human soul anywhere. Anyhow it was certain that it was being inhabited currently by some. So, determined to find out who lived there, the three of them hid themselves in a corner and waited.

As the day wore out, the night started setting in and a sweet angelic aroma pervaded the atmosphere of the place. In a short while the three of them saw standing before them three damsels who looked a marvel of creation and who were in fact *apsaras*, women from the Devaloka who attended to the comforts of the gods at daytime and departed to this place for rest during nights. That day even as they were descending they had spotted the three princes hiding behind a shrub. As they found them to be extraordinarily beautiful, they instantaneously fell in love with them and agreed among themselves that the eldest of them should get hold of the eldest prince, the youngest *apsara* clinging to the youngest one and the middle two to go together.

It was small work for the *apsaras* to decoy the three princes who entered into their arms like a fly into the web. They took to each other so well that the princes entirely forgot their mission – but not the *apsaras*. After enjoying their company at nights, the *apsaras* cursed the princes to become stones during daytime to be revived only at night on their return. For reasons already told, the princes never realized that they were thus made to forget their past.

Months passed in this manner with little change. One night however, the middle prince went out to answer his nature's call. As he was passing a corridor lined by decorated pillars, he heard a cry of distress. Try as he might he was unable to locate the person. Determined to find him out, he walked back in the direction of the sound, but as he crossed a statue carved on a certain pillar, it cried once again "Alas! Alas!"

The prince stopped and asked the statue: "What ails you?"

The statue replied: "There is nothing that matters with me for I am made of stone. But when I think of the fate of you three brothers, my heart breaks!"

"Why do you say so?" asked the prince.

"Don't you realize that you are the bond slaves of the *apsaras* for months now? You do not know that at nights they enjoy your company and fly to heaven after making you become stones. Where is your kingdom and what are you doing here? Did the thought ever occur to you?"

"What you say is correct. O statue, but can you tell me how we can escape from these devils? For, we fear, even if we run away, they can easily catch hold of us. And in daytime we are statues," bewailed the prince.

"Yes" replied the statue, "I shall certainly help you."

Saying this, the statue called the prince and whispered in secret.

46

The Princes' Bid for Escape

THE statue adorning the pillar said to the prince: "Prince, I shall give you seven magic pebbles which you must preserve. This night, all you three brothers must take special efforts to please the women and while they are fast asleep, you must make a bold bid for escape to your native country. You must take the shortest route. Even then, you will not be out of danger. They are likely to catch up with you by their superior powers and drag you back into their clutches any time, throw one of these pebbles, before them. It will cause a big impediment which will take a long time for them to overcome. In the meantime you can ride as fast as you can. You can continue to make use of the remaining pebbles till you reach your place."

"We are much obliged to you, statue! We shall do according to your advice," replied the prince and returned to his apartment wherefrom he managed to contact his two brothers and communicate the statue's advice. All of them agreed that they should lose no time in acting up to it the very same night.

As a result of the ministrations the three divine damsels were soon fast asleep. At a signal, the three brothers collected at the far end of the colony and jumping on their steeds literally flew in the direction of their hometown.

They must have ridden for a couple of hours when one of the women awoke. Not finding her paramour by her side, she peeped into the adjoining room where her sister lay fast asleep. Her lover too was not there. She roused her and enquired if she knew the whereabouts of the two princes. On receiving a negative reply, they together roused the third sister whose lover too appeared to have slipped. They smelt a rat. So using their supernatural powers they mapped the fleeing lovers and rushed with the intention of bringing them back.

The familiar sweet aroma descending on the fleeing princes announced that the damsels were close on them. They looked back and there they stood ready with ropes to tie them. Sensing the danger they were in, the middle prince threw one of the magic pebbles given by the statue between the pursuers and themselves. There rose on the spot a huge impenetrable forest with hills and dales, thick with thorny bushes and impassable rivers and what not. For a time, this proved a barrier and while the damsels were struggling to cross it, the three princes made good their way by spurring their horses to maximum speed.

In less than half an hour the damsels had extricated themselves from the forest and were hot on the heels of the fleeing princes. The middle prince threw one more pebble on the way which created a big gulf in the shape of big seas. The divine damsels had not much difficulty in this case as they took to the air after an initial setback and caught up with the fleers.

The prince threw another pebble which created veritable horde of wild beasts like lions, tigers, bears, jackals, etc. They charged at the three damsels and tried to arrest their progress. The princes, not stopping to look back, redoubled their speed.

Ultimately, the women were more than a match for the beasts and dodging them cleverly, they went in hot pursuit of their paramours. When they were very close, the middle prince threw one more pebble which created a nest of reptiles like snakes, scorpions and similar poisonous creatures. They fretted and fumed against the women, who, although afraid of being bitten manipulated their way and neared the fleeing princes.

Finding the women almost upon them, the middle prince threw one more pebble against them whereupon a flash of lightning descended blinding the women so completely that they could hardly feel their way ahead. The princes, on seeing their predicament, laughed and made quickly for their destination.

Finding that the odds were heavily against them, the women felt greatly worried. At the suggestion of one of them, they prayed to Goddess Saraswati, their patron deity, for help. The Goddess appeared before them and restored their eyesight.

Having recovered their sight, the women discovered to their contrition that it was near daytime and the princes had fled much further. This gave them time for reflection.

The pebbles which created such buffers really belonged to their own house. They wondered how they came into the possession of the princes.

The older girls talked with their eyes and came to the conclusion that the youngest of them was the traitor. In order to live with her paramour exclusively, she had stolen the pebbles and handed over to her paramour; they charged her with that crime; but, poor girl, her protestations were of no avail. So the two older girls, like fiends, killed the youngest and tore her limbs for her supposed treachery and returned to their heavenly abode.

The day broke. The princes, assured that the damsels would have left, returned to the spot where they left them, more out of curiosity. To their horror they found the youngest girl mauled to pieces. Her paramour, the youngest of the princes, wept loudly and, reminded of her affection, could not bear to leave her at that. He bade goodbye to his brothers stating that he would prefer to end his life along with his lady love. No amount of persuasion was of avail with the young prince who appeared to have set his mind.

The older brothers reluctantly left the scene.

Collecting the different parts of the body of one who had loved him as no one could, the young prince started raising a mound of faggots from the forest with the intention of setting fire to her last remains, pitting his own live body in the pyre along with it.

As he was about to set fire, Lord Shankara and Goddess Parvati were passing through the sky just above that place.

Parvati called the attention of her Lord to the tragedy enacted below when Shankara descended before the prince and asked: "My child, why do you want to perish?"

The young prince on seeing the Divine Pair, fell prostrate before them, and prayed: "My Father and Mother! What have I left in this world after losing my heart! Please let me extinguish my soul!"

Parvati looked meaningfully at her Lord whereupon the Lord said: "My son, don't do that. You shall have her back."

So saying He touched the body of the dead woman and vanished.

The young damsel awoke as though from sleep and who can describe the joy of the prince? The young prince related to his sweetheart how he could restore her by the intervention of the Divine Pair. The young lady supplemented the story by relating how her own sisters had murdered her.

The two of them had all the hours of the day and night for themselves oblivious of the past, present or future.

At the closing hours of the night, the young girl remembered her primary duty at Devaloka. With great reluctance she sought permission of the prince for leaving him, saying "My Lord! Don't think I am leaving you for ever. I shall never forget you or my duty. I shall do one thing: I shall leave with you my divine *veena*. Whenever you want me you just raise a tune by playing on it and I shall be there to serve you to your heart's content. But mind you, you must keep that instrument in safe custody and should not allow it to be touched by any other hand when I will not be responsible for the consequences."

So saying, she flew to heaven and brought back the *veena* which she entrusted to the prince. After bidding him sweet adieu, she flew to heaven.

47

Yogis and the *Apsara*

THE young *apsara* on reaching heaven plunged into her duties as though nothing had happened. But when the older girls espied her going about her work, they could not believe their own eyes; but the young one put them at ease by going to them straight and conversing as of old as though nothing had happened, at which the mortification of the older girls became more acute.

Down here, the young prince tried to live without the young *apsara* for a time. But after a few days, her absence started getting on his nerves. He began to fidget; but when he suddenly remembered her *veena*, he laughed within himself for his foolishness in forgetting all about it.

Walking in the direction of his hometown, the young prince reached a charming place studded with green trees in full bloom, a lake of pellucid water and a host of birds chirping and piping their throats in joy. He decided to have his *apsara* then and there. He played a soft tune on the *veena*, when lo! his lady love stood before him in full splendour with a basketful of sweets, drinks, food and flowers. She had great difficulty in disentangling herself from his embrace, after which she set about conjuring a bower. She ran aromatic water for the prince's bath and set up the table. When the prince was ready for dinner, she had perfect establishment ready for him. He partook of the heavenly food, ate *tambul* and for the time being, felt beyond time and space.

The flowers, scents, sandalpaste and other love-materials she had brought from heaven permeated the entire forest for miles around.

Among those who felt greatly disturbed by this exotic atmosphere was a *Yogi* whose concentration collapsed and became a thing of the past. His mind started hankering after things mundane and his legs dragged him in the direction of the prince and the *apsara.*

One look at the young *apsara* made the *Yogi* prostrate before the young prince of whom he begged: "Young man, please make over this young lady to me as I am dying of love for her and I shall in exchange part with this magic sword which knows no defeat."

"Oh, is that sword so powerful? How does one operate it?" asked the prince.

"Just take it out from the scabbard and fling it in the direction of anyone whom you would kill. It will most assuredly kill the man however powerful he may be and return to the sheath on its own accord," replied the *Yogi.*

"Let me see, if you don't mind," said the prince. And the *Yogi* in his eagerness to have his wish fulfilled handed the sword over to the prince. The latter took the sword out of its sheath and coolly flung it at the *yogi,* whereupon it made short work of the *yogi* and returned to its sheath held by the prince.

"Not a bad acquisition," said the prince turning askance at the *apsara* who was looking at him admiringly.

This minor episode did not in any way disturb the equanimity of the pair who had the rest of the night all for themselves.

In the early hours of the morning the *apsara* took leave of the prince and left for Devaloka.

After sunrise, the prince resumed his journey towards his

hometown. He went on looking and admiring nature's manifold ways and appearances. He ate some delicious fruits and drank the sweet water of rippling brooks.

When the sun was about to set he found himself in the midst of a grove which strongly reminded him of the previous evening. So his hand automatically sought the sacred *veena* left by the *apsara* and twanged the strings melodiously. In an instant, his young *apsara* stood before him in full bloom carrying with her a basketful of flowers, sweets, drinks and food.

As on the previous night, the *apsara* created a nice bower with all facilities for spending the night. After bath, the young prince sat down and partook of the delicious food brought by the divine damsel. Laughing and chatting, they partook of *tambul*.

The aroma of the heavenly flowers brought by the damsel started permeating the forest for miles and, as on the previous night another *yogi* who was practising *tapas* felt strangely disturbed and soon completely lost his concentration. A strange power was pulling him in the direction from which the divine aroma was spreading. Ultimately, he located the spot and entered the bower.

Like the previous *yogi*, he too was fascinated by the beauty of the *apsara* that he practically swooned before the couple. The prince came hurriedly and offered him water to drink and gently fanned him. When he regained consciousness, he fell at the feet of the prince and begged. "Sir, please let me have this girl or I shall die."

The prince who had by now become familiar with the waywardness of these half-baked *yogis*, put a smile on his face at the strange request.

The *yogi* continued, "Here, Sir, take this pouch in exchange for her. It is very valuable."

"In what way?" queried the prince.

"You just put your hand in the pouch and ask for any quantity of gold, silver or jewels and you will get them," replied the *yogi*.

"Oh, is that so?" exclaimed the prince and putting out his hand took the offered pouch from the *yogi's* hand.

Having done that, the prince drew the magic sword given by the first *yogi* and directed it against the new *yogi*. The sword cut him into two and returned to its scabbard.

The prince and the *apsara* had a hearty laugh over the episode and with one more valuable acquisition in the shape of the magic pouch, the pair spent the night like the God of Love and his spouse.

48

Princess Amrita in Fairyland

THE young *apsara* woke up before the sun, and bidding adieu to her lover, flew to heaven to attend to her duty at Devaloka.

The prince woke up late. After bathing he helped himself to the food left by his lady love and wended his way in the manner of a vagrant riding, singing and dancing.

By nightfall he reached a grove which strongly reminded him of the previous nights and his heart longed for companionship. So, he raised a tune on the magic *veena* whereupon his sweetheart *apsara* stood before him like full moon.

As on the two previous occasions, the *apsara* improvised a convenient home on the spot with all amenities needed for two love birds like them. From her knapsack, the *apsara* produced divinely flavoured dishes with which she fed her lover with her own hands. The laughter of the pair rang though the stillness of the forest and a divine fragrance permeated the air for miles on end.

They were playing blissfully when to their chagrin, a guest announced himself from somewhere. Although, he was not a *yogi*, in the strict sense of the word, he yet bore marks of some austerity. Apparently, he had been looking at the pair for some time unobserved: for, unlike common guests he asked the prince:

"I am dying of love-hunger; will you give that girl over to me? I shall in return give you something for which you will be grateful."

The prince who had started worrying at the hoodoo that had been pursuing for three days, now, raised his brows and asked: "Revered guest! I am grateful to you for the offer. But before agreeing to it, may I know what that gift is?"

Replied the guest : "I have a pair of magic sandals. All that you have to do is to wear them and think of the place where you want to go however far; they will take you there within the batting of an eyelid."

"May I have a look at it?" asked the prince.

"With pleasure, here they are!" Saying this, the guest produced the pair of sandals from his knapsack.

The prince took them in his hands manifestly for scrutiny but while doing so, he swung his hands on to his hip where the magic sword lay which he flashed on the guest. The sword killed the guest instantaneously and returned to its sheath like a faithful dog.

"Even calamities have their rewards!" he mused as he turned towards his sweetheart who looked at him as though she would devour him. They flew into each other's arms and together they proceeded on to the cosy bed overlaid with heaps of *parijat* and other heavenly flowers.

The *apsara* left the prince in the early hours of the morning in answer to the call of duty. The prince somehow spent the day.

After daylong wandering in the forest on foot and on the saddle, he found that he was very near his capital. The cool evening and the gay atmosphere charming with the noises of birds made him think of his *apsara*. His hand mechanically sought the strings of the magic *veena* and twanged them melodiously. The *apsara* stood before him full of divine beauty as the morning bloom. His hands sought hers and together they walked towards a lovely spot.

As usual the *apsara* opened her knapsack in which she had brought food from Devaloka. They ate it with the relish known only to lovers.

No sooner had they settled themselves on a lawn than a *siddha* appeared before them and stood staring at the *apsara* as though moonstruck. He soon entered into conversation with the prince. Brandishing a cane before the prince, the *siddha* said: "Do you know the value of this cane?"

"No, can you tell me?" asked the prince.

"It cannot be measured in terms even of gold; I consider it only equal to my own life. I got it after lifelong *tapas*. If you touch with it, even the worst mutilated body will get together and be re-endowed with life!"

"That is something wonderful, indeed!" exclaimed the prince.

"You can have it for your exclusive use, if you so desire."

"Suppose I want it?" asked the prince.

"I will ask you a small favour from you in return," said the *siddha*.

"What can be that?" asked the prince.

"Oh, that is but a trifle compared to what I propose to give you," replied the *siddha*.

"Please say that!" Insisted the prince.

"That girl of yours."

For a second the prince closed his eyes at the repellent suggestion but the next moment he opened them and smilingly asked, "May I have a look at the cane!"

The *siddha* gave it and as soon as the prince got it in his hands, he, as before, killed the *siddha* too with his magic sword.

Since interferences like that had become a common

occurrence with them, the pair was little affected by it. On the contrary, they took a delight in being able to overcome them all with perfect ease. They found the hand of God in all those things.

When the time came for her to depart to heaven, the *apsara* prayed to her lover: "May I request you one thing? You have now reached your hometown. You must therefore be particularly careful in calling me up. Please don't call me every now and then and at inconvenient times and places. I have great reason to warn you to keep my *veena* safe and to see that no one else touches it; for you know, I will not be responsible for the consequences. Please be a good boy at least for some time by not summoning me into your palace. Do you hear? Goodbye." So saying she pinched his cheek and departed.

At dawn the prince bridled his horse and made straight for his palace. On seeing him, the entire royal household felt happy and after the usual enquiries, they settled down to their routine.

At home the prince, in view of his special circumstances, chose a rest house which was situated at some distance from the town proper in sylvan surroundings. He put his special acquisitions like the magic *veena*, magic sandals, magic sword and the magic wand in a silken bag which he hung up in the centre and whenever he went out, he locked the place and took the key with him.

It became his custom to summon his sweetheart *apsara* at odd hours – the place being rather secluded – and indulge in love-play with her for hours together. Their *prem* progressed to such an extent that a stage came when the prince appeared to be thinking only of her when she was not near him; he soon became so absent-minded that he even forgot to take any precautions about his precious possessions.

One day it so happened that he had gone out for a walk

in his estate and while going out left the door of the rest house unlocked.

This prince had a lovely sister, Amrita by name. She was particularly fond of him. Not meeting him for days together, she came out to where he lived and finding the door of his place ajar, entered it. She saw to her horror that the place was strewn about with oddments pell-mell. She knit her brow, wondering what had happened to her beloved brother.

The silken bag hanging from the centre attracted her attention. Out of puckish curiosity she put her hand into it and the pair of sandals came to her hands. She threw it down and snatching the bag onto her shoulder with a view to ransacking it more leisurely in her room, she stepped on to the sandals which were daintily made with the intention of walking to her apartment at the palace, but lo! The sandals put on wings and carried her ever so lightly to her apartment!

The thing was so sudden and unexpected and accomplished in so short a time that she became greatly flabbergasted and on alighting into her room, became genuinely afraid lest her brother should scold her. She wanted to return to her brother's place before he knew. Lo! Again the sandals put on wings and carried her like a flower back to her brother's apartment!

Amrita, now bewildered, shuffled off the sandals with awe and put her hand inside the silken bag. A brightly burnished sword came into it. When she started admiring, the sword-began to throb apparently demanding to be released. At that-time she saw a big rat jumping across the room. She thought of trying the sword on it, but instantaneously the blade flew against the rat, killed it, and returned to its scabbard!

Amrita felt like a child left blindfolded in fairyland. Thinking that the dead rat might start stinking soon, she took out the handy cane from the silken bag and lifted the dead rat with a view to throw it out. But to her consternation, the rat came back to life and jumped away to safety, the mortal wound having completely healed!

Amrita's wonder at her brother's unusual collection reached dizzy heights. She felt like singing when her hand touched the magic *veena* which she took out of the bag admiringly and automatically raised a tune.

It was midday and it was never the habit of the prince to summon the *apsara* except at night. So the *apsara* who felt the call of her *veena* came running from heaven thinking that her lover was in some danger. When she pushed the half-closed door of the rest house ajar greatly agitated, she met a pair of feminine eyes staring at her.

49

Maha Sura in Devaloka

IT has been said that a hundred men can live together; but not two women for a day. Jealousy or intolerance, it would appear, is the hallmark of the feminine of the species. The *apsara* was not an exception. So, she asked the princess in a fierce tone "Who are you? Why are you here?"

"I am Amrita, the prince's sister!" she replied in a tone which betrayed her fright.

On hearing that, the *apsara* appeared to cool down for a while but she worked herself up again to high tension, and demanded: "Did your brother ask you to play on that *veena*?"

"No," replied the princess.

"Where is your brother?" asked the *apsara.*

"He is somewhere in the garden," replied Amrita.

"Does he know that you are here?" again the Apsara demanded.

"No." replied Amrita meekly.

"Give me that *veena,*" said the *apsara* and wrested the *veena* from Amrita and grinding her teeth, broke the *veena* to pieces and threw it out of the door. Looking at Amrita fiercely she exclaimed. "Tell your brother that he has lost his love!" and slamming the door walked out of the house on her way to Devaloka which she reached instantaneously.

Amrita who was dumbfounded by the altogether unexpected denouement, quietly walked home without informing anything to anybody.

When the prince returned to the rest house, he looked at the way things were lying strewn about in his room and worst of all, the *veena* broken into pieces. His head reeled and he fell down on the floor with a thud.

It took some time before be recovered his senses, and when he did so, he felt he had lost his heart. He surveyed the scene before him with greater calmness and could not for the life of him think of any one who could have done him this mortal harm.

Slowly, he bestirred himself and tottered home holding his aching head in both his hands. The royal household when they saw the prince in that condition, was alarmed. All sorts of persons ran for all sorts of help. But the prince did not care for any and went directly to his bed in his room.

The brothers sat around him and pacified him. In the end the young prince related to them what had upset him. He asked: "Do you know or have you seen anybody entering my rest house and destroying the divine *veena*?"

The brothers shook their heads in the negative.

Amrita who was a patient listener to this story felt like the thief stung by the scorpion.

The prince then turned towards her and asked: "Amrita, dear, do you know anything about what had happened at my rest house?"

Amrita who had been feeling guilty all the while, broke into tears and said, "I did it all!" amidst sobs.

"What? How did you happen to go there!" asked the others in chorus.

The royal mother went round and hugged Amrita in an effort to calm her. She did so and then the girl related her adventure in detail ending with her encounter with the *apsara*.

No sooner had the narration ended the prince rose and announced: "I am going straight to heaven in search of my *apsara*. If I gain her, I shall return; if I don't this is the last you see of me."

On hearing it, the eldest brother said: "You forget that she lives in Devaloka where an altogether different order of life prevails. If I were you, I will forget the past and get hold of a beautiful girl from our own class here!"

Others also spoke more or less on the above lines. But the young prince would not listen. So bidding them all good-bye, he collected his magic sword, cane other things he could, and stepped on to the magic sandals on his way to Devaloka.

All of them watched him proceeding to Devaloka tearing through space at breakneck speed.

In a short time the prince stood at the gate of Devendra's palace where a dance programme on a mass-scale was in progress. Dumbfounded by the glamour of Devendra's Court, the prince stood at the gate eagerly watching the celestial damsels gracefully portraying the great art.

While everyone was busy watching the performance, the *darwans* who happened to notice the prince from afar, first out of curiosity and later with suspicion, tried to drive him out.

Remonstrated the prince: "What makes you prevent me from seeing the dance?"

Darwans: "You are a mortal and you have no business to be here."

Prince: "What? Do you know how many times your Indra has been saved by mortals?"

Darwans: "Oh, man! Watch your words. This is Devaloka. If you don't restrain your tongue, we shall produce you before our Master for punishment."

Prince: "Do, if you can."

Thereupon the servants lodged a complaint with Devendra against the prince for speaking ill of their master. Devendra in a fit of anger, ordered a number of *rakshasas* to go and kill the prince. They came in high glee. In this melee, the *apsara,* sweetheart of the prince, caught a glimpse of him from afar and became genuinely afraid of his life. But she calmed herself subsequently on seeing him come prepared with his magic sword and the rest of them.

The *rakshasas* came roaring like a sea in an effort to smash the prince out of all recognition. On seeing them all, the prince did not lose heart even for a second, but put out his hands asking them to listen to him for a minute.

"It is meaningless," he said "for you and Indra to attempt to kill me. Why should not a mortal, if he ever can, pay a visit to Devaloka? I have not been disrespectful to you or your master. Please go and advise him to be reasonable."

But the *rakshasa* horde hooted at him and started its onslaught. With no other alternative before him, the prince drew out his magic sword and ordered it to kill the entire *rakshasa* horde which it did in the twinkling of an eye. Blood flowed like river and the carcases of their bodies constituted a small hillock.

Those who escaped from the sword ran in mortal fright and reported to Indra: "My lord, the mortal whom you ordered us to kill does not appear to be an ordinary man. He has killed thousands of us and even now challenges that any more of us can come. What shall we do?"

Devendra who was astounded to hear that, thought for

a moment and became genuinely interested in seeing such a man. So he came down and walked towards the prince. The latter on seeing Indra and his senior officials, folded his hands in obeisance before them.

"Who are you, young man, and why have you come here?" asked Devendra.

"Maha Sura is my name. I am the third son of King Dharmaraja and I have come here to see Your Majesty on some urgent purpose," replied the prince.

"What can that be?" asked Indra.

Whereupon the prince related his story with reference to the three *apsaras* and ended. "I want the youngest *apsara* for myself."

"There are fifty lakhs of *apsaras* here, but if you can identify your sweetheart, I have no objection to grant your request, replied Indra.

Indra then took him around the *durbar* where all the *apsaras* were engaged in dance. Soon the prince identified the three sisters dancing together.

Indra called the three *apsaras* and said: "You three have proved yourselves unfit to be in my service after having loved human beings. I order you therefore to follow this young man to the earth and live as he commands!"

Indra gave the women plenty of jewels and costly dresses to take with them to the earth.

Turning to the prince, Indra said apologetically: "I am sorry I did not reckon your ability when I ordered your killing. I wish you had met me earlier so that the ghastly killing could have been avoided!"

"Devendra," said the prince, "you need not feel sorry about

these, because I shall revive them all now!" So saying the prince touched the dead bodies of all the *rakshasas* with his magic cane at which all of them came back to life hale and hearty.

Devendra was greatly pleased by the exploits of the prince, whom, He therefore honoured by presenting with valuable things from Devaloka.

Followed by the three *apsaras*, the prince was returning to Vishnupuri.

But the youngest *apsara* was anything but happy, for she thought: "I have broken the *veena* which I had given the prince in a frenzy. I don't know what punishments are in store for me!"

The other two girls, equally worried, were thinking: "Now that we are under the prince, we don't know what punishment he is going to mete out to us for murdering our sister – his sweetheart – out of suspicion."

50

Vikrama Rescues Maha Sura

THE parents and brothers of Prince Maha Sura started worrying because he did not return for a long time. They sent for the State astrologer and asked him about the whereabouts of the prince. The astrologer made elaborate calculations and said to the King: "Your Majesty, the mission on which Prince Maha Sura went is a complete success, but on the way back he appears to have been subjected to some serious danger. If I can hazard a guess, I believe that he, along with his followers, are presently being surrounded by a huge forest fire and the chances are that unless rescued immediately the party will be burnt to death. Incidentally, this forest fire is not the making of man. Once a former Devendra made a curse that if any non-Devas succeed in carrying away divine damsels they should be surrounded by a cosmic fire. I feel that our prince has been surrounded by that fire. I advise you to run immediately and arrange for his rescue."

The astrologer also gave them the direction and location of the place where the prince's party was trapped.

On hearing this frightened prediction the two royal princes ordered their best steeds to be brought and armed with weapons, ran in the direction indicated by the astrologer. In a surprisingly short time the rescuing princes reached that spot and were flabbergasted to see the raging fire predicted by the astrologer. From inside that ring of fire came heart-rending cries of the prince and the three *apsaras.*

When the brothers looked about for possible help to gain entrance into the ring, they saw a flashing light emanating from a temple at some distance. Thinking that there might be some help they spurred their steeds in that direction and reached it.

Facing that temple was a huge lake and in the midst of the lake they noticed a ball of fire which was apparently lighting an inscription on a stone jutting from the water. The princes strained their eyes and read: "Any one who climbs the tower of this temple and jumps into this lake at this point will be taken into the Patalaloka where there is the immortal temple of Lord Siva. By praying before Him he can overcome any difficulty that might beset his path or of his friends and relatives. They can get any other of their ambitions too fulfilled by the Lord's grace."

After reading this inscription the two brothers looked at each other apparently expecting the other to jump into the lake.

By that time King and his courtiers who had followed the brothers also came to the spot.

When they saw the fire and learnt about the rock inscription, neither the King nor other members of his family were prepared to jump into the lake and save the prince who was in mortal danger of being burnt to ashes in a short time.

Readers will remember that this story of Maha Sura is being retold to King Vikramaditya by the messenger who returned from the north. The messenger ended: "That is the situation in which Prince Maha Sura finds himself at the moment, when, no one of his relatives is prepared to come to his rescue."

When King Vikramaditya heard this interesting story from the messenger who returned from the north, he felt glad that here was an opportunity to show his mettle.

So he immediately handed over charge of his government to Minister Bhatti and calling his favourite ghoul, went on it to the place where the prince was awaiting scorching death any moment.

Alighting before the temple he bathed in the lake, offered prayers to the deity in the temple, climbed the steep tower and jumped into the spot with scarcely a flicker of thought on the consequences and found himself right before the temple of Lord Siva in Patalaloka as indicated in the inscription.

Vikrama prayed before Him. Lord Siva was greatly pleased by the enterprise shown by Vikramaditya and blessed him with success in his mission.

The Lord further gave him four pebbles which He said he should throw, should he find any difficulty with anything.

Vikramaditya went straight to the spot where the huge fire was encircling Prince Maha Sura and his party. The heat was unbearable even at a distance. He threw one of those pebbles given by Lord Siva, whereupon the fire lost its warmth and became cool as water. Slowly out of the ring came Maha Sura and the three *apsaras* gleaming with gratefulness in their eyes.

On seeing his parents and brothers the prince fell at their feet choked with emotion.

The old king who was witnessing the rescue operations of the stranger who later revealed himself as King Vikramaditya, asked his son to fall at the feet of the great man, who alone was responsible for saving him and his followers.

On hearing that, Prince Maha Sura was greatly delighted and fell at the feet of Vikramaditya who embraced him and blessed him. He said, "Maha Sura, I know all about you and your exploits in Indraloka. That is why I have volunteered to come out and help you."

The party when drove to the palace where King Vikramaditya remained as a guest for a day and at that time on his advice, the *apsaras* were married to the three brothers respectively.

King Vikramaditya also advised Maha Sura to revive the *sadhus* whom he happened to kill and after reviving them, he returned to them the magic sword, the magic cane and the magic sandals.

But when the *sadhus* came back to life, they realised their mistakes in having forsaken their ideal of *tapas* and falling a prey to lust.

They prayed to King Vikramaditya to accept those magic weapons as gifts from them so that they could not thereafter be lured into base actions.

King Vikramaditya approved their suggestion and received the gifts, but handed them over to Prince Maha Sura himself.

Finally King Vikramaditya gave over the remaining pebbles gifted by Lord Siva to Maha Sura to keep them in safe custody to protect against any insurmountable disasters. and blessing them all, returned to Ujjain on the shoulders of the faithful ghoul.

The statuette that was relating this story stopped at this stage and asked King Bhoja: “Bhoja if you too have such a power and are ready to help others in this manner you are welcome to climb this throne, but not otherwise.”

On hearing this challenge, King Bhoja and his Minister Nitivakya bowed their heads in humility and returned to their abodes.

51

Princess Vichitrakala

ON the morning of the thirteenth day, King Bhoja and his Minister Nitivakya woke up early as usual, and after finishing their morning ablutions, said their prayer and distributed different kinds of gifts. Breakfast over, they dresed up for the *Durbar* and marched in the direction of the throne room. On the way Bhoja thought: "I don't know what is in store for me today. For twelve days I have been failed in my attempt to ascend the throne and I wonder if I will succeed today."

On reaching the throne room, Bhoja offered prayers to the throne and started ascending it. As soon as he set foot on the thirteenth step, statuette holding it burst into a sudden fit of laughter and addressed King Bhoja:

"The great King Vikramaditya sat on this throne and ruled the country which under his just rule prospered in an unprecedented manner. May I tell you an incident in the life of that great King for your edification?"

King Bhoja being thus challenged could not help replying in the affirmative; he stood with attention and listened to the story.

Said the statuette:

When the great King Vikramaditya was ruling this country, there was a city in the South named Dakshapuri which was ruled by King Durgeswara. He was very learned and good-natured. His wife who was extremely beautiful was also a learned and devout lady. Under their rule, the city prospered, but the king was sad at heart because he had no children.

On the advice of the learned men of the town, the royal couple undertook a series of fasts and prayers directed to their family deity Parashakti. The latter, greatly pleased with the devotion of the king and the queen, appeared before them and said: "I should say I am gratified by your devotion to me. I am, however, unable to bless you with a son, because of your past *karma;* but you will have a beautiful girl." After saying this she disappeared. From that time the queen showed signs of pregnancy, and for ten months they and the entire city lived in great joy.

In due time a girl was born whose beauty had no parallel. The king and the queen named her Vichitrakala and taught her all the arts and sciences. She turned out to be a great pastmaster in music, dance and other fine arts. When Kala came of age, King Durgeswara was busy looking for a suitable son-in-law.

Kala on her part in the fresh bloom of her adolescence dressed herself in varied patterns and being a hefty girl took great pleasure in games peculiarly suited to women, like playing the ball, picking flowers, swimming in the pools, etc. During one of these sprees, she got into trouble.

Not far from the city of Dakshapuri was a hill by name Mallikarjuna. In one of its caves lived a *rakshasa* known as Mriganka. He was known to be most powerful by virtue of his *tapas* and could make himself invisible to ordinary human beings. It was his practice to roam over parts of the world during day and return to his lair at nightfall. During one of his outings while flying in the skies, he happened to notice Vichitrakala sporting in a bower attached to the palace. Her beauty proved to be a magnet to which his eyes remained glued for minutes together.

When Princess Kala's attendants drew her attention to the hideous monster's gaze falling on her, she looked up and out of terror, ran to her apartment. Her friends who followed her related to her all about the strength and evil nature of the *rakshasa*, whereupon Kala directly ran to her father and reported the incident.

King Durgeswara on hearing this exclaimed: "My God, I don't know what is going to happen to you, because Mriganka is ruthless and he will carry out his intentions at all costs. Personally I am not aware of anybody who could vanquish him because of his power. I can think of no one who could protect you from this danger except our deity Parashakti who gave you to us. Please go to her and pray to her and she will show a way out."

The entire royal household became shaken by this news and the guards were alerted to keep close watch on intruders, although it was well known that the *rakshasa* could not be resisted.

At nightfall, Princess Kala took her bath and carrying the materials of worship, went to the temple of Parashakti, the doors of which happened to be open as the Goddess had gone out on her usual rounds. Princess Kala went inside and bolted the doors. Soon the Goddess returned and on finding the doors closed against her, knocked against it, asking, "Who is inside?" But Kala did not reply for some time; but later opened it and the Goddess entered. As soon as Kala saw the Goddess, she fell at her feet to which she clung and bathed them with her tears.

The Goddess raised her and wiping her tears, asked Kala, "What ails you, my child? Why do you weep?"

Princess Kala started sobbing again. The Goddess embraced her fondly as a mother and comforted her for some time.

Kala said: "Mother, this evening *rakshasa* Mriganka espied me from afar and it appears he is bent on taking me away. Please protect me. I have no other go besides you."

"My child," said the Goddess, "what a misfortune! It is well

-nigh impossible to overcome that *rakshasa* because of the boons he has got from Brahma. There is only one person who can overcome him and he is King Vikramaditya of Ujjain. You go to him straight now and request for his protection."

On hearing this, Princess Kala said: "Mother, if that is your order, I am prepared to go right now, but what shall I do with that demon if he accosts me on the way?"

The Goddess said, "You don't worry about it. I am now making you look like an old woman by my touch. You can proceed to Ujjain in this disguise so that no one can recognize you. On reaching Ujjain, if you want to regain your usual form, think of me and I shall give you back your normal figure. I bless you."

Princess Kala returned home and related to her royal parents the instructions of Parashakti, and with their permission proceeded to Ujjain which she reached not long later. At the outskirts of Ujjain she saw an eating house conducted by an old woman where she took lodgings in the hope of meeting King Vikramaditya.

Princess Kala in the garb of an old woman was waiting for an opportunity to meet King Vikramaditya. But for one reason or other she could not gain entrance into the palace. One night, however, she was singing at the place of her stay a sweet *raga* to the accompaniment of a *veena* merely as a matter of exercise. Since she was a pastmaster in the science of music, her performance was superb. It so happened that King Vikramaditya was going by that side in his usual nocturnal patrol. This song sung by the princess appealed to him so much that he made a mental note of it and returned to the palace. When next morning Vikramaditya started business, the first thing he did was to send word to his Minister to fetch the lady – whoever she was – who sang at the boarding house the previous night. When, therfore, the royal messenger asked her to accompany him, Kala felt that it was the hand of God, which drew her to the King's presence. So she gladly went.

King Vikramaditya on seeing her rose from his throne and respectfully conducted her to a seat of honour and in the presence of all of his courtiers requested her to give the audience some of her wonderful songs. Princess Kala felt greatly honoured and being in high spirits, she brought into force all her abilities and gave a performance which enthralled the whole audience including the King.

King Vikramaditya at the close of the performance was lost in deep thought. He could not reconcile such a voice with an oldish appearance. Feeling that there was something unusual about the lady, he called her aside and asked her: "Dear lady, who are you?" What is your name? Where are your noble parents? Why should you come here in this form? I request you to tell me the truth."

On hearing this, Princess Kala replied: "Noble Sir, I am Vichitrakala, the daughter of King Durgeswara of Dakshapuri. A *rakshasa* by name Mriganka wanted to carry me away and consequently I prayed before our family deity Parashakti to protect me from the demon; but the Goddess asked me to seek protection under your venerable banner and by way of interim protection, the Goddess gave me this aged form."

King Vikramaditya was satisfied with the reason adduced by Princess Kala, and replied to her: "Dear lady, I am so glad you have come to me. Please be free of all fears. I shall remain your protector. You may, therefore, remove your aged appearance and become your usual self. I shall myself marry you as soon as Uttarayana starts."

On hearing this, Kala was greatly overjoyed and by contemplating on Parashakti she cast off her elderly form and became her real self. On seeing her charming figure King Vikramaditya felt more than justified in having taken an interest in this immortal beauty.

King Vikramaditya appointed a team of maids to look after Princess Kala's comforts and placed at her disposal a most charming palace which he ordered to be heavily guarded against all intruders.

While everyone was expecting the return of Uttarayana, the turn came for King Vikramaditya to go on his half-yearly self exile to the forest. In view of the precious protection given to Princess Kala, King Vikramaditya called his Minister Bhatti and told him all about Kala, and instructed him to protect her against the *rakshasa* Mriganka. Handing over charge of the kingdom to Bhatti, King Vikramaditya went into exile in the company of his favourite ghoul.

While Kala was thus being protected by Bhatti, Mriganka was searching heaven and earth for the princess; for, when he came back to Dakshapuri the next day with the intention of carrying her away, he was surprised that she had completely disappeared. But he did not lose heart, because he was conscious of his great strength and his ability to travel anywhere he liked. He, therefore, made a plan of action that he should search every nook and corner of the world.

After searching many a part of the country, he came to Ujjain and knowing well the valour of King Vikramaditya, entered the city with great trepidation. He thought of a plan and accordingly he disguised himself as a merchant selling bangles which, are exclusively worn by women of high society. He had with him a particular set of two pairs of bangles which were very costly and which would be purchased only by a royal household.

As he was coming around the city showing the bangles, some palace attendants happened to notice those beautiful bangles and one of them suggested that the costly pairs could well form a present for King Vikramaditya's new bride Princess Kala. As the other attendants also agreed, the matter was taken to Bhatti who was in charge of the kingdom. In deference to the wishes of the women, Minister Bhatti sent for the merchant and when he saw the bangles he too was greatly taken in by their workmanship and decided to buy them as presents by the great monarch for his lady-love: Bhatti bargained for the price and fixed it at two lakhs of gold coins for the two pairs.

When it was about to be handed over, Mriganka felt that once the bangles left his hands he would not be in a position to look out for Vichitrakala. So he suggested to Bhatti: "Respected sir, may I submit that these bangles being very precious, I should be given the honour of putting them on the princess's hands myself?"

When Bhatti heard this request, he knit his brows and felt that as long as the money was paid in full, the merchant had no right for any other interest. Suddenly a thought struck him whether there could not be any fraud and whether the merchant could not in reality be Mriganka in search of Princess Kala.

Great diplomat that he was, Bhatti brought the situation into control by saying: "Now that we are talking of the final arrangements for purchase, I feel it would only be fair if we wait for King Vikramaditya himself – for him to personally put them on to the hands of his queen. I also feel that in such transactions where huge sums are involved, I had better take his personal sanction. Could you, therefore, be kind enough to wait for a few months till the king returns?"

Mriganka was a little taken aback by the reply, but protested. "If you people say like this, how can I expect to sell such precious jewels? It is meant only for the royal household. But you see, I am travelling from place to place and it is manifestly unfair to ask me to wait here for months together. If I go from here, I do not know whether I will be back at the time of the King's return. I propose a compromise. If you can tell me now where King Vikramaditya is, I will myself go to him personally and get his permission for purchase. Do you agree?"

"You are quite right," replied Bhatti. "King Vikramaditya is at present in the Dandaka forest. You are quite welcome to meet him and get his approval."

On hearing this Mriganka, the fake jewel merchant, made straight for the place indicated by Bhatti where King Vikramaditya was spending his exile. In a suprisingly short time, Mriganka located him. On seeing King Vikramaditya, the fake merchant fell at the feet of the King and said: "Great King, Minister Bhatti sent me to you on a small job. I showed these bangles to him and he approved of them as fit presents for your new queen. But since the amount involved is over two lakhs of gold coins, he thought it better to get your prior approval. I volunteered to get it for him. Here it is, you can have a look at it yourself." Saying this, Mriganka handed over the precious jewels to King Vikramaditya. The latter was, no doubt, greatly impressed by their workmanship and quality, but what exercised his mind was this: "Bhatti is in entire charge of my kingdom and that being the case, why should he seek to get my prior approval for this small piece of transaction? Bhatti is too clever and he could not have done this, had it not been that he suspected some fraud, and as I remember, possibly this man has something to do with Mriganka, that *rakshasa* who has threatened to carry away Princess Kala, because this ornament is meant for women. I shall put him to test." So thinking he called his favourite ghoul which was always invisible and asked it:

"Tell me now, who is the man before me?"

The ghoul being gifted with superhuman knowledge easily identified the merchant as the *rakshasa* Mriganka himself. So it told king Vikramaditya that the merchant was in fact Mriganka in disguise. This conversation was held in mysterious language by signs and hence could not be noticed or deciphered by the fake merchant. When King Vikramaditya knew that he invoked the blessings of his favourite deity Mother Goddess of Ujjain and whipping out his magic sword, flung it at the neck of the fake merchant whose head rolled down on the mud in a pool of blood.

Taking the precious bangles from the fake merchant, King Vikramaditya waited till the completion of his six-monthly exile; and when he returned to Ujjain, with his own hands he put those bangles on the hands of Princess Vichitrakala.

By that time, Uttarayana had come and King Vikramaditya married Princess Vichitrakala with whom he lived for many years.

The statuette which was telling this story stopped at this stage and asked King Bhoja. "Bhoja, if you think you are as clever, intelligent and valiant as our King Vikramaditya you can climb on this throne, but not otherwise."

King Bhoja on hearing this, bent his head down in humility, and walked back to the palace accompanied by Nitivakya and other courtiers.

52

Vikrama Helps Dharmasheela

ON the morning of the fourteenth day, King Bhoja and his Minister Nitivakya woke up early, went through their morning routine and followed by other courtiers went to the divine throne and started ascending the steps.

Nothing happened till he crossed the thirteenth step and at the time of setting foot on the fourteenth, the statuette holding it suddenly became animated and clapping its hands heckled, saying "Ho, ho, Bhoja, I thought you had become wiser after listening to the story related by my sister yesterday. But now I see that there is not much difference between an ordinary man and yourself insofar as your ambition goes. Perhaps, I may be able to succeed where my sister appears to have failed. Could you listen to another episode from our Emperor Vikrama's life?"

Bhoja who had now become familiar with the technique to meet the setbacks with equanimity put on a bright smile on his face and intimated his readiness to listen to the story.

The statuette began:

When our great emperor Vikramaditya was ruling over this country from this throne, once he felt a weakness to know what other people thought of him. This may be thought excusable in a great monarch; but it was not born out of any desire for hearing his own praises; on the contrary he wanted to know if people found out any fault in his administration or if he had further scope for being of use to his subjects.

Whatever the motive, he called his confidant aide, the ghoul, and said, “Ghoul, would you do me a favour? I would like to have a first-hand report of what people at large think and speak of me and my regime in their heart of hearts. You may call it a weakness of mine. But I would like to have a faithful account from you.”

“With great pleasure,” replied the ghoul and went out to examine each cross-section of society.

By and large it heard men from all parts of the country praise King Vikramaditya for his valour, courage and justness. They were inclined to believe that the enormous prosperity which the country enjoyed under his benign rule was in a very large measure due to his *Dharma*. There were pretty little misdeeds in the country and much less godlessness.

The ghoul went round the sphere of women; they liked Vikramaditya for his beauty and personality. They worshipped him as their idol.

After hearing these, the ghoul went to Kashi for purpose of making personal enquiries from people there about King Vikramaditya. In that city the ghoul heard a curious incident. A very wealthy merchant by name Dharmasheela had ordered a tank to be dug for purposes of providing water to the public, by employing an army of workers for a number of days. It so happened that, however deep he had it dug, there was no prospect of water coming from any quarter in that area. This made the merchant sick at heart. He almost became mad for having spent enormously on an unproductive job.

One day he become so lost, that he decided to end his life in that waterless land. When he made himself ready to carry out his intention, he heard an unseen voice from the sky saying “Dharmasheela, what a foolish act do you propose to do? If your efforts did not prove fruitful, it is because of the sin you have committed in your past life. If you want to atone for that and to get your object fulfilled, you must sacrifice a man who has all the thiry-two marks of a great man on this spot; then water will well up in this tank.”

On hearing this voice, Dharmasheela became immensely happy; because with his enormous wealth he could buy out an ideal person for sacrifice.

For that, he made an icon of a man possessing all the thirty-two *lakshanas*, from gold, diamonds, emeralds, pearls and other costly jewels, placed at the base of a huge column, also made of gold and nine kinds of gems. On that column he had a golden plaque inscribed, "anybody who possesses the thirty-two *lakshanas* who offers to sacrifice himself will have the icon and *stambha*, which are worth crores of gold coins, gifted to his heirs or whomsoever he likes them to be given."

This offer interested the ghoul so much that it told Vikramaditya about it when it returned to Ujjain and reported all that it had heard about him. King Vikramaditya who heard the Kashi incident was fascinated by the merchant's offer, not because of its reward, but because of the intention behind the offer.

He thought, "What a golden opportunity for me to be of help to millions of pilgrims who go to Kashi by providing good water, if I could sacrifice myself at this spot."

King Vikramaditya then and there decided to proceed to Kashi and with the aid of the ghoul, went straight to the spot and read the plaque.

There was a temple of Lord Shiva near that dry tank. When Vikramaditya went inside to offer worship to the deity, he saw a *yogi*, immersed in meditation and Vikrama was very much impressed by that great man.

The *yogi* woke up from his trance and addressed Vikramaditya: "Great Vikramaditya, here lies before you a wonderful opportunity in which you can prove your greatness, by offering yourself to be sacrificed; you will be establishing a great *Dharma* which will have no parallel in the annals of history. Go right now and cause your blood to flow on the dried-up depths of the tank when divine water will gush from the bottom and make the spot a glorious *pushkara*. Go now."

King Vikramaditya who heard those words, took them as a blessing and prostrating at the *yogi's* feet returned to the spot after offering his worship to the deity of the temple.

Standing before the golden column and the plaque, King Vikramaditya thought within himself not merely of the happiness of devotees flocking into the city of Kashi, but also of the happiness that will surge in the heart of the merchant prince Dharmasheela who was mainly responsible for the great act of *Dharma*. He thougt of himself as merely a tool or a help in carrying out that great act of merit.

Allowing himself no further reflections, he drew out his magic sword and slit his own throat wherefrom blood flowed profusely down and wetted the driedup surface of the barren lake.

No sooner did the blood touch the ground, than Lord Siva appeared and touching Vikramaditya, brought him back to life. Said He: "My son, I very much appreciate your sense of unselfish sacrifice. Ask me any boon you like and I shall grant."

King Vikramaditya fell down at the feet of Siva and prayed: "My Lord, I have no other boon to ask, except to satisfy the wishes of the merchant Dharmasheela who wanted this lake to flow with nectarine water."

"So be it," said the Lord and disappeared and in a second, water was gushing from the depths of the barren lake and in a very shortwhile the entire area was filled with water overflowing from the *pushkara*. After seeing this, King Vikramaditya straightaway returned to Ujjain.

Next day, the entire city had flocked round the *pushkara* where a miracle had happened. The lake was overflowing with water although there was not a single drop of rain overnight. The wealthy merchant, who saw this, was mad with joy. He prayed before the deity and started dancing deliriously when the same unknown voice from the sky announced:

"Dharmasheela, know that the great King Vikramaditya of Ujjain allowed his own blood to flow down and wetted the driedup depth of the tank last night in answer to your public request by cutting his own throat. Lord Siva was so pleased with him that He offered him a boon and the great king asked of the Lord that this lake should overflow with water. This is the story of how this lake is now overflowing like *pushkara.*"

On hearing this, Dharmasheela's joy knew no bounds. He was at a loss to know how he could adequately thank the great monarch. It was manifestly impossible for him to send the gifts of the golden statue and the golden column to King Vikramaditya, for they were nothing for the great man in no uncertain terms.

Thinking thus he called five of his confidant messengers and sent through them ten valuable gems which were collectively worth a crore of gold coins. Calling his messengers to his room and handing the gems, he said, "My friends, you must carry these ten gems and place them at the feet of the great King Vikramaditya of Ujjain. Please convey my eternal gratitude to him and tell him that a million voices join me in blessing him for a long and prosperous life."

The five messengers mounting on horses, started towards Ujjain.

In a short time they announced themselves before the gates of King Vikramaditya's place.

As soon as they were taken to the King's presence, they placed those gems at the feet of the great monarch and conveyed in identical terms the eternal gratitude of their master Dharmasheela to him for an act no parallel in the history of the world.

They added: "My lord, on the way, robbers caught hold of us and in order to carry out the behest of our master, we had to swallow these gems before they stripped us of all our belongings."

King Vikramaditya on hearing this, was in great joy and he said: "I very much appreciate your sense of responsibility and now I present you one each of these gems as a mark of my appreciation of your sense of loyalty. Here, take the *pitambar* which was given to me by Devendra as a gift from me to your master Dharmasheela and offer him my compliments."

Those attendants returned to Kashi to report to their master, carrying with them the *pitambar* carefully.

Immediately after the messengers had departed, five poor brahmins in an effort to improve their economic condition, sought audience before King Vikramaditya. The king on finding them to be really needy, gifted them with the remaining five gems which Dharmasheela had sent. Vikram also gave away other valuable presents and gold to those brahmins.

At this stage, the statuette which was relating the story said: "Our King Vikramaditya was helping people like the cloud which empties its bowels on earth with no thought of reward or return. I, therefore, say if you too start helping the people in like manner, you will have the credentials to ascend this throne and not before that."

On hearing this exalted story, King Bhoja and Nitivakya felt themselves so small before the august King Vikramaditya whose exploits they listened to with rapt attention that they returned to their respective quarters without a word.

53

Vikrama Liberates *Brahmarakshas*

ON the morning of the fifteenth day, King Bhoja woke up early and after completing the morning routine, went to his Darbar followed by Minister Nitivakya and other courtiers.

He prostrated before the Divine Throne there and prayed within his heart that he should somehow succeed in ascending it. He walked up the first fourteen steps confidently, but when he set foot on the fifteenth, the statuette holding it suddenly broke into a fit of laughter and addressed him: "Bhoja, you seem to be unusually confident today. But do you think you are qualified to sit on this throne? I do not think that anybody other than our great Emperor Vikramaditya can sit on this throne because no one can possess such valour, such good qualities and sacrifice. Listen to one more incident from his lofty *charitra* which should be an eye-opener to you."

Bhoja, arrested in his progress thus, could not help standing petrified and listening to the story.

Said the statuette:

In one of his self-imposed half-yearly exiles King Vikrama went to the banks of the Ganga for the purpose of listening to the *pravachanas* of the great men who came there. At that time, the king of Ayodhya by name Mantrasena had pitched his tent on the banks of the Ganga along with selected courtiers and a batch of army personnel. Being a devoted man, Mantrasena was preparing to have a holy dip in the sacred Ganga uttering holy *mantras*. The priests chanted the holy words and after bathing, he dressed himself in holy attire and sat upon an improvised throne and the holy men assembled there blessed him with holy *akshatas*. After that, that senior pundit started *pravachana* of the *Puranas*.

At a certain stage, the pundit was saying, "For anyone born as a human being the greatest assets are valour like that of a lion, character and compassion towards women, children and animals. People should be ready to help the pious ones, children, women, etc., even at the cost of their lives."

As the pundit was exhorting thus, the people asembled there heard a pietous cry calling for help. All eyes turned in that direction. A brahmin who had entered the waters of the Ganga for a sacred dip was caught by a crocodile and was struggling in its clutches: every minute he was being dragged to the deeps.

On seeing his plight, the brahmin's wife who was standing on the bank, raised a hue and cry. She shouted for help crying, "O king and ministers assembled here! Is there not a single individual who can save my husband and grant me my *mangalya*? The *Sastras* say that a woman in distress should be given all help. You have just been listening to the pundit's exhortation to that effecct. Is there nobody to come forward to save my husband?"

Still none of those assembled came forward to help the poor brahmin. Left helpless thus she wept profusely rolling on the mud, and the woman beating her breasts, wailed, "I have lost my husband on the banks of the Ganga where I came to cleanse my sins, Oh God!"

King Vikramaditya who was present there in disguise was witnessing this scene. Seeing that none had offered to help her struggling husband, he thought: "When the elephant Gajendra was in similar plight he too appealed for help. The Lord then ran to his rescue and saved him. It is now my duty and privilege to help that man out of danger and save his wife's *mangalya*."

With these thoughts he plunged into the river with no consideration of self and killed the crocodile with his magic sword.

The poor brahmin who was thus saved from certain death came out with gratefulness flowing through his eyes. His wife seeing her husband coming out safely, embraced him and the pair felt like having a second life.

The brahmin who was choked with emotion said, "O rescuer! It is impossible for me to repay my debt of gratitude. All that I can say is that I will cherish you in my memory even as I do my father, mother and my *guru.* I know that your action is beyond repayment and that you, like the cloud, do not expect others to do so. Even so in my small way, I want to express my gratefulness towards you. Please say that you will accept it."

King Vikramaditya replied apologetically, "Please do not mistake me. I only did my duty and it is not in my nature, as you have rightly guessed, to expect any return. I will, therefore, request you not to bother yourself with return. You should not, and I would not expect the same."

The brahmin felt wounded by this refusal and so he said, "Am I such a sinner as not have the privilege of even symbolically expressing my gratitude to my life's saviour? I would in that case rather not preserve this body which you have so generously saved from the jaws of death." Saying this, the brahmin ran towards the river with the intention of falling again into the waters.

King Vikramaditya ran after him and caught him. "Oh, holy man! I am extremely sorry for having offended your sentiment. If you are serious about repaying the debt, please teach me any *mantra* which you might have accomplished."

The holy man beamed with joy. He had accomplished a mountain of *tapas* and *japa.* Consequently, he taught King Vikrama a *mantra* which he cherished as the life of his life. After teaching Vikrama the *mantra,* he said "if recite the *mantra* nine times, the *pushpaka,* the aerial vehicle of

Devendra, will come down and stand before you. You can ascend it and go anywhere you like. You can, for the mere wish, have tons of money which you can enjoy. May you live long." After blessing King Vikramaditya the brahmin couple went their way.

King Vikrama thereafter left the banks of Ganga and walked towards a hillock nearby on top of which was a dense forest. He had no particular intention but he simply wanted to amuse himself in the solitude and secrecy of the forest.

As he proceeded along uncharted paths, he felt tired and took rest beneath the shade of a big peepul tree.

He had laid down for a while. Then a *brahmarakshas* which had made that tree its abode descended from it on seeing the human figure lying down. King Vikrama who noticed its descent asked nonchalantly, "Who are you? What do you want?"

The *brahmarakshas* which had for a long time the only experience of frightening others felt frightened for once.

It said, "I am surprised that when the Devas and *rishis* run away from me, you seem to have the audacity to question me. I know that you are king but a mortal all the same. Let me see.

Saying this, the *brahmarakshas* assumed a menacing form. Its face reddened; then blackened. Twisting its huge arm which looked like a hose pipe, it prepared to belabour Vikrama.

But the latter looked on without a flicker of his eyes and taking out his magic sword, flashed it against the the evanescent *brahmarakshas*.

The *brahmarakshas* had met its equal. It thought, "He is really a courageous man. I should think he is not an ordinary mortal. He should have been blessed by the Devas."

So thinking, the *brahmarakshas* assumed a small but beautiful human form and stood before the King submissively.

On seeing this metamorphosis, King Vikramaditya, although amazed, sternly asked, "O *brahmarakshas*, how is it that you have shed your hideous form and assumed this human form?"

The *brahmarakshas* replied, "O King! I was born in this world and became learned in the *Vedas* and *Sastras* but I started abusing the great and the good, religion and God. The *rishis* whom I started troubling by my superior attainments, cursed me to become a *brahmarakshas* for a thousand years. Frightened by this curse, I fell at their feet and asked for pardon. Taking pity on me they said, "It is not possible to entirely revoke the curse. All that we can do is to time your life as *brahmarakshas*; when you come across a mortal who without being frightened by you, actually instills fear in your mind, this curse shall cease to operate. But you must leave your wicked ways." I promised. For years I have been languishing on this tree looking for my deliverance till I met you. I am grateful to you for liberating me."

King Vikrama who listened to this history felt happy that he was able to liberate another soul from a life of misery.

The liberated scholar said: "King Vikrama now that I have been saved from the life of a *brahmarakshas*, I do not know how I am going to lead my future life. Can you not help me in chalking out a life for me?"

King Vikrama said, "O learned man, you can follow your rightful profession and regain your own promised life. You are learned, you can teach others, and you can be of immense help to others. But, if however, you have any particular wish which you would like to be fulfilled, tell me and I shall do it."

The scholar replied: "I am greatly obliged to you for giving me thus an opportunity. A few days back you saved a brahmin from the jaws of a crocodile in the Ganga. That brahmin, out of gratefulness to you, taugt you one *mantra*. If you can kindly part with that *mantra* to me, I shall have no difficulty in pursuing a normal life. This is the only boon I ask of you."

Without hesitating for a second, King Vikrama taught the scholar the precious *mantra* he learnt from the brahmin and added, "You can command all that you want in life and you have little reason to be anxious about your future. If you repeat the *mantra* nine times you will get an entrance into the *pushpaka* and can take a round of the world if you feel so. I hope that the lessons of the life you have just been liberated from will not be lost on you and will prevent you making any more mistakes. May God bless you."

The *brahmarakshas*-turned-scholar blessed King Vikrama. In Vikrama's very presence he chanted the *mantra* nine times whereupon the Divine vehicle sortied before him and he boarded and flew heavenward in all glory.

The Devas showered flowers at this sight.

After this, King Vikrama returned to Ujjain and resumed his royal duties sitting on this throne.

"If you think," said the statuette, "You are capable of as much valour and generosity as our great king, you can proceed further on the remaining steps."

On hearing this King Bhoja and Nitivakya silently retraced their steps to their quarters.

54

Danseuse Kamalarekha

KING Bhoja and his Minister Nitivakya woke up early on the morning of the sixteenth day and after completing the morning routine, went to the throne room followed by other courtiers.

As had become the wont, he offered due prayers to the divine throne and ascended the first fifteen steps without any obstacle.

When he set foot on the sixteenth step, the statuette holding it stood up, and said: "Ha-ha, great king, listen to me before you proceed further. You know King Vikramaditya was ruling this country from this throne to the universal happiness of his subjects. At that time, a warrior came from the nether world and told King Vikrama something in confidence. Immediately King Vikrama called the ghoul and riding on its shoulders hurried out of the palace."

"O statuette! Can you tell me what was the secret that made King Vikrama leave the palace in such a haste?" asked King Bhoja.

The statuette on hearing this, burst into a fit of laughter and replied, "You are itching to hear that secret aren't you? When you do not have that much of patience till I tell you, how do you expect to ascend this throne and rule on it?

King Bhoja, thus humiliated, kept quiet.

Continuing, the satuette said: "Listen then: this is what that warrior told King Vikrama. In his country there was a danseuse by name Kamalarekha. She was so beautiful that even *napumsakas* would fall in love with her. After entering her chamber at night her lovers invariably came out as corpses next morning. Nobody knew how or why. The warrior wanted King Vikrama to come and see what the matter was with that danseuse.

King Vikrama in the company of that warrior reached the land of the *patala* in a short time and instituted enquiries in the town about that girl. All that he heard was, from the time she came of age, the girl was meeting all her suitors, none of whom returned alive from her. Over thousand had thus lost their lives. The people recounted the names of those persons who met their end at her hands although each one of them knew very well what was going to happen. The funny part of the whole affair was she herself was unable to account for the death of her visitors.

King Vikrama there and then made up his mind to investigate the truth about her, and accordingly sent word to Kamalarekha that he would be visiting her that night itself.

At this stage, King Bhoja intervened: "O statuette! How is it that, although people knew pretty well that death would overtake them, they still offered to visit her?"

The statuette kept mum for a moment and said: "Bhoja, have you not understood yet that in each case the infatuation for her prevailed over fear of death? I am surprised at your poor comprehension. How do you expect to ascend this throne and reign? Now, let me ask you: When each of the fifteen statuettes have uniformly dissuaded you from ascending on this throne, why have you come again for the sixteenth attempt? Don't you realize that an infatuated man loses his reason and sense of shame? Just as you are doing now, people went after her. That is all!"

The statuette continued the story. When Kamalarekha received the news of the visit of King Vikrama, she felt very happy. She arranged her bedroom in such a way that even angel could be charmed. On one side of the table were spread a hundred varieties of delicious dishes: on the other, were kept ornate vessels of *attar* and rose water which made the entire room smell fragrant. Further off were kept fruits, *tambul*, and milk boiled with kesar. Every corner of the room was brilliantly lit.

As the time drew near for the King's visit Kamalarekha became expectantly uneasy and kept looking out of the balcony.

At the appointed hour, King Vikramaditya made the appearance and ascended the steps. As soon as he entered the chamber, Kamalarekha fell at his feet in the traditional manner and led him by the hand on to the cot which was spread with exquisite mattresses. But Vikramaditya said, "My dear, I do not like to sit or lie on cots. I am not used to them. Perhaps, if I do, I may lose consciousness and possibly lose my life. Please, therefore, spread the mat on the floor itself so that I may comfortably sleep."

On hearing this, Kamalarekha just let a sparkle of muffled laughter escape from her rosy lips from which peeped a part of her pearly denture. King Vikramaditya understood the significance of her laughter and kept quiet. He sat down on the matted floor.

King Bhoja interjected: "O statuette! Could you tell me why Kamalarekha laughed and what your great King understood from it?"

"Bhoja, I am sure you will never sit on this throne, because you are unable to see this simple thing. I shall tell you now why. Her laughter was like the laughter of a butcher who offers luscious grass or leaf to the goat before cutting its throat, because he knows fully well that in a few moments the goat will roll down on mud. At least our King Vikramaditya understood it in that way."

The statuette continued:

Till about midnight Kamalarekha was amusing King Vikrama with extraordinary solicitude. She bathed him in warm water made fragrant with *attar*, she caused him wear costly clothes and jewels. She smeared aromatic sandalwood paste and unguents on him and sitting beside him, offered him delicious *pan*.

When they thus settled down, Vikrama gave her the thousand gold coins being her fee. On receiving it, Kamalarekha embraced him fondly and tried to kiss him on the cheek. But King Vikrama pulled himself away from her and dodged all her further guiles to entice him into the bed.

When they were thus spending the night in a game of wits, down below, people had assembled with the usual paraphernalias for funeral obsequies. There was the barber, the priest and the rest of them with the utensils, wooden poles, etc. They were expecting the paramour's body to be brought out in the morning to be removed to the crematory.

In Kamalarekha's chamber time wore out heavily. Till the very late hours of the night the danseuse was entertaining the King with sweet melodies on defferent musical instruments and retiring to bed for sleep. Invited to accompany her, King Vikrama also pretended to follow her. He placed his pillow by the side of hers. When Kamalarekha started sleeping, King Vikramaditya jumped out of the bed, placed the pillow by her side and quietly hid himself at a distance in the shadow of a pillar.

Within a few minutes of sleeping, a hissing sound came from her and out of nostrils, came a small but ferocious looking serpent with a golden hood which turned to her side and looking fiercely bit the pillow which Vikrama had placed by her side.

King Vikrama was stunned at the sight for a second. What would have been his fate if he had succumbed to her guile, he thought.

Within the twinkling of an eye, King Vikrama whipped out his magic sword and cut the traitorous snake into two lest it should creep back.

In this melee, the danseuse Kamalarekha woke up and when she saw King Vikrama with sword in hand and a snake lying slain before them, she was completely nonplussed. She rubbed her eyes fast and looked at the King who did not open his mouth.

She asked, "What is all this? Where did the snake come from?"

King Vikrama explained how the snake had emanated from her nostrils and how he killed it! Her body shivered at the revelations.

He asked: "What would have been my fate if I had laid down by your side?"

The danseuse fell at the feet of King Vikrama and shed tears of gratefulness. Said she: "You have saved me from a great slur. People have been calling me a murderess. God knows my innocence.

Now that the killer had been removed, King Vikrama had no compunctions in yielding to her persuasions and spent the remaining part of the night with her.

Early next day he completed his morning ablutions and dressing himself for departure, came out of the house, when he was pleasantly surprised by the crowd of obsequial visitors with the materials for cremation at the door.

When they saw Vikrama coming out hale and hearty, they were taken aback for a time, but soon recognized him to be King Vikrama. They asked him in one voice how he could come out unscathed when thousand who had visited her met with death.

King Vikrama explained to them how Kamalarekha was not consciously responsible for the death of others and showed them the pieces of the killed snake.

All those assembled praised the King for his valour. King Vikrama after making large gifts to the danseuse and others left for his capital Ujjain.

The statuette asked, "Bhoja, do you think after hearing this story, that you can be as capable as our Emperor Vikramaditya? Then only this throne can carry you, not otherwise."

King Bhoja and his ministers went away without replying. The sun set on their back.

55

Nava Mohini

ON the morning of the seventeenth day, King Bhoja, as usual, went to the throne room accompanied by his Minister Nitivakya and other courtiers. After offering the customary worship to the divine throne, Bhoja tried to ascend it.

As soon as he set foot on the seventeenth step, the statuette holding it became animated and said:

"Harken, Bhoja, to the story of our great King Vikramaditya, before you proceed further. While he was ruling the earth from this throne, on one occasion he had sent messengers to all parts of the world to find out if there were anything extraordinay in those parts. Those who had been sent east, west and south drew blank; but the fouth from the north came with an interesting report which is as follows:

In the north there is a city by name Makarapuri which was ruled by King Soma Pratapa. That king was so punctilious in the discharge of his duties that people looked upon and cared for him as their own eyes. So much so when he set out on his state-round of the city, people used to offer prayers for his safe return to the palace.

Indeed at the close of each such perambulation numerous women used to take out *artis* of pearls, *praval*, rice, etc., round the king's person seated on the elephant, and throw them in the air in the north-east direction. But what they threw never came down. On enquiry it was found that some demons lay in wait in the air for swallowing the rice balls and carrying away the pearls, *pravals*, etc., to their abode via a huge banyan tree. This was a regular practice.

When King Vikramaditya heard this strange story, he became eager to investigate the truth. So calling the faithful ghoul he rode on it to Makarapuri which he reached quickly. He waited for the next day for royal parade at the close of which the usual *artis* were taken out by beautiful women and were thrown in mid-air. He saw those throwaways being literally gobbled and grabbed by fierce-looking demons which climbed up an ancient banyan tree and vanished into the air.

King Vikrama who saw the phenomenon decided to explore further along the path of the demons. So he prayed to his favourite deity Mahakali of Ujjain and drawing out his magic sword climbed the tree in hot pursuit of the vanishing demons.

Since Vikrama was also a *siddha purusha* he had no difficulty in following the demons. He found himself soon in a new world in mid-air which had all the allurements of a *gandharva loka.*

On one side he saw a beautiful swimming pool in which *apsaras* could enjoy playing in water. On the other were groves of flowering plants which spread enthralling perfumes. Further on, were streets beautifully laid out with towering mansions, temples with huge towers, theatres, etc; yet he did not meet any live beings.

He came across a palace which was large and more beautifully furnished than others. He surmised that it should belong to the king or leader of that community, whoever it was. He decided to enter and investigate it which was completely unguarded.

After crossing the front portion of the mansion he saw before him what looked like a bathtub which was filled with warm water. By the side of it was a glolden platter which contained aromatic soapnut powder. He decided to take his bath making use of them which were so readily kept.

Drying himself up with a soft towel hanging by a stand, Vikrama proceeded to the next apartment.

It contained a huge metallic mirror done most artistically and by whose side were kept scented sandalwood paste mixed with *attar* and rose water, unguents, flowers, etc. He helped himself liberally to those things and proceeded further on.

The next apartment invited him with a variety of delicious dishes. As Vikrama had not eaten a morsel of food since starting from Ujjain, he plunged into the heap of dishes and ate them to heart's content and ate fragrant *tambul.*

When he went further inside, he saw a brilliantly lit hall with soft curtains hanging all around and in the centre was placed an exquisitely decorated couch spread with mattresses made of swan's feathers. The lamps made of the nine kinds of gems were such that they burned eternally. *Agarbattis* tickled the nose mysteriously. This was too much for Vikramaditya to resist and in the then state of his body and mind, he threw himself on the luxurious cot and slept divinely.

It so happened that the mansion belonged to one Nava Mohini, a prominent denizen of that mid-air world. She had few equals in beauty, accomplishment and wealth.

When she came from outside to have her bath and food, she was surprised to see the bath empty, even as the dishes and other vases.

Her brow rose first in surprise and knit in anger as she imagined an intruder.

She walked inside briskly and was stunned to see a man drawn to full length in deep slumber on her cot!

She was not, however, unimpressed with the masculine beauty and the thiry-two *lakshanas* of the man.

Yet, it was sacrilege to interfere with her privacy and so she conjured up a fierce-looking demon and ordered it to lift the man bodily and throw him out beyond the limits of her domain at the foot of the banyan tree.

The demon obeyed and in the midst of being carried, Vikrama woke up. He instantaneously realized his position and undeterred by the demon, he drew his magic sword and slew the demon into two and retraced his steps to the palace from where he had been so unceremoniously expelled.

By the time he had reached the palce back, it was heavily guarded by a host of demons which offered resistance to reentry. But King Vikrama fought with them and hacked them all to pieces. When he had killed the last of them, he had a wash and entered the sanctum sanctorum where he saw the damsel fast asleep on the luxurious couch.

King Vikrama grinned at the sight and calling his faithful ghoul, ordered it to carry her along with the couch to Ujjain. The ghoul did so and within a few seconds, the party descended on the lawns of the palace grounds of Ujjain.

When Nava Mohini woke up, she was chagrined to find her self on earth in the presence of the handsome man with drawn sword.

The first thought that arose in her mind was one of surprise: how could she become the prisoner of one whom she had driven out of her house for once! Her second thoughts were how to escape from the man. As she thought furiously, it dawned upon her that a man who could bring her from her divine mansion to his pleasure ground would surely be capable of restraining her. And the man did not look bad at all.

So, thinking that descretion was the better part of valour, she put on a broad smile on her face and asked : "Sire, may I have the pleasure of knowing who you might be?"

"I am King Vikramaditya of Ujjain and Emperor of the world and you are in his palace grounds presently," replied Vikrama.

"I am so obliged to you for bringing me down all the way from my world."

Soon the pair felt like old friends and bantering pleasantly they entered the palace where Bhatti and other courtiers received them in an appropriate manner.

In commemoration of Mohini's arrival, King Vikrama ordered the sixteen kinds of gifts to be given away liberally to the pious and the learned of the country.

As the *danas* were being given away, one of the recipients went straight to King Vikrama and prayed before him: "Mighty King! I had been a *brahmachari* all three years because I did not meet a woman who appealed to my conception of beauty. After all I have met her today!"

"Tell me, sir who she is and I shall have her married to you this minute!" replied Vikrama.

The brahmin laughed sheepishly and pointed to Nava Mohini who was standing by his side.

Not moving an inch of his face, King Vikrama took the hand of Nava Mohini and placed it on that of the brahmin and at that instant had them married according to *Shastras* and gifted away large sums of money and jewels to the pair to the utter consternation of all those assembled.

Do you think, Bhoja, you could do like that and give away a girl, a peerless one at that from heaven, for whom you had braved a host of demons and what not, for the asking of a poor brahmin? Such was the generosity of our great King Vikramaditya. If you think you are as good as he, you can ascend this throne, but not otherwise."

King Bhoja and his Minister Nitivakya, on hearing this absorbing anecdote from the life of Vikramaditya returned home wihtout giving any reply.

56

Vikrama Interprets a Will

IT is more easy to imagine than describe the state of mind of King Bhoja when he started ascending the steps of King Vikramaditya's divine throne on the eighteenth day.

It was a tribute to his persistence in his attempt to occupy the throne despite successive setbacks caused by the adroit narration of episodes from King Vikrama's life which made him always look small.

With hope poised against trepidation in his heart, he set foot on the eighteenth step, when the statuette holding it clapped its hands and said: "Stop, Bhoja, and listen to this story of our Great Vikrama before you proceed further."

Arrested thus, Bhoja did not have the courage to ignore the statuette's call.

Further he sicerely believed that he could yet learn much from the life of exalted ones like Vikramaditya.

The statuete started:

There was a city called Alakapuri in which lived a merchant by name Nitipara. He had four sons, Para Datta, Maru Datta, Dhana Datta and Charu Datta. The family lived in comparative affluence. In due course, their mother and father went the way of all human beings. One after the other.

For a time, the brothers lived together amicably. Soon, however, the proverbial family discord started showing its head, and they had perforce to split the joint family and live apart if they wanted to stop further unpleasantness.

Then began the great partition. Every little item in the family was counted and distributed among the brothers equally.

It was when they opened their father's account book that they got the shock of their life. All along they were living under the impression that their father had amassed a lot of money and that was why they could live comparatively happy. But the account book bore no traces of cash or any investment. On the contray, it bore the follwing written passage:

"To my sons:

"Share without quarrel the contents of the four copper pots placed underneath the four legs of my cot; don't spill the gold; give away the cows as gifts; find your level like water."

This read like a riddle at which they became exasperated.

"What became of all my father's wealth?" Shouted one, obviously thinking that one or more of the others had whisked it away before the old man died.

At which the other remonstrated with equal fervour : "You must be knowing it better!"

"Ah, the wily old bandicoot!" ejaculated a third.

But all these altercations led them nowhere near the truth. In the end they decided to refer the document to King Vikramaditya and request him to unravel the mystery, each wishing at the same time that the other would be found guilty and punished.

Accordingly they sought audience before King Vikrama who readily granted it. Vikrama received them with courtesy and before he could open his mouth, the brothers vied with one another to catch Vikrama's eye first, so that he could lay the blame squarely on the other.

It was not difficult for King Vikrama to gauge the atmosphere and so smilingly he said: "I have one request to make before you start and that is, only he should give me the reply whom

I ask. Upon that condition I am willing to listen to your plaint."

They agreed and King Vikrama asked one of them: "Now, you can make your representation."

He said, "Our father was a rich man by all standards. He was paying a large amount to government by way of taxes. Your Majesty may be knowing. He died last month. When we started examining his books, we do not find any mention of any holding. As it is, we are left penniless. We therefore suspect some foulplay."

"Is that your case too?" asked Vikrama of the other sons, each of whom nodded "Yes."

"Now," said Vikrama, "let me have a look at the account book your late father maintained."

The eldest son produced the book which was completely blank except for the writing already mentioned on the first page.

King Vikrama thumbed the pages carefully and not finding any more entries, started reading the first page containing the said writing which read like a will. He read it twice, thrice. Afterwards he sat quietly for a few seconds and said: "I think I can help you provided you promise me, all of you, to abide by my decision."

"Yes." replied all.

King Vikrama asked then to take him to their house. They gladly agreed and all of them went in the royal carriage.

King Vikrama asked for the room and the cot which the old man used. They showed them. Asking to remove the cot, he ordered them to dig the floor at the places occupied by the four legs of the cot.

Each of them brought a pickaxe or whatever he could lay hands on and started digging till a metallic sound rose from each. After making sufficient space round the object, they excavated four metallic pots, one from beneath each leg.

Expectations ran high, but King Vikrama who took hold of them examined them carefully.

The first he took was found to contain lumps of charcoal, the next a number of bones; the third contained a small quantity of sand and the fourth water!

Disappointment was writ large on the faces of the brothers on this discovery as they found their King no better.

But King Vikramaditya kept on smiling.

He said : "Now I should once again remind you of your promise to abide by my decision."

"What is there to decide? We are not anxious to divide these precious gifts," interposed one of them.

"Wait and see!" said Vikrama.

Taking out one lump of charcoal from the pot, he rubbed it on the floor and lo! it was pure gold! All those assembled gasped in wonder. The brothers looked at one another meaningfully.

King Vikrama examined the next pot which contained bones.

He counted them and said : "You must give away as many cows as there are bones here, to brahmins. That is the wish of your father!"

The brothers looked at each other and with grateful feelings replied: "Yes, we shall certainly do so."

King Vikrama took up the third vessel containing sand. The grains were of a fairly large size and so he counted them. He said: "You have as many items of articles in your house as these sands and it is the wish of your father that you should divide them equally between you. Am I right?"

"Yes, you are quite right. The number is correct as we checked it only yesterday. We have divided the artticles exactly as you want us."

"That is splendid," replied King Vikrama.

Taking out the last of the vessels, he saw in it nothing but cool water.

Clearing his throat King Vikrama addressed them all : "As I have said, your father in his will has given certain directoins which it is your duty to fulfil. I have explained some of the clauses. What remains I shall presently explain. It is the express wish of your father that you should live amicably as a joint family. He has made it perfectly clear that the wealth of the family should not be dissipated by litigation. He has therefore enjoined that the eldest among you should keep custody of the family wealth which consists of this pot of gold, the charcoal is really gold bars and the rest of you should go out in the wide world and work without worry, as water find its own level, thus helping the family wealth to grow. Only in this way, can peace return to your family along with prosperity.

All the brothers immediately regained their lost faith in each other and fell spontaneously at King Vikrama's feet. The King blessed them all and repaired to his palace.

All the brothers immediately made arrangements for the *dana* of cows enjoined in their father's will. Having done that their hearts became pure and happy. Thereafter they lived in perfect amity and prosperity.

The statuette asked King Bhoja: "You know very well that the King is entitled to half of all hidden treasures recovered. But King Vikrama had the magnanimity not only to help the brothers find the hidden wealth but also forego what by law belonged to his State. Do you think you belong to the category of kings who do not long for subjects' wealth? If you have that magnanimity alone are you entitled to rule from this throne and not otherwise."

King Bhoja on hearing this immortal account returned to his palace along with his Nitivakya without making any comment.

57

Vikrama Gifts a Princess

UNDETERRED by setbacks King Bhoja returned to the throne room on the morning of the nineteenth day with the intention of successfully climbing on the throne this time.

He offered prayers as usual and started ascending the steps.

Nothing happened till the eighteenth step, but when he set foot on the nineteenth, the statuette holding it became animated and addressed him: "King Bhoja, you can sit upon this throne only if you have the capacity and qualities of our King Vikramaditya, but if you do not have them you will be thrown out."

"Oh, is that so?" replied Bhoja. "Can you tell me what was it that made the great Vikramaditya so outstanding?"

It said, "Our King Vikrama had many great men lining around him. One of these men was a brahmin priest of the name Surasena. One of these men was that, in the early part of his life, he had been a thoroughgoing man of the world and he had enjoyed life as anyone did, but as he grew older he had a change in his outlook which made him look upon the material comforts of this world with scorn. He learnt the *Vedas* and *Sastras* thoroughly, killed the three-fold desires, overcame the six-fold enemies and bidding adieu to his friend, the King, started on a pilgrimage round the world like a *Sanyasi*. He journeyed throughout the land visiting holy places and bathing in holy *thirthas*.

In the course of his journey he visited Prayag, bathed in Yamuna and Ganga and carrying their holy waters returned to Ujjain. On the way back, he came across a city by name Sringarapuri. He entered the city and while he was looking around, he came across a Kali temple on the north-east side. When he entered it with the intention of praying before the deity, he was surprised to see a small crowd of people at the portico standing near a huge cauldron in which oil was boiling. Out of curiosity he asked of one who appeared to be the leader as to what might be the reason for boiling such a huge quantity of oil.

The man replied: "The king of the city, Vratasheela, has a daughter by name Veeralakshmi. She is greatly accomplished and she has come of age. With the idea of marrying her the king sent out invitations to the leading princes of the country for a *swayamvara.* But when those princes and others turned up for the *swayamvara*, the princess refused to choose any one of them.

The king insisted she should marry one who was very highly educated. The queen said she should marry the prince of the largest country. In this clash of interests, none of the guests prsesent appeared to them to be a suitable husband for their beloved daughter. The king therefore announced in a fit of temper the following conditions for the suitor for his daughter's hand: "Whoever successfully jumps into this boiling cauldron of oil will marry my daughter."

"On this announcement, all those invitees fled away. We have since then been waiting here for the man who would have the courage to accomplish the feat and claim the hand of the princess. We have not been able to meet one till today."

On hearing this strange story, Surasena smiled within himself and reflected: "Whoever can accomplish this feat except my gracious King Vikrama?"

Thinking thus, he came posthaste to Ujjain. King Vikrama was greatly pleased to see his old friend return from his holy wanderings, carrying pots of holy water on his shoulders. King Vikrama paid him the customary worship and gave him large quantities of money, and jewels as presents to be disposed of in good causes.

Just at that moment an old brahmin came to the palace dragging a girl by his hand seeking audience with the King. He was allowed immediate permission to see the King. Vikrama on seeing them asked "Holy man, what is the trouble with you? May I help you?"

The brahmin replied: "O mighty King! This girl is my daughter. She has come of age. I want to get her married, but I have no money. Further, this girl has been possessed by a devil. You are the only person who can cure her of her malady and help financially in getting her married away."

On hearing this, King Vikrama looked at the face of the girl sternly. Unable to face him, the girl started shrieking "I am running. I am running."

Vikrama held the girl by the hand and beckoning to his faithful ghoul, asked it to accompany the girl. He also instructed the ghoul to drive the devil out of her body and get the girl married to a suitable bridegroom. He gave some jewels and cash for the purpose. He took out one of the ornaments he was wearing and gave it away to the girl to wear. No sooner did she wear it than the devil that possessed her quit her crying "Now that Your Majesty has cast on her the jewel you had been wearing. I see no reason for possessing her."

By way of compensation the devil further gave some more riches to the girl and the bridegroom-to-be.

After expressing his gratefulness to the King the old brahmin went away with his daughter followed by the ghoul.

With all the gifts given by King Vikrama and with all the disabilities cleared, the girl who was really pretty had little difficulty in finding a suitable groom for herself. The marriage was celebrated in a grand manner at the conclusion of which the brahmin adequately thanked the ghoul for all the help it had rendered.

The ghoul immediately returned to King Vikrama and related the happy tiding of the marriage of the girl.

One day King Vikrama during the course of his conversation with the old brahmin friend asked, "Did you have your bath in the holy Ganga?" Have you brought the water of the holy Ganga? Had you been to Rameshwara? What all did you see and hear in the course of your pilgrimage? If there is anything worth mentioning. please tell me."

"With the blessing of great men like you I had the good fortune of visiting almost all the sacred places and having dips in the sacred *thirthas* and rivers of this country. There is only one particular incident which I think is worthwhile for your hearing. There is a city on the way down here called Sringarapuri. I went to worship the Mother Goddess in that famous temple of the city. To my surprise I saw a concourse of people standing round a boiling cauldron of oil looking as though they were expecting someone. On enquiry I learnt that whoever jumped into the boiling oil and came out alive would be given the hand of the princess of that State and would also be crowned as king. At that time I could only think of you."

"Anything else which you think will be of interest to me?" asked King Vikrama.

"Not that I know of," replied the brahmin.

Without waiting for anything King Vikrama called his faithful ghoul and accompanied by Surasena started in the direction of Sringarapuri reaching it quickly.

He went to the temple of Kali and saw the officials standing there waiting for the successful candidate to the princess's hands.

Vikrama offered himself to them and completing his routine

prayer, he bathed and went round the Kali's temple thrice and prayed lying on all fours before her. Then he walked towards the boiling cauldron and with no thought of his life jumped into the boiling oil. The way in which he enjoyed swimming in it made one think that the oil had become cool like the waters of Ganga.

Everyone assembled there was greatly impressed by the performance of that unknown person. News went round and the king of the city came running to the spot followed by his daughter and courtiers, all of whom nearly fell at the feet of King Vikrama who revealed himself.

According to the king's proclamation, the princess as well as the rule of the kingdom were placed at the disposal of King Vikramaditya, but, do you know what our mighty King did? He did not even look at the girl nor at the deed transferring the kingdom to him. He simply handed over both of them to his brahmin friend Surasena whom he made king of that country and to whom he gave away the princess in marriage with his own hands.

After seeing them installed satisfactorily, Vikrama returned to Ujjain.

You will now be able to see that this throne was holding a man of such extraordinary powers and generosity. You will realize that you cannot occupy this throne for obvious reasons.

On hearing this, King Bhoja returned to his palace followed by his Minister Nitivakya.

58

Kali's Gift to Vikrama

WHEN King Bhoja came back on the twentieth day, to make a further attempt to climb the divine throne, the statuette holding the twentieth step stopped him as did the previous ones and told him the following story:

When the great Vikramaditya was ruling this country justly, the Goddess of *Dharma* walked with all her four feet. *Varnasrama* never faltered. Elders blessed the younger ones who showed them all respect. Temples of Gods were like the pole star guiding erring humanity. Anyone who thought ill of others was blasted. Rain poured thrice in the year. People lived healthily. Rogues perished. The King's rule was upright like the staff of the mast.

It was at this time that the ubiquitous ghoul brought a disquieting news to King Vikrama. It was this. A king by the name of Chaturavan ruled over Sagarpur. He was fatally bitten by a serpent and his wife was about to commit sati. This was enough grist for the mill of Vikramaditya. He immediately jumped on the shoulders of the ghoul and made a dash for Sagarpur. He arrived there just in time to stop the queen from falling into the pyre ready to be lit for her husband's body. Vikrama said: "Tarry, Madam, I shall, with God's grace, revive your husband from the fatal bite."

Struck mute by his assurance, the queen desisted for a while, while the royal minions moved the body of King Chaturavan from the pyre and deposited it on a sheet of grass. King Vikrama prayed to Goddess Kali of Ujjain and touched the inert body with his magic wand all over when Chaturavan sat up like one gone on deep slumber! The joy at the sight of this occurrence was indescribable. King Vikrama raised Chaturavan by the hand which he placed on the hand of (Chaturavan's) queen, thus uniting them for the second time. Tears flowed from the eyes of the pair.

When Chaturavan recovered sufficiently, he and his queen prostrated before Vikramaditya and prayed: "It is impossible to repay our debt of gratitude we owe to you. The utmost we can do is to place our entire kingdom at your gracious feet and to beg of you to accept us as your servants."

Visibly moved by this spirit on the part of the royal pair, King Vikrama gladly accepted the gift and after releasing them from what they chose to call as their debt, he gifted the entire kingdom back to the king and bade them adieu.

By that time, the calendar showed that King Vikramaditya's half-yearly exile period had commenced. So he straightaway proceeded towards the forest. On the way he came across a city by name Shambhu Surya. While he was walking through the streets, he saw a temple by the side of which was a tank. The portico of the temple was multi-pillared. From the chimes and the smoke escaping from the kitchen of the temple, it appeared that the deity of the temple was being worshipped regularly according to schedule and that the annual festivals were being celebrated regularly. He made enquiries of the people who went inside and out of the temple about it which only confirmed his surmise. He further learnt that the name of the deity was Shambhu Surya and that the city derived its name from that God. All these informations gladdened his heart. He went inside the temple.

Just as he was returning after praying before the deity, he saw a few persons dragging another, after tying both his hands at the back. The victim appeared to be of noble birth while his persecutors looked ruffian-like.

Any act of injustice was anathema to Vikrama, so it was not surprising that his blood boiled at this outrage. He called out in a stentorian voice: "Stop, all of you there! Why do you torment the poor man?"

Vikrama's imperious stature instilled fear into the minds of the persecutors who instantaneously folded their hands in supplication.

At this, the victim was emboldened to address Vikrama: "Great sire! May I know the name of my well-wisher?"

Laughingly the monarch replied: "Vikrama of Ujjain!"

"Can that be true? Oh, Lord! My troubles are at an end."

"Please tell me the cause of your difficulty."

"How shall I express it, sir? I am King Singara of Rajamahendra. As ill-luck would have it, I had too many foes. I was careful to keep them at bay all along. Not being able to vanquish me in open battle, they conspired of devious ways. They sent to me a wily brahmin who ingratiated himself into my confidence. He invited me to a game of dice in which I am also an expert. But by loading the dice covertly and other means the brahmin defeated me in a series of games in which I was made to pawn my country, wealth and my own people. Having thus stripped me bare, my foes further arranged to send me to this place like a convict and they propose to lock me up in one of the great vaults of this temple. There is none but God to save me now!" and the man wept loudly.

King Vikrama moved by the heart-rending story ordered the persecutors to untie the chord wound round the wrists and free him. Taking Singara along with him on the ghoul, he reached Rajamahendra. He called an assembly of all the feudatories who conspired to dislodge Singara and made him challenge them for a return game of dice. By the help of the ghoul, Singara learnt each clandestine move of the opponent, and thus succeeded in regaining his lost country and wealth.

Addressing all the mystified feudal lords, King Vikrama said: "Know me to be Vikramaditya of Ujjain. I am now personally anointing Singara as King of Rajamahendra. Now tell me, are you in a mood to rebel against him or live in amity after paying him your subsidies? You must make up your mind right now or you will not live to do it again!"

When the feudatory chiefs came to know that it was King Vikramaditya who was addressing them they fell at his feet saying: "Who would dare to defy your bidding, Mighty Monarch? Gone are our jealousies. We shall live united in peace. We shall do as you order."

Installing Singara once again as King of Rajamahendra and ordering all other chiefs to pay him annual bounties, King Vikrama returned to Shambhu Surya.

By the side of that city was a hill of the name of Indrajit. He climbed it and at the top of it saw a temple of Kali. Going inside it he found the idol of Kali surrounded by eight other idols studded with diamonds. He wondered how such *murtis* came into being at that place.

At the time his eyes fell on a rock on which was an inscription which ran: "In this *peeth* of Parasakti, there are untold treasures. Any one who wants to possess them must offer his or any other human head to Goddess Kali."

The proposition interested Vikrama very much. In that desolate place, however, not a human soul could be seen for miles around, so he decided to offer his own head.

With that idea, he bathed in a tank nearby, and after praying before Kali, drew out his magic sword with the intention of slitting his own throat. As the sharp edge of the knife touched his neck, Goddess Kali herself appeared and caught hold of the arm holding the sword.

Kalimata said: "Vikrama, my son, I am delighted by your courage. I have laid open all the hidden treasures before you It is for you to take all of them," and disappeared after granting him further boons.

Just in front of him the hollow of the earth opened, as it were, and there lay a whole heap of untold treasures beneath.

Vikrama dug out all the hidden wealth and tying them up, loaded them on the ghoul. Together they returned to the palace of King Singara to whom he gave away all the treasures as gift.

He further enjoined on Singara to worship Goddess Kali at the hill-top as his family deity.

Having performed these exploits, King Vikrama returned to Ujjain after the completion of his exile period.

Asked the statuette: "Bhoja, if you think that you are as valorous and selfless as King Vikrama you can ascend the throne, and not otherwise."

King Bhoja and Nitivakya returned to their palace as usual after hearing the story."

59

Vikrama Honours a Great Magician

THIS is the story related by the statuette holding the twenty-first step of King Vikrama's divine throne when King Bhoja returned on the following morning to ascend it.

On one occasion when King Vikrama had been visiting Varanasi, he had, as usual, the sacred dip in the Ganga in the company of his ministers and courtiers. He went into the temple and had *darshan* of Lord Visveswara, Mother Visalakshi and Sri Kalabhairava and afterwards ate his breakfast. Since he was off duty, he went into a nearby grove to whileaway his time. His close attendants also followed him.

As he was enjoying the cool shade, the fragrant air and the multi-voiced chirps of endless birds that had taken shelter in it, a beggarly looking man appeared before him and stood bowing.

"What can I do, old man?" asked King Vikrama.

"My Lord! you are master of all the eight *siddhis (anima, nahima, garima, laghima, prapti, prakamya, isitvam, vasitvam)* and it has been my life's ambition to demonstrate the little knowledge I have of *indrajala.* I beg of you to give me permission to do so," requested the old man.

"Sure. I shall be pleased to see your power!" replied King Vikrama.

"I shall just come with my paraphernalia," said the man and turned his back.

No sooner did he do so than appeared there before the King a remarkable white steed bearing a young warrior in full panoply and a very good-looking woman seated behind him. The warrior bowed elegantly at Vikrama and stylishly getting down from his charger said: "My lord, I was for long serving the Pasha at the head of his cavalry. As a result of some misunderstanding, I had to leave his service. Having heard of your great name and fame, I could only think of your kingdom where I could get a suitable job. We are only two; me and here, my wife."

King Vikrama was greatly impressed by the bearing and delivery of the young warrior, and no sooner had he decided to appoint him in his service than a babel of voices arose from the north following by the sound of war drums! The dust that arose in the sky indicated a holocaust all of which made Vikrama wonder: "Who could that enemy be who wants my blood?" For, as far as he could see, he had no enemies at all!

The young warrior opposite to him stood in attention and begged: "My lord, that is the enemy horde, no doubt. May I beg of you to give me this chance to break the knee of the enemy?"

"That is right. You had better take care of them, whoever they are," ordered the King.

"One more request, my lord! During the time I shall be away, may I entrust my wife to your care? You are like a father and mother to both of us."

"Yes; that is all right!" replied King Vikrama.

The warrior jumped on the exquisite-looking horse which did not wait for the spur to gallop and both of them vanished into the distant sky.

As King Vikrama sat thinking, resting his chin on his palm he could hear the progress of the war and see the trunks, heads, hands and limbs of men and carcases of animals fall from above with the smell of fresh blood which poured like rain. The cries of the contending armies and drums deafened the ears.

As he sat there, he was shocked to see the heads and trunks of both the young warrior he had despatched and his white steed fall before him cut into two by the marauders.

The warrior's wife who was looking on, fell into a swoon as she saw her husband's fate. Soon she regained consciousness but rolled in the mud pietously crying, "Ah! This should be my fate where I took shelter! I must follow my husband! O men! Won't you light a fire for me? I must enter it!"

The courtiers who were flabbergasted at the sight of all that was happening, were not in a mood to oblige the lady. But she was not to be outdone; for, by her own hand she lighted up a fire which rose sky-high. Crying bitterly at her fate, she entered the fire cursing: "The onus of bringing this fate on me shall lie, squarely on you, King Vikramaditya!" Afterwards the woman was burnt to ashes instantaneously by the marathon fire.

All assembled were greatly agitated by the uncalled for accusation on the part of the lady, but their surprise knew no bounds by the appearance of the same warrior on the same horse before them with the trophy of success in his hands. After smartly bowing before the King, the warrior related how, with God's grace, he had been able to beat the enemy blue and massacre the entire army.

King Vikrama thereupon complimented him on his bravery.

As the warrior politely stepped back, his eyes roved in search of his wife. With great difficulty, the courtiers conveyed to him the death of his wife and the circumstances under which she died.

"What! I can't believe this cock-and-bull story. My wife is not that sort of woman. King Vikrama, tell me truly what happened to her!"

"You have heard the correct version!" replied King Vikrama.

"That can't be, mighty King! I suspect foul play. Was her beauty the cause of her undoing? Please reply," challenged the warrior.

King Vikrama asked his courtiers to deliberate over the matter and give a suitable answer to the warrior.

As he said so, a messenger appeared before Vikrama and said: "My Lord, the Great Pasha has been pleased to send you these bounties which he requests you to accept," and placed before him a cart-load of precious jewels, clothes and gold. This was followed by five thousand horses and five hundred elephants.

King Vikrama expressed his gratefulness to the Pasha which he wanted to be conveyed to him.

After suitably honouring the messenger and sending him away, the King turned to the warrior and said: "My young man, I am so pleased with your performance. You really are a gem and you have mastered *indrajala* perfectly. I present you with all the gifts the Pasha has really sent to me," said Vikrama, handing them all over to him.

That warrior, after bowing before King Vikrama, went a little way off and fell at the feet of the old beggarly looking man who had come to Vikrama at first.

All those assembled looked at them with open mouthed wonder.

King Vikrama explained to them that all that they had been witnessing over the past hour was a demonstration of *indrajala.*

The warrior-looking *chela* took hold of his wife who had made herself visible by then and after bidding adieu to all, returned to his place.

King Vikramaditya too returned to Ujjain followd by his courtiers.

Said the statuette, as usual, in the end: "If you feel you are as great as King Vikramaditya, you may ascend the throne."

King Bhoja returned to his place followed by Nitivakya and other courtiers.

60

Navamohini

WHEN King Bhoja returned on the morning of the twenty-second day to ascend King Vikramaditya's divine throne, the statuette holding that step narrated the following story:

A very rich merchant by name Dhanapati lived in Ujjain. He was a multi-millionaire but had no children. So he spent all his wealth in charitable activities like construction of temples, choultries, tanks, schools, etc. At last he went to Kashi.

As he was returning after *darshan* of Lord Bhairava, he saw before him two beheaded children, a boy and a girl. By the side of this gruesome tragedy, oil was boiling in a cauldron. A scroll of palm leaf lay nearby. Taking it he read: "If anyone possessing all the thiry-two *lakshanas* of a great man were to jump into this cauldron and come out alive after staying there for a couple of hours, these children will come back to life."

Dhanapati came home and reported to King Vikramaditya about this strange announcement. King Vikrama who was ever willing to help where his help was needed, flew to Kashi on the shoulder of his faithful ghoul and after successfully swimming in the boiling oil, restored the two children to life.

The statuette holding the twenty-third step related the following story to King Bhoja on the following day:

During one of his self-imposed exiles, King Vikramaditya

stayed beneath a giant banyan tree for a night. On that tree lived Sanjeevi, the *garuda* which was the king of birds. At night, Sanjeevi asked of the others if they had anything to report to Ujjain where King Vikramaditya rules like Indra in Heaven. Prosperity and amity reign supreme there!"

"If that is so, why not we leave this forest where the *rakshasa* yonder kills a hundred of us each day, and migrate to Ujjain? If he too is unable to protect us, we shall go to a far off place to some lone island," said Sanjeevi.

As King Vikrama was listening to this conversation, a cow chased by a tiger came racing and fell at his feet. Vikrama at once whipped out his magic sword and dashed against the pursuing tiger killing it with one stroke.

Afterwards, he came near the frightened cow, caressed it and drove it to a pool to make it allay its thirst.

The birds living on the tree witnessed this scene and considering that he should be a *mahatma*, they flew round him in formation and saluted him. King Vikrama asked them: "What can I do for you?"

Sanjeevi replied: "To the north of the mountain there lives a *rakshasa* by name Prakash. He catches a hundred of us each day for his meals. He is so powerful that no ordinary human being can punish him. We pray that you save us from him?"

"I shall certainly do so," replied King Vikrama. As he said so, he mounted on his ghoul and flew across the lair and arduously, Vikrama killed him. Returning to the birds, he told them of the death of *rakshasa* and advised them to live there for ever free of all fear.

The statuette holding the twenty-fourth step told the following story:

A brahmin by name Lakshmi Sanmana performed *tapas* for long before Mahakali of Ujjain. One day Kali Mata appeared before him in his dream and said: "O, brahmin, go to King Vikrama right now. He is in his pleasure-garden surrounded by his queens and is in a particularly happy mood. Ask him whatever you want, he will grant all," and disappeared.

The brahmin accordingly ran to the garden which was lit like Indraloka and the chimes of dancing women kept time for the warble of the cuckoo. The brahmin had no compunctions, because Kali Mata of his frolic, noticed the brahmin from a distance and even before asking, divined what the man wanted and gave away in profusion what all he wanted. The brahmin blessed the King and returned the happiest man.

The statuette holding the twenty-fifth step related the following story:

In the city of Vijayanagara, a brahmin boy lived. As he was wayward in his behaviour, his father one day explained to him the need for learning the *Agamas* and *Sastras* without which one was a mere animal. The boy became ashamed and went to the city of Vindhya where he sat at the feet of a great scholar and learnt the *Sastras* quickly. After study, he returned home.

On the way, the Shastri had to pass through Kalahasti. He went into the famous temple of the place and after having *darshan* of the Lord, was returning through the streets. It was dusk. From the balcony of her house, a famous danseuse of the place – Navamohini – was looking out for paramours. Finding the young Shastri passing along with the look of a newcomer, she aimed her bow and arrow of charms in his direction and the lad's feet started dragging him towards her house.

As he was making his way for her house, people sitting near called him and said: "Shastriji! You seem to be a newcomer to this place. Don't you know that whoever seeks her company does not return alive? A *rakshasa* lifts her visitors bodily and swallows them. Begone, if you want to save your life!"

The young Shastri got the fright of his life on hearing this well-meant advice and ran home.

One day this Shastri went to King Vikrama's *durbar* to pay his respects. Asked by the King how he fared, the young Shastri related to him the Kalahasti episode.

As usual Vikrama immediately started for Kalahasti on the ghoul accompanied by the brahmin. He went straight to Navamohini's house. On seeing a noble man like him, the danseuse's joy knew no bounds. After suitably entertaining him, she confessed: "Noble sir, I am so happy to receive you because no one dares to visit me because of a curse I lay under. Whoever visits me is carried away by a *rakshasa*; I have not been able to see it or prevent it."

King Vikrama revealed to her his identity and his resolve to release her from the *rakshasa* that very night. They waited patiently for the *rakshasa* who appeared at midnight. King Vikrama hacked the monster to pieces by his magic sword to the great relief of the woman.

After that, King Vikrama brought his friend the Shastri and handed Navamohini over to him saying: "Now, you had better make merry without fear," and returned to Ujjain.

61

Vikrama's *Dharma*

WHEN King Bhoja returned to ascend the throne on the morning of the twenty-sixth day, the statuette holding the step told the following story:

On one occasion King Vikramaditya ordered the ghoul to go and find out if there was any event in any of the world worth knowing. The ghoul went out and returned with the following account.

"There is a hill called Chitragutti. On the side of that hill, is a temple of Mahakali which is built of *spatika*. In front of that temple ghee is falling in *dhara*. A brahmin by name Mantragyani is performing *havan* or *homa*. He has been doing it for a hundred years now and the ashes that have accumulated by his sacrificial fire are like a hillock. That brahmin observes a vow of silence and he would not speak of his objective to anyone,"

On hearing it, King Vikrama started towards that hill on the ghoul which brought him in a trice. Wondering at the unceasing fall of ghee, King Vikrama thought it was Kali Mata's *leela* and he therefore bathed in it. But as the ghee touched King Vikrama's body, it turned into milk! King Vikrama on seeing it concluded that that too was a *leela* of the deity.

This attracted the attention of the brahmin who appeared to be interested in the King. The latter therefore approached the brahmin and asked, "Holy sire, may I know the object of your *havan* and how long are you performing it?"

The brahmin replied: "Noble sir! I am performing this *homa* for the last hundred years for the purpose of seeing Kali Mata in person. But as ill-luck would have it, I have not yet been successful!"

On hearing it, King Vikrama bathed in the brook running nearby, performed Shiva *puja* and going inside the Kali temple prayed before the deity for appearing before him. There was no response. Thereupon, Vikrama pulled out his magic sword and was about to cut his head off as offering to Kali. At that time Kali Mata appeared before him and asked: Vikrama! What do you want?"

Vikrama fell at her feet and begged: "Mother! Why is it that although this devout man has been propitiating Thee for a hundred years now, Thou hast not been pleased to accede to his request?"

Kali replied: "Oh! That man was thinking of a thousand matters at the time of *havan* and not even for a few minutes did he concentrate on me. That is why I have not cared to appear before him."

King Vikrama thereafter pleaded on behalf of the brahmin that she should accede to his request and grant him all the boons he wanted. In response to the King's request Kali Mata granted the brahmin all he wanted and the King helped him to carry them all to his home.

The statuette holding the twenty-seventh step told the following story:

There was a city by name Sambhukapuri. In it lived a big diamond merchant called Dhanadatta. One day he offered some precious stones at the feet of King Vikramaditya. The latter accepted them and asked the merchant, "Have you any other gems of higher value?"

The merchant replied: "Yes sir, I have ten most precious stones. They are very very costly."

"How costly?"

"With your permission, sir, I will say this. If you take one of them and fling it at the sky, it will go up to some height. Now if you heap gold to that height, that gold will be the cost of each stone!"

King Vikrama was fascinated by the proposition, so he ordered the merchant to go to his city and bring those ten stones for which he was willing to pay the cost. The King however gave him only eight days to return.

Taking a few soldiers with him as guards, the merchant went. On their return journey, however, they had to cross a river which had risen in spate. It was dangerous to cross it without the aid of boats. So they called a boatman. The boatman, however, refused to take his life and that of his family.

In view of the King's order to return within eight days, the merchant agreed to part with five of those precious stones he carried to the King as the fee for carrying them across and the merchant handed over to the boatman the stipulated five gems.

Reaching Ujjain, the merchant handed over to the King the five gems. Vikrama was charmed by those stones. Asked he: "Where are those remaining five stones?"

The merchant narrated the circumstances in which he had to part with those five gems.

King Vikrama overwhelmed the merchant by his praise for parting with those five precious stones and paid for all the ten stones.

This is the story narrated by the statuette guarding the twenty-eighth step.

There was a brahmin by name Soma Swamin in Ujjain.

He had married a good-natured girl called Gunavati. Although she was twenty, Gunavati did not conceive. This made her unhappy. One day she asked her husband: "My lord! You are very learned and know the stars upside down. How is that we have had no children so far?"

He replied: "My love! A man who is clever will fend for himself. A man who is devout and prayerful will surely beget children. Why do you worry?"

On hearing it the lady became more pious. She interested her husband in propitiating God on *Sanitrayodasi.* Soon a son was born to them. He grew up wonderfully. They taught him all the *Sastras* and when he came of age, himself left for the forest to do penance.

The boy too grew up in age as well as attainments. He too set up a cottage in the thick forest and started contemplating on God.

One day King Vikramaditya had gone hunting. In the wilds of the forest he lost his path, and he and his associates were dying of thirst. At that time, Vikrama chanced to notice the boy's hut which he reached.

The boy was so overwhelmed with the visit that he fed the party with food and water and helped the party to reach home. King Vikrama took the brahmin youngster to Ujjain and gave him rich presents, gold and ornaments.

Soon after, the King was having his lunch with his queen. At that time Vikrama's young son was found missing. Some palace official said they saw the brahmin from the forest taking the child away. This made the King wonder. Soon he sent guards to seek the brahmin youth and find out about his son. The guards reported: "The forest brahmin says he killed your son, having been enamoured of the *ratna-hara* the child wore."

The King's sorrow knew no bounds. When the abductor was brought before him the King thought: "Poor man! I would have given thousands of such ornaments if he had told me! Alas! in the ordinary course, I should have ordered this man to be killed. But I have eaten his salt. I shall be going against *dharma* if I sentence him."

The King therefore sent him away advising him not to go against *dharma* in future and gave him more gifts and gold.

Turning round, the brahmin said: "King! I have not killed your son. I only wanted, in my curiosity, to see how far you are wedded to *dharma*. Your son is safe in my cottage. I shall bring him quickly. I have now known a King who has no equal in all the three worlds."

62

Last Days of Vikrama

WHEN King Bhoja came on the twenty-ninth morning to ascend the throne, the statuette holding the twenty-ninth step stopped him and told the following story:

At the time when our King Vikramaditya was ruling this country, a king by name Prasanna ruled the city of Mallikapur. He had a daughter, Chitrarekha. She loved to play on the top of the palace which had seven storeys. She had further vowed that she would marry Lord Vishnu alone.

In that city was a brahmin lad by name Souri. He was so enamoured of the princess that he decided to marry her by hook or crook. Having come to know of her vow, he decided on a plan. He propitiated Vishwakarma and by his help, got a wooden *garuda* which had the power of flying in the air. Dressing himself in the likeness of Lord Vishnu, he ascended the *garuda* and entered the *zenana* of the princess. He explained to Chitrarekha that he was Lord Vishnu come to marry her. Chitrarekha who believed him directed him to her father. The King too believed him under the circumstances and gave his daughter away in marriage to him.

One day a rival King invaded Mallikapur and Prasanna's armies took to fight. At this the king asked his daughter to persuade her husband to help him to rout the enemy since he was Mahavishnu. Chitrarekha in turn requested her husband who became flabbergasted. He felt that his game would be up unless he got the help of King Vikrama.

So he ran to our King and explained to him the circumstances under which he was obliged to help his father-in-law.

King Vikrama graciously acceded to his invitation and mounting the ghoul, started for Mallikapur followed by Souri who accompanied him on his *garuda*. King Vikrama successfully routed the enemies and returned to Ujjain.

The same statuette told another story which was as follows:

Once our King Vikramaditya performed *Asvamedha Yaga*. At that time he sent messages of invitation to all the kings. One of those invitees was the King of the Oceans. The messenger who carried that message, went to the seashore and called out the Ocean King. Finding no response, he started returning. But the Ocean King, recalling that the messenger was from King Vikramaditya, suddenly appeared before the messenger and handed him four gems to be given to Vikramaditya. He explained that one of them would give all riches, the next ornaments, the third armies and the fourth all pleasures.

The messenger duly handed them over to the King. Vikrama, however, presented one of those gems to the brahmin messenger, keeping the rest to himself. The brahmin requested, "Sire, please give me the other three too. I will show them to my relatives and return them to you." The King agreed and gave them.

The brahmin took all the four gems to his home and handing them to his relatives, explained the powers of each gem. On hearing their powers, his relatives refused to return them. Thus ensued a quarrel. The messenger who became frightened dragged all the relatives before the King and filed a complaint against them. King Vikrama had a hearty laugh over this quarrel and generously gave away the three gems to those relatives who would not return them.

The statuette holding the thirtieth step related the following story when Bhoja returned to the throne the next morning:

In a village near Ujjain a wild boar from the forest was doing havoc by destroying the crops and killing those who came to drive it away. The people collected some *shikaris* from the neighbouring village who too failed to drive the boar away.

Greatly afraid, the people reported the matter to King Vikrama who, arming himself, straightaway went to the village. He was however disappionted to find that the boar had returned to its lair in the forest. King Vikrama went to the forest and by beating the drums tried to stir the beast. The boar, frightened by this hullabaloo, started killing people indiscriminately. But King Vikrama followed it wherever it went, ultimately the boar jumped into the mouth of a cave on the side of a hillock called Chandragiri.

Leaving his horse and other habiliments at the mouth of the cave, King Vikrama entered the cave with drawn sword but was surprised to find the cave leading him to a far end which was shining like daylight. When he went near, however, he was intrigued to find a big mansion made of gold and shining by the light of inlaid gems. He opened its door and entered the building which was palatial. He saw large pavilions and bathing pools. At the central pavilion was seated a *rakshasa* king surrounded by courtiers. By the side of that king was an orderly who was telling his king: "I had been to the earth and started killing people. King Vikrama came chasing me and I jumped into Chandragiri. Look! There he comes in hot pursuit of me!

The *rakshasa* king, on seeing Vikrama, ran towards Vikrama and embracing him, said: "Mighty monarch, pardon me. The fact is, I myself played this hoax on you. On hearing your great exploits, I wanted to meet you, but thinking that you would not respond to my invitation I sent one of my messengers in the shape of a boar to lure you."

The *rakshasa* king took Vikramaditya to Patala Loka and showed him the temple of Lord Dakshinamurty and the great Mahabali doing his job, who embraced King Vikrama saying "What a great fortune! What a great fortune!" King Mahabali entertained Vikramaditya with the best food and gave him a pot of divine nectar for his use and several *nagaratnas*. Accompanied by a guide King Vikramaditya returned from Patala Loka.

On his way to Ujjain, Vikrama met a brahmin whose son was suffering from a wasting disease as a result of which the child's entire body was split like an overripe cucumber. The King was moved to pity and he gave the boy some of the nectar he had brought to drink by which the boy was not only cured, but made deathless. Vikrama also presented that family with several gems and jewels.

Our king used the nectar he brought from Patala Loka in restoring all persons and crops killed and destroyed by the boar.

This is the story narrated by the statuette holding the thirty-first step of Vikrama's divine throne.

King Vikrama had a Minister by name Yuktisekhara. The latter had no issues for a long time. So he performed all the propitiations enjoined by the *Sastras* as a result of which he got a son whom he named Gokul Nandan but unfortunately the child grew to be an imbecile. People wondered how such a clever man begot such a foolish son.

Not being able to bear the ignominy, the young boy left Ujjain on a pilgrimage. In the course of his travels he came to a village by the side of river Kauveri. There was a temple of Aghora Virabhadra. He entered it and to his surprise found at the back of that temple a rivulet whose water was steaming hot. The steps leading to the temple were made of *sphatika*. There was no sign of any living creature. The boy, however, managed to stay in that place for a few days.

One day, he saw eight *apsaras* coming to that temple and offering worship to the deity. They kept on coming everyday for that purpose. One day, however, the leader of the group discovered the young Gokul Nandan. She took him to ask for staying there unawares and explained to him that it was a dangerous place as even *rishis* feared to tread their path. She was however so fascinated by that lad that she expressed her desire for his company. But the boy resolutely refused her telling that he was on a pilgrimage whereby he could set at nought the infamy that he was a born idiot. The damsel was greatly pleased by the boy's resolve and blessed him to become a very clever and erudite man. Thanking her, the boy returned home as scholar to the great joy of his parents.

One day Minister Yuktisekhara took his son to King Vikrama before whom he exhibited his powers. The King was greatly pleased with the lad's performance which made him ask how he got those abilities. Gokul Nandan faithfully reported the circumstances whereupon King Vikramaditya took the boy along with him and went to the temple of Virabhadra.

Hiding themselves at a distance, King Vikrama and the lad saw those eight damsels coming to the sanctum of the deity and worshipping. King Vikrama however took the risk of following them and ultimately spotted them at the abode of eight *Siddha Purushas* whom they were serving. The *Siddhas* on seeing King Vikrama asked him how he happened to come that way. King Vikrama explained how he owed that pleasure to his minister's son. The *Siddhas* blessed the King and gave him a gem each which they said will give the owner whatever he wanted. The damsels also blessed the King.

After receiving the gems, King Vikrama asked them: "How is it that the water in the rivulet is steaming hot?"

The *Siddhas* explained that a part of the divine Ganga flowed through the third eye of Lord Shiva which was that river and that was why the water was hot. After bidding adieu to the *Siddhas*, the King returned to Ujjain. The first thing he did was to present all the eight gems to the brahmin boy.

King Bhoja came to ascend the last step on the thiry-second day. On that day also the statuette refused to permit him. Asked by Bhoja how Vikrama came to depart from this world, the statuette replied as follows:

Towards the close of the 2000 years of Vikrama's life, there lived in a village on the banks of Kauveri a brahmin by name Avadhani. He was greatly learned in the *Vedas*. He was married to a girl by the name of Divya Chintamani. The learned man of the place forecast that if he joined his wife exactly after twelve years he would beget a son who would rule over the world. Consequently, Avadhani started on a pilgrimage with the intention of returning on the last day of the twelve years.

Accordingly, he arrived near his village on the last day of the twelfth year and had a river to cross to reach his home to accomplish the millennium. Unfortunately, on that day the river had risen in spate. Until dusk there was no sign of abatement of the floods.

A potter who was witnessing the brahmin's dilemma asked him why he was so uneasy. Avadhani explained to him the circumstances.

The potter replied: "Sir, it is not possible for you to cross the river before daybreak. If you do not want to waste a heaven–sent opportunity, I will request you to sleep tonight in my house. I have a marriageable daughter whose company you can keep."

The brahmin felt that the request was not unreasonable and so he accompanied the potter and after staying with his daughter for the night he returned to his village in the morning.

As forecast, the potter's daughter gave birth to a son who came to be known as Salivahana. Starting from a potter he rose to become the Minister of King Vishwanatha of Mysapur. The king owed allegiance to King Vikramaditya of Ujjain.

At the suggestion of Salivahana, Vishwanatha refused to pay his bounty to Vikrama whereupon the latter invaded Mysapur. Salivahana who had anticipated this had prepared a number of earthen soldiers and cavalries and kept them ready on the route of Vikrama. As soon as he sighted Vikrama's army, Salivahana directed power and life into the earthen army by his skill whereupon they took Vikrama's army unprepared and routed it.

Vikrama who led the expedition asked Minister Bhatti: "What has happened to my prowess?"

The latter replied that hardly a few days were left of his 2000 years.

Foiled thus for once, King Vikrama beat a hasty retreat to Ujjain.

Sitting for the last time on the divine throne, he addressed the thirty-two statucttes: "Listen all of you. Five hundred years after my demise a king by name Bhoja will discover this throne from the earth and he will attempt to sit on it. All of you must relate to him my exploits. After that, you may return to your abode in heaven."

After saying this, King Vikrama dug a pit in an open space and concealed the throne for posterity.

One of his last acts was to release the ghoul from his service and remove its curse, thus enabling it to take its own brahmin form. The grateful brahmin went after blessing King Vikrama.

In the meantime Salivahana's astras came in hot pursuit to King Vikrama whose head it cut asunder. The head fell in the midst of Vikrama's queens. On seeing the King's severed head all the queens lighted a fire and immolated themselves in it.

Bhatti, not willing to be killed by others, released his life by *yoga.*

Salivahana on hearing the demise of King Vikrama and Bhatti, helped his suzerain to become the king of the entire country. Viswanatha ruled the country for 1000 years.

Ujjain soon became a deserted place.

The statuette concluded: "Now we have done our duty. Permit us to return to heaven."

King Bhoja replied: "You have regaled me with the exploits of King Vikramaditya all these days. He was such a large hearted person that you should certainly have imbibed some of his qualities. Now won't you permit me to sit on this throne and rule for some time at least?"

The statuettes agreed to Bhoja's request and permitted him to rule from that throne for only one year and afterwards returned to heaven.

Bhoja and Nitivakya felt happy that their perseverance had borne fruit.